Beginning InfoPath™

Beginning InfoPath™ 2003

F. Scott Barker

WILEY

Wiley Publishing, Inc.

Beginning InfoPath™ 2003

Published by
Wiley Publishing, Inc.
10475 Crosspoint Boulevard
Indianapolis, IN 46256
www.wiley.com

Copyright © 2005 by Wiley Publishing, Inc., Indianapolis, Indiana

Published simultaneously in Canada

ISBN: 0-7645-7948-7

10 9 8 7 6 5 4 3 2 1

1B/ST/QS/QV/IN

No part of this publication may be reproduced, stored in a retrieval system or transmitted in any form or by any means, electronic, mechanical, photocopying, recording, scanning or otherwise, except as permitted under Sections 107 or 108 of the 1976 United States Copyright Act, without either the prior written permission of the Publisher, or authorization through payment of the appropriate per-copy fee to the Copyright Clearance Center, 222 Rosewood Drive, Danvers, MA 01923, (978) 750-8400, fax (978) 646-8600. Requests to the Publisher for permission should be addressed to the Legal Department, Wiley Publishing, Inc., 10475 Crosspoint Blvd., Indianapolis, IN 46256, (317) 572-3447, fax (317) 572-4355, e-mail: brandreview@wiley.com.

LIMIT OF LIABILITY/DISCLAIMER OF WARRANTY: THE PUBLISHER AND THE AUTHOR MAKE NO REPRESENTATIONS OR WARRANTIES WITH RESPECT TO THE ACCURACY OR COMPLETENESS OF THE CONTENTS OF THIS WORK AND SPECIFICALLY DISCLAIM ALL WARRANTIES, INCLUDING WITHOUT LIMITATION WARRANTIES OF FITNESS FOR A PARTICULAR PURPOSE. NO WARRANTY MAY BE CREATED OR EXTENDED BY SALES OR PROMOTIONAL MATERIALS. THE ADVICE AND STRATEGIES CONTAINED HEREIN MAY NOT BE SUITABLE FOR EVERY SITUATION. THIS WORK IS SOLD WITH THE UNDERSTANDING THAT THE PUBLISHER IS NOT ENGAGED IN RENDERING LEGAL, ACCOUNTING, OR OTHER PROFESSIONAL SERVICES. IF PROFESSIONAL ASSISTANCE IS REQUIRED, THE SERVICES OF A COMPETENT PROFESSIONAL PERSON SHOULD BE SOUGHT. NEITHER THE PUBLISHER NOR THE AUTHOR SHALL BE LIABLE FOR DAMAGES ARISING HEREFROM. THE FACT THAT AN ORGANIZATION OR WEBSITE IS REFERRED TO IN THIS WORK AS A CITATION AND/OR A POTENTIAL SOURCE OF FURTHER INFORMATION DOES NOT MEAN THAT THE AUTHOR OR THE PUBLISHER ENDORSES THE INFORMATION THE ORGANIZATION OR WEBSITE MAY PROVIDE OR RECOMMENDATIONS IT MAY MAKE. FURTHER, READERS SHOULD BE AWARE THAT INTERNET WEBSITES LISTED IN THIS WORK MAY HAVE CHANGED OR DISAPPEARED BETWEEN WHEN THIS WORK WAS WRITTEN AND WHEN IT IS READ.

For general information on our other products and services or to obtain technical support, please contact our Customer Care Department within the U.S. at (800) 762-2974, outside the U.S. at (317) 572-3993 or fax (317) 572-4002.

Wiley also publishes its books in a variety of electronic formats. Some content that appears in print may not be available in electronic books.

Library of Congress Control Number: 2004029500

Trademarks: Wiley, the Wiley Publishing logo, Wrox, the Wrox logo, Programmer to Programmer, and related trade dress are trademarks or registered trademarks of John Wiley & Sons, Inc. and/or its affiliates, in the United States and other countries, and may not be used without written permission. InfoPath is a trademark of Microsoft Corporation in the United States and/or other countries. All other trademarks are the property of their respective owners. Wiley Publishing, Inc., is not associated with any product or vendor mentioned in this book.

About the Author

F. Scott Barker, a Microsoft MVP, has worked as a developer in the database field for over 16 years, and with Visual Basic, SQL Server, and Microsoft Access for the last 12 years. Scott is currently working on a major InfoPath project for Toyota, converting a largely manual paper form production quality control system to InfoPath forms. Scott worked at Microsoft in the Access and Foxpro teams. Since leaving he has been contracting with Microsoft developing in-house tools used throughout Microsoft. Scott is a writer for a number of VB/Office magazines as well as a columnist for DotNetJunkies.com and is the author of a number of books.

Credits

Acquisitions Editor
Jim Minatel

Development Editor
Howard A. Jones

Senior Development Editor
Kevin Kent

Production Editor
Pamela Hanley

Technical Editor
Wiley-Dreamtech India Pvt Ltd

Copy Editor
Foxxe Editorial

Editorial Manager
Mary Beth Wakefield

Vice President & Executive Group Publisher
Richard Swadley

Vice President and Publisher
Joseph B. Wikert

Project Coordinator
Kristie Rees

Graphics and Production Specialists
Carrie A. Foster
Lauren Goddard
Denny Hager
Joyce Haughey
Amanda Spagnuolo

Quality Control Technicians
Leeann Harney
Jessica Kramer
Susan Moritz

Proofreading and Indexing
TECHBOOKS Production Services

I want to dedicate this book to my oldest son, who has fast become a man. Chris, stay true on the path and there will be nothing you can't accomplish!

Contents

Contents

Contents

Contents

Contents

Contents

Contents

Acknowledgments

As a father of five, I think I can safely say that every book I write is like going through pregnancy. By the end of it, you are ready just to be done. Just as with a pregnancy you need a good coach to get through it with a positive attitude. There are a number of people I want to thank at Wrox and Wiley for helping get me through another book with encouragement throughout the endeavor: Jim Minatel, who has got to be one of the easiest acquisition editors I have worked with. He can prod you on, yet ease pressure from you at the same time. Howard Jones, by far the best development editor, who encourages you with every phone call and has you looking forward to every page of red marks. My thanks also go to the technical editors for their positive remarks and keeping me honest.

I want to thank good friend Mark Woodlief, who worked on the Security chapter and case study and provided examples in a pinch when I was brain dead.

At Microsoft I want to thank Ned Friend for recommending me for the task and providing answers to my questions when needed. Thanks are also due to the MVP leads Rita Nikas and April Dalke for being quick to get resources when needed, and also just for being good friends. You two are awesome and give Microsoft a great name.

Thanks again for Woodinville Starbucks #2, for keeping my seat warm and latte hot.

As usual, I have to of course thank my patient, if unruly, family for putting up with me in the writing mode again. Especially my lovely wife Diana, who puts up with so much.

Introduction

If you have heard of Microsoft InfoPath but never had the chance to work with it, you are in for a treat. Microsoft has really outdone itself coming up with a tool that gives the power user a forms tool they can use right away, and the developer a forms tool that can be taken to the next level. This book guides you in taking advantage of this very cool new product.

While using InfoPath is fairly straightforward, there are features and concepts that may confuse or deter you from getting as much out of InfoPath as you could. This book was written to save you from any confusion or frustration. As you read it you're likely to get more and more excited about InfoPath because you'll see all that can be done with it.

InfoPath is very unique in that it works well as standalone, yet dovetails into enterprise use with products and technologies such as XML Web services, Windows SharePoint Services, and BizTalk. By the end of this book you will see the necessary steps to use these technologies, and read some real-world case studies of major institutions that have used them.

Who This Book Is For

Beginning InfoPath was written with both the power user and developer in mind. A power user is a user who has a fairly good handle on most of windows functionality, working with the Office applications, and creating small Access or Excel applications for their own groups or departments. A developer creates applications using .NET technologies or something similar. They may be developing solutions for:

- ❑ Their own use.
- ❑ Department use.
- ❑ IT Department use.
- ❑ Independent Project for someone.

Once they start reading this book, power users will learn how to crank out fairly sophisticated forms very quickly. The power user may get by just by reading the first two sections (chapters 1 through 9) if they are not interested in creating code behind their InfoPath forms or working with InfoPath at the enterprise levels.

Developers will want to read this book cover to cover. Because InfoPath is so new, they will want to read the first two sections to get a handle on the user interface, and see how to create forms that are as streamlined as possible. The last two sections of the book contain the most useful information for developers.

With the inclusion of InfoPath in the growing number of products to take advantage of managed code and .NET, this book helps the developer take advantage of using Visual Studio for writing code, or learn how to use their favorite scripting language. Developers also get some experience with enterprise-wide use of InfoPath.

What This Book Covers

First and foremost, this book gets you, the reader, comfortable with creating forms in Microsoft InfoPath 2003, including the features that come with the latest service release 1.1.

The databases Microsoft Access and SQL Server are mentioned, with Access databases being used for sample purposes.

.NET Technologies such as Visual Studio 2003, the C# programming language, and XML Web Services are discussed. Other ways of coding using scripting are covered in later chapters, as well as enterprise products such as Biz Talk and SharePoint covered.

Finally, you will be presented with two Case Studies featuring InfoPath deployment with Windows SharePoint Services, SQL Server, and Microsoft BizTalk.

How This Book Is Structured

The book has been broken up into four parts to give you as much value for your investment as possible and to give you the best information you need for the stage you are at in your InfoPath journey.

Chapters 1 through 6 introduce you to InfoPath, and what possibilities exist for using it as a development tool.

- ❑ **Chapter 1: InfoPath – The Journey Begins**: This chapter discusses how InfoPath became the product it is today. Also discussed is how you can use InfoPath in various scenarios to meet your various forms needs. Ways to use data are discussed, including XML technology, Access and SQL Server databases, and XML Web services. Deployment requirements are reviewed, and finally a typical InfoPath form is examined.

- ❑ **Chapter 2: Getting Started Designing with InfoPath**: This chapter starts off with a tour of the InfoPath form editor, showing you the various tools that make up a very versitile editor. It examines one of the many sample forms that come with InfoPath and shows you how to access more form templates from the Web. By the end of this chapter you will have all the information you need to use most of the tools on the task panes.

- ❑ **Chapter 3: Understanding Data**: This chapter gives you an overview of relational databases, and how you can use them with InfoPath. By the end of the chapter you will have a good understanding of what databases are used for, and how data is represented in them. Microsoft Access and Microsoft SQL Server are highlighted and discussed, as you're provided with a brief look at XML.

- ❑ **Chapter 4: Creating an InfoPath Form from an Existing Data Source**: This chapter walks you through creating an InfoPath form working against an existing database. You see how to use multiple (related) tables from the same database, where they are used in a form, as well as how to refresh the data source if it has changed.

- ❑ **Chapter 5: Utilizing XML and Web Service Data Sources**: One of the things that can be pretty intimidating is the thought that you may have to use XML for a data source. This chapter removes any concerns you have about using XML because the majority of the work is done by

InfoPath. You will see how to create a form with an existing XML document as the data source, and how to create a new InfoPath form, specifying the XML document (schema).

❑ **Chapter 6: Working with Controls in General**: This chapter provides a great overview of what controls are available in InfoPath. It lays out when you will want to use which type of controls for the data you are using. You will read about the different ways you can put controls onto your InfoPath form. Also discussed are ways to enhance the user's experience while controlling what data goes into your form by using default values and data validation. Lastly you also will see how to use conditional formating to highlight specific data conditions, and use formulas on calculated fields.

Chapters 7 through 10 take you from the basics to creating some useful InfoPath forms, then show how to publish those forms for other users' use.

❑ **Chapter 7: Looking at Some Useful Controls and Techniques**: This chapter highlights some of the very useful controls that let you work with data on your forms. You will see how to use the Drop Down List Box control to give users controlled choices in the data they enter. Additional data sources will be discussed, as well as entering the information in your list manually if desired. You will also see how to base drop downs on other drops, and work with other controls such as the Rich Text Box Control.

❑ **Chapter 8: Working with Sections:** InfoPath forms are created using various types of sections, whether they are a main section of table information, or a repeating section of related data. This chapter explains how to work with the various types of sections, taking advantage of different properties and creating master/detail sections. You will even see how to "trim" sections based on the users security level.

❑ **Chapter 9: Managing Views:** Instead of using multiple forms to organize data as traditional applications do, InfoPath enables you to manage various types of data using multiple views in one form. This chapter discusses in further detail the concept of views and shows you how to manage them. You will also see how to switch between views using built-in menu choices and custom task panes.

❑ **Chapter 10: Publishing InfoPath Forms**: Once you have created your forms, you may have to have other people use the forms as well. This chapter shows you several ways to deploy your forms for other people to use, including putting the form out on a file server that other users can access, and emailing the form to other users. You also see how to merge data from multiple forms so that you can aggregate and study the data that different people have inputed.

In chapters 11 through 14 you're shown various ways to add code behind your InfoPath forms. Besides giving the fundamentals of coding you will see some real-world examples that you can use in your own forms.

❑ **Chapter 11: Working with Code in Your InfoPath Form**: This chapter introduces you to the world of coding behind InfoPath forms. While InfoPath does a lot for you regarding common data tasks, there are some times when you just need to code it yourself. In this chapter you will see the various choices you have when it comes to coding behind your InfoPath forms. You will also read about event programming and get a better understanding of that.

❑ **Chapter 12: Getting Started Using Script**: Introduces using the Scripting languages behind your form. The default scripting language, Jscript, will be featured. You will see how to use the scripting editor to create and edit your code. You also will get a chance to work on some tasks, and run the code with your forms to test them out.

❏ **Chapter 13: Working with .NET Managed Code**: .NET is Microsoft's new development platform, offering a number of different languages for coding applications. With Service Pack 1.1 InfoPath has joined a grower number of applications that allow developers to use C# behind their forms instead of scripting. This chapter shows you how to set up an InfoPath project in Visual Studio, create the code behind your InfoPath form, and run it.

❏ **Chapter 14: Real World Tasks and Coding Examples**: Now is where the work in the preceding chapters pays off with creating real world examples yourself. You'll see routines for date calculations to use behind your forms, handling data submission on a form offline then synching it up with a database, and many more.

Chapters 15 through 18 take you through the various technologies that you can use with InfoPath to have your data used throughout the enterprise, including using technologies such as Windows SharePoint Services and BizTalk. You also will be able to read a couple of real-world case studies where InfoPath has been used successfully at an enterprise level.

❏ **Chapter 15: Creating and Working with Web Services**: In earlier chapters you saw how to attach a data source to a Web service; in this chapter you see how to create your own. You will have a greater understanding of what Web services are, as well as how to create them and test them using Visual Studio 2003. Lastly, you will see how to publish them so that you can access them over your intranet.

❏ **Chapter 16: Implementing Security**: As with every other application where you are working with data, Security is very important. This chapter shows you how to set security up for other users, specifying trust levels in Windows. You see how to create an MSI and use digital signatures to secure forms. You're also shown how to secure the designer so that only you can modify the structure of a form.

❏ **Chapter 17: Working with InfoPath with Windows SharePoint Services**: Windows SharePoint Services is a collaborative Web site software published by Microsoft. When used with Microsoft InfoPath, it's a great way to get information consolidated for a company, aggregate results, and maintain forms for a common purpose. This chapter provides an overview of WSS and how to set up a WSS site. You are then shown how to publish InfoPath forms onto the site, specifying fields from the form to list as columns in the browse display of the site. Other features such as totalling, sorting, and filtering are covered as well.

❏ **Chapter 18: Manufactoring Plant Case Study**: This chapter is a culmination of all the techniques you have seen throughout the book, and is used with the real world showing how InfoPath is used with SharePoint. Also shown is how to take the data inputed using InfoPath and displaying it on an ASP.NET Web site.

What You Need to Use This Book

The majority of this book covers Microsoft InfoPath 2003 with Service Pack 1.1. This service pack is required because Microsoft InfoPath 2003 is a 1.0 product, and as a result, a substantial number of changes and improvements have been made to it. You can download the Microsoft InfoPath 2003 Service Pack 1.1 at http://office.microsoft.com/officeupdate/.

In the second half of the book you will read about creating code behind your InfoPath forms. You will be able to use VBScript or Jscript without any additional software. If you choose to use the managed code samples, you need to install the .NET Framework and Visual Studio 2003 with C# included. These last two products also are required if you wish to create XML Web services, as described in this book.

Lastly, some of the last chapters cover enterprise products such as BizTalk and Windows SharePoint Services, which, besides the products, require Windows Server 2003. Here you also will want to download the InfoPath 2003 SDK to use InfoPath with BizTalk. You can download the SDK from `http://www.microsoft.com/downloads/`, then supply InfoPath for the product/technology, and SDK for the keyword.

Conventions

To help you get the most from the text and keep track of what's happening, we've used a number of conventions throughout the book.

> **Boxes like this one hold important, not-to-be forgotten information that is directly relevant to the surrounding text.**

Tips, hints, tricks, and asides to the current discussion are offset and placed in italics like this.

As for styles in the text:

- ❑ We *highlight, or in this book italicize,* important words when we introduce them
- ❑ We show keyboard strokes like this: Ctrl+A
- ❑ We show file names, URLs, and code within the text like so: `persistence.properties`
- ❑ We present code in two different ways:

```
In code examples we highlight new and important code with a gray background.
The gray highlighting is not used for code that's less important in the present
context, or has been shown before.
```

Source Code

As you work through the examples in this book, you may choose either to type in all the code manually or to use the source code files that accompany the book. All of the source code used in this book is available for download at `http://www.wrox.com`. Once at the site, simply locate the book's title (either by using the Search box or by using one of the title lists) and click the Download Code link on the book's detail page to obtain all the source code for the book.

Because many books have similar titles, you may find it easiest to search by ISBN; for this book the ISBN is 0-764-57948-7.

Once you download the code, just decompress it with your favorite compression tool. Alternately, you can go to the main Wrox code download page at http://www.wrox.com/dynamic/books/download.aspx to see the code available for this book and all other Wrox books.

Errata

We make every effort to ensure that there are no errors in the text or in the code. However, no one is perfect, and mistakes do occur. If you find an error in one of our books, like a spelling mistake or faulty piece of code, we would be very grateful for your feedback. By sending in errata you may save another reader hours of frustration and at the same time you will be helping us provide even higher quality information.

To find the errata page for this book, go to http://www.wrox.com and locate the title using the Search box or one of the title lists. Then, on the book details page, click the Book Errata link. On this page you can view all errata that has been submitted for this book and posted by Wrox editors. A complete book list including links to each's book's errata is also available at www.wrox.com/misc-pages/booklist.shtml.

If you don't spot "your" error on the Book Errata page, go to www.wrox.com/contact/techsupport.shtml and complete the form there to send us the error you have found. We'll check the information and, if appropriate, post a message to the book's errata page and fix the problem in subsequent editions of the book.

p2p.wrox.com

For author and peer discussion, join the P2P forums at p2p.wrox.com. The forums are a Web-based system for you to post messages relating to Wrox books and related technologies and interact with other readers and technology users. The forums offer a subscription feature to e-mail you topics of interest of your choosing when new posts are made to the forums. Wrox authors, editors, other industry experts, and your fellow readers are present on these forums.

At http://p2p.wrox.com you will find a number of different forums that will help you not only as you read this book, but also as you develop your own applications. To join the forums, just follow these steps:

1. Go to p2p.wrox.com and click the Register link.
2. Read the terms of use and click Agree.
3. Complete the required information to join as well as any optional information you wish to provide and click Submit.
4. You will receive an e-mail with information describing how to verify your account and complete the joining process.

You can read messages in the forums without joining P2P but in order to post your own messages, you must join.

Once you join, you can post new messages and respond to messages other users post. You can read messages at any time on the Web. If you would like to have new messages from a particular forum e-mailed to you, click the Subscribe to this Forum icon by the forum name in the forum listing.

For more information about how to use the Wrox P2P, be sure to read the P2P FAQs for answers to questions about how the forum software works as well as many common questions specific to P2P and Wrox books. To read the FAQs, click the FAQ link on any P2P page.

InfoPath — The Journey Begins

InfoPath is a new journey for both users and developers. If you are like many people, you may have many questions about just what InfoPath is and how it will help you in your work. That is what this chapter is all about. In it you will:

- ❑ Learn what InfoPath is, and how it can be used for various solutions.
- ❑ Read about different ways to connect data to InfoPath.
- ❑ Understand deployment requirements of InfoPath forms.
- ❑ Take a look at a typical InfoPath form.

What Is InfoPath, and How Can It Be Used?

InfoPath is a forms management tool that enables you to create forms and publish them in a number of different ways. InfoPath enables you to use forms that are attached to various types of existing data, and to use data that is self-contained within the form. Before going into more detail, take a look at what the problem was before InfoPath came about.

The Challenge of Forms Management

Over the last decade there have been a number of attempts, both inside and outside of Microsoft, to enable users to create forms quickly, yet responsibly, to work with data. You can see this with database systems such as Access, and the form tools in Word and Excel. However, these tools have either come up short in helping users control and share their data, or they are too confusing to use to create forms that can handle data made up of more single-table solutions.

To be useful for other systems, data needs to be manipulated or combined with other data. IT departments tend to cringe when a system like Microsoft Access is used to create a standalone or medium-sized solution because they have no control over the data.

The IT manager of one large corporation figured that the corporation had at least 40,000 Access databases throughout its enterprise. These are databases that are not controlled by the IT departments until the authors (developers) of these databases transfer from or leave the company. Then the IT department has to assign its own developer to learn and work with the system and control the data.

Users create their own standalone or group databases because IT departments don't have the time and manpower for smaller projects. Traditionally, trying to create an application that the department knows would work for their needs, with a large backend database, has been something of a struggle. So, the question remains: What is a solution to this set of challenges?

Various companies, such as Adobe and Oracle, have created their own form packages that attempt to resolve the issue of forms management. The problem with these packages is that they are either limited to the product they come with, such as Oracle forms, or to other proprietary data storage.

Even Microsoft has a number of possible forms packages, depending on the products you are using. In fact, some of them are pretty robust and powerful. Access has a great forms package built in that gives you the power you need when working with Access, or even SQL Server, data. Word and Excel have more limited forms packages. But again, these packages are somewhat limited in how they are bound to data of different types.

Microsoft InfoPath changes all that — not only by using the quickly becoming universal Extensible Markup Language (XML) standard for its base file structure, but also because of its expanding base of ways to connect to different types of data.

Microsoft's Solution: InfoPath

Microsoft's solution is InfoPath. Although there have been a number of forms packages from Microsoft in various products, InfoPath is the most intuitive, yet full featured, to date. With InfoPath, you can quickly create forms, either by using existing data or by creating the new data structure when you create the form itself. Now IT departments can create the backend database for the users and let the users create their forms based on the data. An example of an InfoPath form can be seen in Figure 1-1, where an Absence Request form has been filled out by an employee.

This form is one of the many sample forms included with InfoPath.

Try It Out   Opening the Sample Absence Request InfoPath Form

If you have already played with InfoPath forms, then you can skip this example. Otherwise this is a good way to get the feel for how users fill out an InfoPath form. After you have installed Microsoft InfoPath:

1. From the Windows Start menu, choose Microsoft Office ⇨ Microsoft Office InfoPath 2003. The Fill Out This Form dialog box appears, as shown in Figure 1-2.

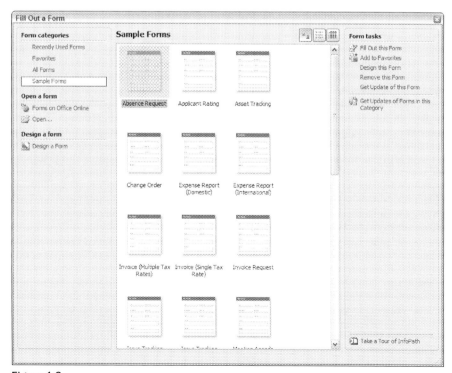

Figure 1-1

Figure 1-2

2. Select the Absence Request form.

3. Click on the Fill Out This Form task in the Forms Tasks task pane. The Absence Request form opens, ready to be filled out.

Take time to move around the form and get used to the way to enter data. You will notice a number of very nice features in the InfoPath form. The next section discusses some of those features.

> Besides the sample forms included with InfoPath, Microsoft offers some additional forms on the Office Online Web site. To get there, click on the Forms from Office Online task, located on the Open a Form task pane on the Fill Out a Form dialog box displayed in Figure 1-2. Once on the Web site you can search for InfoPath in the search field, and all the available templates (forms) will be displayed.

Side Trip: Installing the InfoPath 2003 Service Pack 1.1

If the Fill Out a Form dialog box presented in Step 1 doesn't look the same as the one displayed in Figure 1-2, this means that you probably have not installed Office 2003 Service Pack 1, which you can download from Microsoft. To download and install the service pack, go to `http://office.microsoft.com/officeupdate` and download and install the service pack.

InfoPath Features

You can see just how powerful InfoPath is as you continue through the book. Here are just a few of the many things InfoPath enables you to do:

Create Attractive Forms Quickly

The designer provided in Microsoft InfoPath enables you to create forms that are pleasing to the eye, while being functional and very powerful, with very little extra work. Controls are provided automatically for specific tasks and types of data. For example, when you have a date type field, and place it on your form, InfoPath places an icon beside it in the shape of a small calendar. When you click the calendar icon, a small calendar appears, allowing you to pick a date to enter into the field.

Forms are laid out using a table and section format, with various types of tables available to choose from. You can create your own custom tables as well.

Prevent Data-Entry Errors

Through the use of field properties for the various controls, you can easily help users prevent data entry errors. Some of the ways to prevent data entry errors are by using:

❑ **Default Values**: Default values ensure that fields are not unintentionally left blank.

❑ **Data Validation Conditions**: Data validation conditions allow you to specify values that are okay to enter, including ranges. Based on the data, you can either have InfoPath give an error message or run code to handle issues that arise.

❑ **Rules**: Rules can be applied that cause InfoPath to perform a set of actions based on the data entered.

Consistent and Conditional Formatting

You can apply formatting to fields and color schemes throughout a form and throughout multiple forms. This makes for a more consistent and comfortable experience when inputting data into forms.

Conditional formatting also can be specified to let users know when field values are negative (making them red) or when a field is invalid for some reason.

Combine Data from Multiple Forms

When you create a standalone form, you can e-mail that form and have the form e-mailed back to you. Once you have received one or more forms with the data filled in, you can merge the data with other forms that use the same form template. This is very useful, for example, if you are compiling data, such as evaluations from a presentation, and want to provide a report with all the data in one form.

Generate Different Views of Data

You can have multiple views with one form, switching between those views by using a task pane on the form. Task panes are a section of the form that include hyperlinks you can use to pick other tasks to perform. Besides the task pane in the InfoPath designer, Access and Excel both include task panes.

While the information displayed and edited could be different views of the same data, it makes more sense to create forms that contain different types of related data. An example of a form that includes multiple views is a form created for an auto repair shop. Here is way the views could be laid out:

1. **Customer Information**: This information would be entered once for a customer and could be pulled up into future forms that are filled out for the customer.

2. **Description of Issues**: This allows the customer and mechanic to list what the issues are. This form could include the make and model of the car as well as current issues.

3. **Mechanics Bid**: Pulling forward the information from the description of issues view, hours and dollars can be assigned and the bid presented to the customer.

4. **Final Invoice**: The final invoice can be displayed here and printed for the customer.

While it is not mandatory to break your forms into separate views, it can help with organizing the data for the user.

Features Introduced in Service Pack 1.1

The service pack has enough interesting features that it is well worth mentioning. With the additions listed in the next sections, the service pack has enough new features, rather than just bug fixes, to make it a 2.0 release. The following sections outline some new features and enhancements.

Ink Enabled for Tablet PC

With the release of Service Pack 1.1 of InfoPath, Microsoft has made InfoPath ink-enabled for use on tablet PCs. Microsoft has added additional support for the tablet environment, including special input boxes that appear in which users can write their entries for their InfoPath forms and then convert the information into text. Additional ink controls also are included for displaying images such as pictures and enabling the user to annotate the images. All of these features are included without the need for any additional programming.

Additional Controls

There are a number of new types of controls that were added with the Service Pack 1.1. They fall into a number of different areas, and you will see their value as you use them throughout the rest of the book.

- ❑ **ActiveX Control**: This enables you to utilize standard ActiveX controls that can be used in a number of different applications and languages. This control enables you to use Window's standard controls such as file open dialog boxes, TreeView controls, and more. There are literally hundreds of ActiveX controls available on the market.

- ❑ **Choice Group**: This allows you to replace an option at the time you are filling out a form — for example, if you wanted to replace a person's cell phone with his or her office phone as the contact phone.

- ❑ **File Attachment Control**: Enables you to attach files to a form being filled out.

- ❑ **Master/Detail Control**: Allows you to use data from two different tables, such as a Customer table and Orders, displaying and editing the data easily without any additional programming.

- ❑ **Repeating Recursive Section**: This can be inserted within itself, bound to nested reference fields, and repeats. This is extremely useful when you need to create hierarchical content.

- ❑ **Scrolling Region**: This allows you to scroll through text inside fields.

- ❑ **Vertical Label**: This specifies that text should appear at a 90-degree angle in the form.

Control Enhancements

There are a number of control enhancements that we take for granted in other applications that have been around for a while, such as Microsoft Access. For example, you can now highlight and edit multiple controls and modify their properties all at once.

Data Enhancements

The biggest improvements in the area of data enhancements is probably in the way that InfoPath handles data used as the source for forms. Besides being able to populate list boxes with choices by using secondary data sources, you can now bind controls to those secondary data sources. You can then use these controls to submit data to and query the secondary data source. In InfoPath 1.0, you could not submit data to the secondary data source. Data sources and secondary data sources are discussed in Chapter 4, "Creating an InfoPath Form from an Existing Data Source."

In addition to the data enhancement just mentioned, Windows SharePoint Services support has been greatly increased, and you can now submit forms using an e-mail program by attaching the form.

These are just a few of the enhancements with the Service Pack 1.1. You will be experiencing the features just mentioned and others as you progress through this book. For now, the next section walks you through a condensed set of steps you will take when working with InfoPath forms.

The InfoPath Form Process

When working with InfoPath you can accomplish creating and entering the data in a 2 to 4 step process in some cases. The steps are:

1. **Create the Data Source**: In some cases, the data source will have already been created, so all you have to do is connect to it during the next step.

2. **Design the Form, Using the InfoPath Designer**: This designer is a powerful, yet simple tool that uses a table layout.

3. **Publish the Form**: If you are using the form for your own purposes, you can skip this step altogether.

4. **Fill Out the Form with Data**.

Microsoft has created InfoPath so that it both stores and manipulates data using XML, as specified by the World Wide Consortium (WC3). XML is to data what HTML (Hypertext Markup Language) is to displaying information. This opens up the structure of InfoPath forms, allowing developers to work with the data and forms, and use the data with other business systems when necessary, in a nonproprietary way.

The beauty of working with InfoPath is that you don't have to have a computer science degree in XML to create some very powerful and useful forms. In Figure 1-3, you can see a simplified overview of how InfoPath uses XML to let you enter data. InfoPath puts that that data into your database, in this case Access, where you can then generate reports.

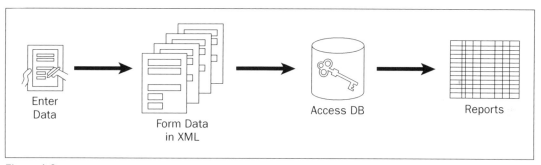

Enter Data

Form Data in XML

Access DB

Reports

Figure 1-3

The InfoPath forms editor does most of the work for you. This doesn't mean that you are limited to what the editor gives you for controlling your form. Like database systems, there are underlying languages that can be used to extend the power of what Microsoft gives you in InfoPath. In InfoPath, you can use script languages, such as Java or VBScript, or if you are using Visual Studio, you can even use C# .NET, Microsoft's newest language.

Ways to Use InfoPath

The various ways to use InfoPath forms is limited only by your imagination, as shown by the number of sample forms included in InfoPath (refer again to Figure 1-2). The following sections outline some of the major uses for InfoPath.

Single User

You can create an InfoPath form that is just used for your own use. This form will be stored on your own computer, be it a desktop, notebook, or tablet PC. You may want to use this to create an expense report for yourself and print it or export the information to Excel.

Published for Others' Use

You can create forms to share with other users. You can place the form on a server, and others can use it as a template for their own data. An example of this is a form that inspectors pull off a network and use for their reports. Using this method of development provides each report with a common look and feel, but allows them to contain autonomous data.

Collaborative Efforts

There are several ways to collaborate in InfoPath forms. The first method is to e-mail a form around the company, which still requires you to have a common share where the users of the form can find the template for the form.

Another method of collaboration is to use a SharePoint Team Service Web site to store common forms, where the user can fill out forms, leaving the filled out forms on the Web site, with lists being generated from the completed forms. There's more detail about using InfoPath forms with SharePoint in Chapter 4.

You can use InfoPath forms with various methods of data storage, depending on your needs. One of those methods is to store them locally, using XML.

Ways to Connect Data to InfoPath

Designing a form with InfoPath is a lot easier than with databases such as Access, because you drag and drop the fields onto the form, and InfoPath creates the underlying form definitions and defaults to whatever type of data the field is. There are three ways that you can connect data to InfoPath.

❏ **Standalone XML**: This has been mentioned before; the data is stored in a separate XML file by itself. The XML file (and schema) can already exist, or be created on the fly at the time the form is being designed. Creating an XML schema is discussed in Chapter 5, "Utilizing XML and Web Service Data Sources."

❏ **Connecting to an Existing Database**: This could be as complicated as SQL Server or Oracle, which are called client/server databases and are used for large-scale data storage. Or, it could be as easy as an Access database, which can even travel with the document. Connecting to an existing database is discussed in Chapter 4.

❏ **Using XML Web Services**: This sounds scarier than it is. An IT department, or you, can create routines that provide access to data over the Internet. When you connect to an XML Web service, the fields will look the same as when you are connecting an existing database or XML file. Creating and connecting to XML Web Services is discussed in detail in Chapter 15, "Creating and and Working with Web Services."

Deployment Requirements for Designing and Filling Out InfoPath Forms

To design or deploy InfoPath forms, each user needs to have InfoPath on their computer. You can post a read-only version of a form on the Web and users can read it without owning a copy of InfoPath.

InfoPath is considered a Microsoft Office application, but it can only be purchased by itself or as part of the Office Professional Enterprise Edition 2003.

When deploying forms for common use, you need to have the templates available on a network share or on a Windows SharePoint Services Web site. Deploying InfoPath forms in the various ways other than SharePoint is discussed in Chapter 10, "Publishing Your Forms." SharePoint and deploying InfoPath forms on a SharePoint site is discussed in great detail in Chapter 17, "Working with InfoPath and SharePoint."

Taking a Look at a Typical InfoPath Form

There are many aspects to an InfoPath form that make it powerful, yet convenient to use. Returning to the first example, in Figure 1-4 you can see the Absence Request form, which is a typical InfoPath form, with some of the features highlighted.

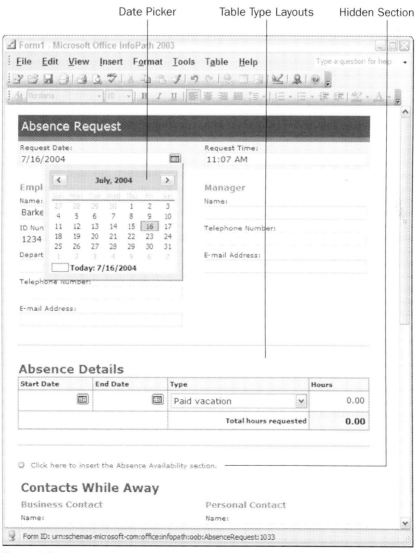

Figure 1-4

In Figure 1-4 you can see a few of the common features of an InfoPath form. These include:

❏   Common colors can be assigned at the view or control level. Note that the summary column is a different shade than the other fields.

❏   Data is laid out using tables. Those tables can range in size from one column to as many as you want. You can also embed tables within tables using drag and drop.

❏   Controls such as the Date picker are automatically placed on a form, based on the type of data you are using.

❏   You can create multiple sections, and those sections can be hidden. When a section is hidden, InfoPath displays a message telling users to click a spot to redisplay the section. Groups can be repeating, based on the type of data you are using. You can see this in Figure 1-5.

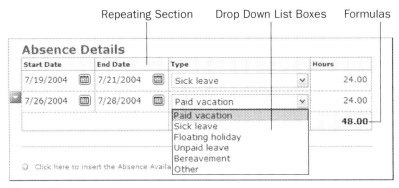

Figure 1-5

❏   Drop-down list boxes enable you to control the data that is going into a field. In Figure 1-5 you are limited to a list of types of absences.

❏   Fields can use formulas to display the summation of data.

❏   Sections can be redisplayed, as shown in Figure 1-6.

Try It Out   Testing the Features of the Absence Request Form

After looking over the bullet points mentioned over the last couple of pages, open the Absence Request form once again, and test the features for yourself:

1.   From the Windows Start menu, choose Microsoft Office | Microsoft Office InfoPath 2003. The Fill Out This Form dialog box will appear.

2.   Select the Absence Request form.

3.   Click on the Fill Out this Form task in the Forms Tasks task pane. The Absence Request form will open, ready to be filled out.

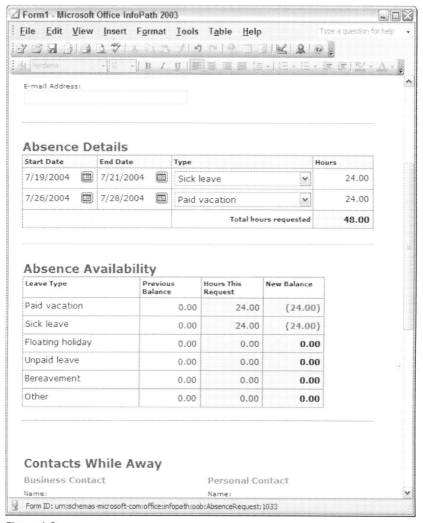

Figure 1-6

4. Click on the date picker control, next to the request date field.

5. Pick a date, and click OK.

6. Fill in some entries for the absence details. As you place the cursor over an entry, a gray down arrow icon appears to the left of the section. Clicking on this arrow gives you the choice of inserting items above or below the current item, or removing the item. You can also choose to cut, copy, or paste data. You can see the menu in Figure 1-7.

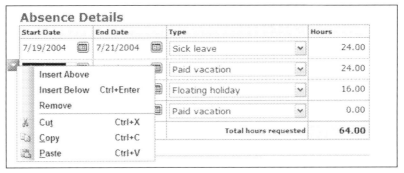

Figure 1-7

Summary

This chapter has introduced you to InfoPath and how to use it. InfoPath is a forms management tool that provides users with a means of creating attractive forms that control how data is entered, while also letting them use their forms for existing or new data. There are a number of very power features in InfoPath, such as the ability to merge data from multiple forms, to provide multiple views in a single form, and to work with data from many sources.

You can base your forms on one of the of sample forms providing with InfoPath out of the box. Or, you can go online and use one of the forms that Microsoft provides on the Web. While the InfoPath editor lets you create forms that accomplish a great deal, you also have the ability to use scripting or code .NET-managed code if needed.

Exercises

1.   What is the main deployment requirement for InfoPath?

2.   What are the two scripting languages supported in InfoPath?

3.   Which .NET language is supported in InfoPath with the Service Pack 1.1 release?

4.   What are the three main ways to use InfoPath?

5.   What are the three ways that data sources are utilized in InfoPath?

6.   Name the two databases to which you can directly connect an InfoPath form.

7.   What are the main steps in the InfoPath form process?

8.   Name two of the controls used on an InfoPath form.

Getting Started Designing with InfoPath

The forms, or form templates, you create with InfoPath are actually XML files. You could create a form by specifying the XML commands in a file if you wanted to, with the extension of .xsn. However, this is cumbersome because you would be editing Extensible Markup Language (XML) in either an XML editor or a text editor. Microsoft realizes that for most business developers and users, who just want to create forms to take care of their business, this is not a practical answer.

In an effort to make life easier for InfoPath developers and users, Microsoft came up with a very robust designer, set up in a very logical manner for the way that you create InfoPath forms. With the designer, you can specify the layout, insert data intelligent controls, assign scripts or code to events related to the form, and much more.

This chapter is all about getting going with the InfoPath Designer. In this chapter you will:

- ❑ Take a tour of the InfoPath Designer.
- ❑ Learn about ways to create InfoPath forms.
- ❑ Discover the tools in the task panes.
- ❑ Work with the Layout task pane.
- ❑ Create your first InfoPath form.

Touring the InfoPath Designer

To examine the InfoPath Designer, a good sample form is necessary to show off the various features available. For this reason, the Absence Request form should be opened in design view. This is a good form that includes various controls and provides a good overview of various designer tools.

When first starting Microsoft InfoPath 2003, the Fill Out a Form dialog box opens. After picking Sample Forms from the Form categories on the left, the Absence Request form is highlighted. One of the tasks in the Form tasks is Design this Form, shown in Figure 2-1.

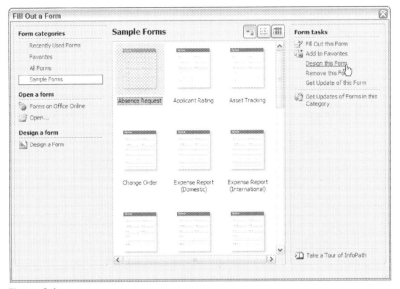

Figure 2-1

After clicking the Design this Form task, the Absence Request form opens in the InfoPath designer, as shown in Figure 2-2.

As can be seen in Figure 2-2, there are three main areas within the form designer:

❑ **Menus and Toolbars**: It contains the standard setup of menus and toolbars, which change depending on the task you are currently performing.

❑ **Main Design Layout**: This is where the design of the form is laid out. Elements are dragged from the various task panes and are laid out in table format.

❑ **Task Panes**: These tasks panes will display different tasks when various categories are chosen. The various categories are described in the next section.

> The last option displayed in the Task Panes panel, Publish Forms. . ., is not a task pane unto itself, but a task. If you click it, the Publishing Wizard will open. This wizard will be covered in Chapter 10, "Publishing InfoPath Forms."

Menus and Toolbars   Main Design Layout   Task Panes

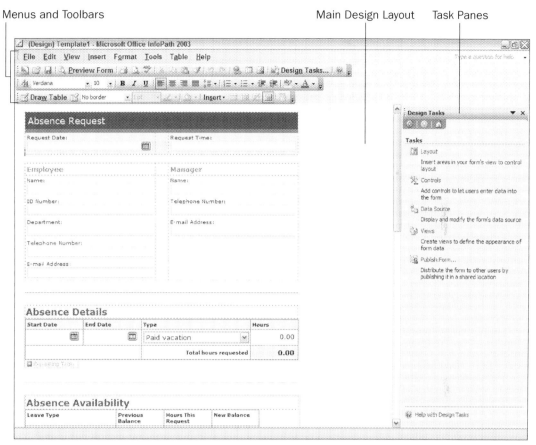

Figure 2-2

Overview of the Task Panes

In Microsoft Office applications, such as Word and Excel, you are using task panes when you choose to open or create new documents. InfoPath takes things a step further by displaying a task pane constantly when designing forms using the various categories of tasks.

Layout Task Pane

The Layout task pane contains tasks that help build the base structure of the form. The various layout tasks mainly have to do with specifying table layouts with different numbers of columns, as shown in Figure 2-3.

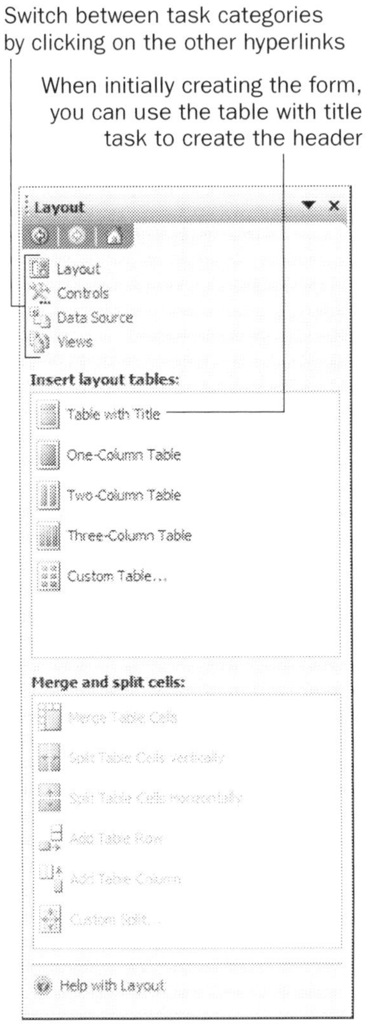
Switch between task categories by clicking on the other hyperlinks
When initially creating the form, you can use the table with title task to create the header
Layout
Layout
Controls
Data Source
Views
Insert layout tables:
Table with Title
One-Column Table
Two-Column Table
Three-Column Table
Custom Table...
Merge and split cells:
Help with Layout

Figure 2-3

Control Task Pane

The Control task category will be used to insert the various controls that you can use on your forms. Controls are used to control or insert data into your forms. While some controls are automatically inserted into the form when you choose your fields from data sources, there will be times when you will want to add special controls to your form. Some of these controls can be seen on the Control task pane in Figure 2-4.

In addition to the two control categories displayed in Figure 2-4, Standard controls and Repeating and Optional (sections), there are two other categories: File and Picture controls and Advanced controls.

You will see more on the various controls and how to use them in Chapter 6, "Working with Controls in General."

You can add custom activex controls
to accomplish additional tasks

When checked, as you drag a
control onto the form, a data
field is added to the data source

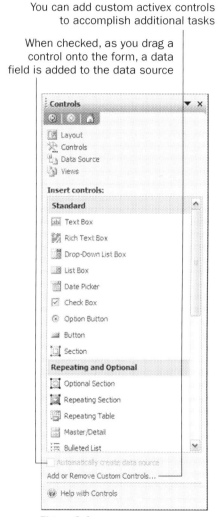

Figure 2-4

Data Source Task Pane

The Data Source task pane is where you specify and work with the data sources you will use as the base for your form. You can see the data source, in this case an XML schema (data structure), displayed in Figure 2-5. If you are adding a data source, or specifying one for the form such as a database, you will use the Data Connections command on the Tools menu.

You will learn about databases and XML in the next two chapters.

Clicking the add button enables you
to add new data fields to your structures

When checked, details
about each field will be
displayed such as data type

Figure 2-5

Views Task Pane

The Views task pane manages the various views you have in your forms. As mentioned in Chapter 1, a form can have multiple views where you are organizing your data. You can also have views to query data and others to manage the data. Figure 2-6 displays the single view choice in the Absence Request form.

Views will be discussed in great detail in Chapter 9, "Managing Views."

Note that if you want to get back to the original choice of task panes displayed in Figure 2-2, you can do so by clicking the Design Tasks toolbar button, located on the far right of the toolbar.

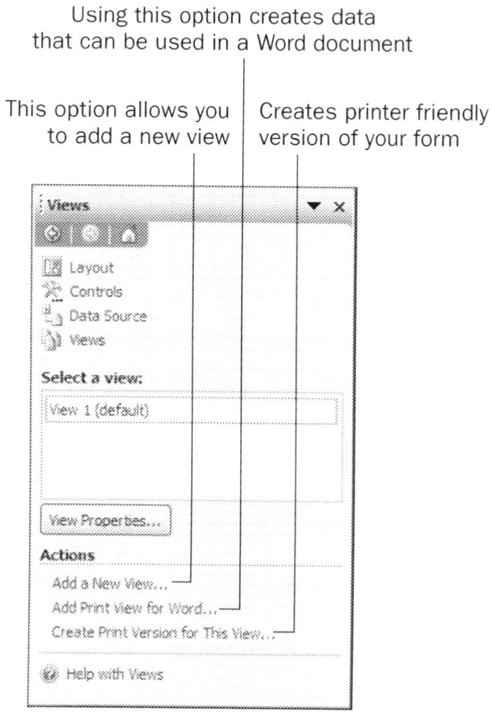
Using this option creates data that can be used in a Word document
This option allows you to add a new view
Creates printer friendly version of your form
Views
Layout
Controls
Data Source
Views
Select a view:
View 1 (default)
View Properties...
Actions
Add a New View...
Add Print View for Word...
Create Print Version for This View...
Help with Views

Figure 2-6

Creating Your First InfoPath Form

In the prior sections in this chapter you were introduced to the various task panes and the tasks contained within each pane. Now it is time to get to work and perform some of those tasks. In the next sections, you will create a new form, adding a few tables and controls by dragging and dropping them from the various areas on the Layout and Controls task panes. To create this form, the top section of the Absence Request form will be replicated, shown in Figure 2-7.

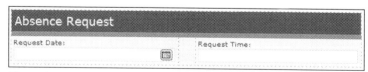

Absence Request
Request Date:
Request Time:

Figure 2-7

Try It Out Creating a New InfoPath Form

1. Open InfoPath by choosing All Programs ➪ Microsoft Office ➪ Microsoft InfoPath 2003 from the Start menu. The Fill Out a Form dialog box is opened.

2. Click on the Design a Form task. You will then see the Design a Form task pane with a blank design layout. The Design a Form task pane can be seen in Figure 2-8.

Figure 2-8

3. Click on the New Blank Form task. The designer now displays a blank form, with the Design task panes open.

How It Works

When a form is created using the InfoPath editor, you visually see what you are putting on the form, such as tables and controls. Under the covers InfoPath is creating a number of XML documents. To see the actual documents, you can choose File ⇨ Extract Form Files. InfoPath then displays a dialog box asking where you want to put the files. After you browse for the folder and click OK, InfoPath stores the files described in the following table:

File Extension	Description
manifest.xsf	The manifest file ties all the other files together, you will see all the other files listed in this file at one point or another.
myschema.xsd	This file defines the data schema (structure) as you add controls to your form. Used with myschema.xsx.
myschema.xsx	Holds information about the schema for the designer surface.
sampledata.xml	Stores any sample data that may be used in a form.
template.xml	XML file contains information about overall forms data sources, if created.
view1.xsl	Contains information about individual view.

Don't use the File ↔ Extract unless you are very comfortable with XML. Even then, there is a good chance that you could break a form if you tweak it under the covers incorrectly. Be careful!

Exploring the Ways of Designing a New Form

Taking a closer look at the list of tasks under the heading Design a new form in Figure 2-8, you can see that there are a number of ways to accomplish creating a new form, depending on your needs. While you will be using the various ways throughout the rest of the book, here are the ways listed with descriptions of their purpose:

❑ **New from XML Document or Schema**: XML Documents are files that contain data and describe that data in a specific format. When you get an XML document from a source, InfoPath will read it and use it as a data source, so you can add the data fields to your new form. More on using XML documents can be found in Chapter 5, "Utilizing XML and Web Service Data Sources."

❑ **New from Data Connection**: Frequently the data you want to work with already exists in a database of some kind, such as Access or SQL Server. This option enables you to connect to the databases just mentioned, as well as to Web services.

Web services, also called XML Web services, work as a shell around a database, limiting views and access to the data and giving access to those databases over the Internet or intranet. Where InfoPath can only connect directly to Access or SQL Server, you can use a Web service to work with other types of databases such as Oracle. You will read about databases in general in Chapter 3, "Understanding Data," and Web services are discussed in Chapter 15, "Creating and Working with Web Services."

❑ **New Blank Form**: The option you currently are using, this form creates a blank form that has no data connected whatsoever. You can create an XML schema or connect to data once you have started a form using this method of creating a new form.

❑ **Customize a Sample:** This is a great option when you know that one of the samples included in InfoPath is very close to the form you want to create. When you choose this option, a new template is created based on one of the samples.

> Remember also that there are additonal templates at Office Online. If you want to look at these templates, click the Customize a Sample task, and then click on the button labeled Form Templates at Office Online in the Custom a Sample dialog box.

❑ **Import a Form**: If somebody you know has created a form that is what you need or even a similar one, you can import that form with this option and modify it as needed.

Now that you know the various ways that you can create forms, you're going to continue with creating your first form, which you started using the New Blank Form task. It is time to add some new tables, so let's get busy.

Working with Tables

As mentioned previously, tables play a big role when designing InfoPath forms. Controls are placed within tables as are other tables to organize the layout of the form. For convenience, there are a number of different table layouts that you can drag and drop onto the designer layout area. To create the heading portion of the form displayed in Figure 2-8, two table layouts are used: Table with Title and Three-Column Table.

Adding a Table

Adding a table to your form is fairly straightforward. When you want to add a table, you place the cursor in the area you want the table to appear, and then choose from the list of table layouts in the Insert layout tables tasks.

To insert a table into another table, place the cursor in the cell of the table where you want the second table to appear. Next, under the Insert layout tables tasks, click the table with the number of columns you want to use, or click Custom Table . . . to specify the number of columns and rows you want in the new table yourself.

Try It Out   **Adding the Tables**

1. Continuing with the form you created in the last Try It Out, click on the Layout design task. The Layout task pane is displayed.

2. With the cursor located at the top of the blank form, click the Table with Title task in the Layout task pane. The table is then displayed in the top of the layout area of the form designer, as shown in Figure 2-9.

    > Note that Figure 2-9 has the title (Design) Template2 at the top of the form. This may differ from yours, depending on if this is your first form or if you have been experimenting and creating your own forms.

3. Click in the area labeled Click to add a title, and type in **Absence Request**.

4. Place the cursor in the area of the table labeled Click to add form content.

5. Click Three-Column Table in the Insert layout tables tasks. You now see three columns displaying Click to add form content, shown in Figure 2-10.

How It Works

That's all there is to it. As you add the tables, they show up in the location where you place the cursor. You can then size the columns and rows as you see fit. The nice thing is that you can embed as many tables as you need to. However, don't add unnecessary tables. This will just clutter your forms.

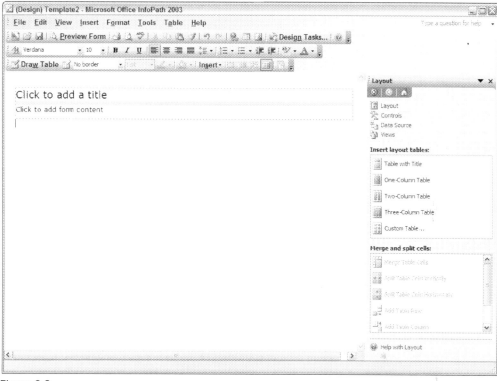

Figure 2-9

Figure 2-10

Resizing Table Columns and Rows

Before adding controls to your form, it is a good idea to resize the table, columns, and rows to the sizes you ultimately want them to be. While you can resize all three with controls in them, that just makes it a bit more cumbersome. To resize the columns and rows, as well as the borders of tables, you will move the cursor over the frame you want to resize, and the cursor will change into crosshairs with arrows pointing up and down.

Press and hold the left mouse button, and then drag the cursor in the direction you want to resize. When the particular edge is where it is supposed to be, release the left mouse button. This works the same way that resizing objects such as Word tables or Excel cells works in other Office applications.

Try It Out   **Resizing Elements**

1. Place the cursor over each of the inside column edges, pressing the mouse button when the cursor changes.

2. Drag the edge in the direction in which you need it to go. Then release the mouse button.

3. Repeat Steps 1 and 2 for the bottom edge of the 3-column table. You can see what this step will look like in Figure 2-11.

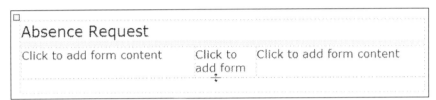

Figure 2-11

The table will now be resized to the desired dimensions.

> The text "Click to add form content" in the individual cells of the table will disappear as soon as you place (click) the cursor inside the individual cell. So, if your screen doesn't have this text, you probably accidentally clicked in the cell or cells. Also, don't panic if you have clicked in the cell, removing the text, and afterwards chose Edit ➪ Undo with no effect. Once you have clicked in the cells, the text will not return regardless of what you do. It will not affect your final form, because the text is not displayed in any case.

Setting Fonts and Adding Text to the Form

With many applications, such as Access, when you want to add text to your forms, you do so by adding controls called *labels*. With InfoPath you just type the text where you want it, first setting the font and size of the text from the Format toolbar, located at the top of the form, as displayed Figure 2-12.

Figure 2-12

Once you have set the font, font size, and any other attributes such as underline, color, and so on that you want to use, type the text to be displayed. This is how you add the label information about the controls you are adding to the form.

Try It Out   **Setting Font Information and Adding Text**

1. Place the control in the cell of the table you want to place the control in. In this case, it will be the first column of the three-column table you added.

2. Click on the font you want to use — in this case Verdana font, size 8.

3. Type **Request Date:**

4. Press the Tab key twice to jump over to the third column.

5. Once again set the font to Verdana and size to 8.

6. Type **Request Time:** Your form should now look like Figure 2-13.

```
Absence Request

Request Date:                    Request Time:
```

Figure 2-13

Seeing how to add text to the form is a big step in creating forms. With literal text you can create not only labels for individual controls, but also section headings and form instructions. However, forms are not much good with just a bunch of literal text on them; you need to have a way to accept data as well as display text. To accept data you need to add controls.

Adding Controls to the Form

Adding controls really isn't any different from adding tables. Once you have placed the cursor in the cell where you want the control to be inserted, choose the control you want from the list in the Controls lists. You can also drag and drop the control into the location you want it to be on the form. Just click on the control, and holding down the left mouse button, drag the control where you want it and release the button. The control is displayed in the location where you placed it.

While a number of the controls will be displayed and be set up as needed just by dropping them onto a form, some controls will need to be adjusted by setting either their width, height, or other necessary properties. Which properties need to be set will depend on the control.

You can also resize controls using the same steps you used to resize table columns and rows. Place the cursor on the edge of the control, and when you see the double arrow cursor, hold down the left mouse button and drag the cursor (and edge of the control) in the direction you want to resize. Note that one difference is the look of the cursor. The control resize cursor is simply two double arrows, versus two double arrows with a bar in between them, which is used with table resizing.

> If you are resizing a table to be smaller than the control or controls contained within, you need to resize the control (or controls) first. Otherwise, the control will be larger than the table cell that contains it, and the controls won't act correctly.

To move a control, or a table for that matter, move the cursor over the top left corner of the table or control, and when you get the four arrows, hold down the left mouse button and drag the object where you want it.

Adding Controls

1. Place the cursor in the cell of the table where you want to add the control. In this case it will be the first column of the 3-column table you added, under the text reading "Request Date:".

2. Click on the Controls task list.

3. Click on the Date Picker.

4. Using the same steps outlined for resizing table elements, resize the Date Picker control you just added to the form.

5. Repeat steps 1 through 4 and add a Textbox control under the test "Request Time:". When completed the form looks as displayed here in Figure 2-14.

Figure 2-14

When laying out controls this way, the data is not going to be added into a database because you are not binding the controls. Data binding of controls will be discussed in Chapter 4, "Creating an InfoPath Form from an Existing Data Source." An XML document is being created, although specific field names are not being used.

Setting a Color Scheme

The form is looking good as far as replacing the Absence Request form heading. One last thing remains: to change the color scheme to match the colors on the original form. Changing colors is actually easier than it sounds. While you can set the background color for a view, and the individual colors for text and controls, it is a lot easier to set all the necessary colors using a color scheme.

Set the Color Scheme

1. With the cursor anywhere in the form, choose Format ⇨ Color Schemes. You then see the color scheme chart shown in Figure 2-15.

2. To match the color scheme used in the Absence Request form, click on the Blue color scheme.

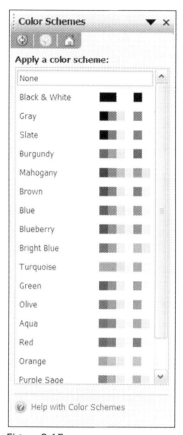

Figure 2-15

There you have it. The form will now match the Absence Request form.

Summary

After reading this chapter you have seen various aspects of the InfoPath designer. Microsoft created the designer to make InfoPath developers' and users' lives easier when trying to create InfoPath forms.

Using the InfoPath designer you are able to control the layout using tables of various sizes (rows and columns) based on your needs. The designer supplies a set of task panes to handle the different tasks and objects you need to add to your forms such as tables, text, and controls.

You can also apply a color scheme to your form, so that you don't have to set the individual colors.

Exercises

1. What are InfoPath forms made up of?

2. Name the four main task panes that you use in the InfoPath Designer.

3. What is the fifth choice that appears when you are on the main Design a Task pane?

4. What is the first step when adding an object, when you are just clicking on the the control (or table) to add it to a form?

5. What is the other way to add an object to a form, other than the one just mentioned in the last exercise?

Understanding Data

Getting to know the InfoPath Designer is very important if you're going to get the most benefit from the program. Getting to know and understand data is just as important. One of the main obstacles occurs when the data is not set up correctly, or logically.

A lot of users, and developers for that matter, treat the data side of forms management as they would Excel spreadsheets or Word documents. This is not said as a slam against either the products or the people. It is just truth. The reason for this dilemma is that people don't know any better. Users feel they don't have the time or capacity to learn the ins and outs of databases, and some developers feel they already know it enough.

This chapter covers data — primarily data used in databases. While you can use data without managing whole databases, having a good understanding of what databases, or in this case relational databases, are and how to work with them will help you create forms that are more logical, powerful, and easy to work with. In this chapter you will

- ❏   Be given a quick database primer.
- ❏   Read about the databases to which InfoPath connects.
- ❏   Be given an overview on XML.
- ❏   Be introduced to Web services.

A Quick Database Primer

As you work with computers, you quickly realize that everything you do on a computer deals with data in one sense or another. Whether you are creating a Word document or crunching numbers with Excel, it is all data. However, not all data belongs in a database, and not all programs are meant to be used as databases, although if you look at some people's documents and worksheets, you may wonder if they are trying to use them as databases. This section explains a few things about databases and shows how you use real-world databases everyday.

If you have been using Microsoft Office products for a while, you have probably had some experience with or at least heard of databases. In fact, even if you haven't used databases on the computer, you have used them in real life.

Databases in the Real World

In the real world there are a never ending number of tasks and subjects that work as an example of databases. Every day from the time you get up until the time you go to bed, you are dealing with databases of one kind or another. Here are just a few examples of real-world data:

- ❑ Mailing lists
- ❑ School registrations
- ❑ Checking account information and history
- ❑ Membership lists
- ❑ Customer information

And the list goes on and on. While some of these items look like simple topics in themselves, undoubtedly each topic could be fleshed out with additional data so that more than one topic, (what are called *tables* in database jargon) would be necessary.

The last entry in the preceding list is a common example of a real-world database and is worth discussing further. Customer information is stored as business records in manila folders, usually located in a filing cabinet. In the manila folders customer information is stored, with either:

- ❑ One customer's information stored in each folder
- ❑ All customer information sheets in one folder

Electronic databases can be analogous to either of these methods, which have been used for years in the real world.

In accessing the real-world customer database, you:

1. Open the file cabinet
2. Search through the cabinet for the folder you are looking for
3. Pull out the folder
4. Look through the folder for the information for which you are searching
5. Take the piece, or pieces of paper, containing the information
6. Read the data on the page
7. Modify the data as necessary

At this point, you also could also add new information by filling out a new form or delete information by throwing away information. Of course, nowadays you would most likely shred the information for security reasons.

It should be noted that the following terms are generic as far as the various database systems are concerned. These terms will be discussed in greater details in the next section.

Tables are used to store data in databases. Fields (columns) are used to store individual pieces of data such as customer name, address, and so on. The information supplied in all the fields makes up a record (row) in the table. So in this instance, all customer information such as name, address, city, state, and so on makes up a record (row). These terms are used interchangeably when discussing various database products such as Microsoft Access (fields, records) and Microsoft SQL Server (columns, rows).

Database Models

Various models of databases exist, two of which are flat file and relational databases. Nowadays, the relational model of databases is the most commonly used model for desktop and Web development. However, before going deeper into the relational database model, you'll read about the flat file model, including how these databases store data and their drawbacks.

Flat File Model Databases

Flat file model databases store information in single tables, including repeated data. For example, if a store were selling different kinds of coffee and wanted to track customers, invoices, invoice items, and suppliers, it would organize information as shown in Figure 3-1, which is a flat file style table.

Customer	Invoice Date	Invoice #	Product1	ProductSupplier1	Product1Cost	Product2	ProductSupplier2	Product2Cost
John Smith	9/1/2004	3443	French Roast	Starbucks Coffee	$10.95	House Blend	Starbucks Coffee	$11.95
Sally Jones	9/1/2004	3445	Sumatra	Starbucks Coffee	$11.95	French Roast	Starbucks Coffee	$12.95
Harry James	9/1/2004	3445	Columbia	Seattles Best Coffee	$12.95	Columbia	Seattles Best Coffee	$12.95

Figure 3-1

If you look at this figure closely, you may notice that it looks as if it was created in Excel, which it was. A lot of developers and users store data in Excel spreadsheets, thereby creating flat file tables and databases without realizing it.

There are a number of problems with the flat file database model. Here are just a few of the issues:

❏ **Redundant Data**: Often Entries are repeated, taking up more space than necessary. In Figure 3-2, there is no reason to spell out the names each time, taking up more space.

❏ **Error Prone**: When data has to be repeated, there is more of a chance of entering erroneous data into the table.

❏ **Limited Columns**: Currently, only two products and their information can be entered using the table structure displayed.

❏ **Extra Work to Update**: With the redundant data issue, if you want to make any updates, you will have to make sure that you parse through the other fields and update those values to match.

In addition to these issues, reporting on the data can be problematic. Now take a look at the relational database model.

Relational Database Model

Unlike the flat file database model, which stores all data, including related data, in a single record and table, the relational database model uses tables that are related to each other to store information. For example, instead of having your coffee invoices all stored in a single table called tblCoffeeInvoices, the information would be stored in related tables with customer information being stored in one table, invoice information being stored in another, product information in yet another, and so on. Figure 3-2 shows an example of how the flat file table in the previous section could be restructured into a relational model.

Figure 3-2

This figure was taken from Microsoft Access and is a shot of the tables in a database called Coffee.mdb, located in the Chapter 3 folder. The figure shows the structure with the data from the single table separated out into multiple tables. The process of normalizing a database is discussed later in the chapter, in the section titled "Normalizing Your Data."

Take a look at some of the benefits of using relational databases. They are pretty much the opposite of the issues found in flat file databases:

❑ **Nonredundant Data**: Because entries are entered once, and other tables point to the data, there is less redundant data.

❑ **Less Error Prone**: When data is entered once in lookup tables, data is then picked from lists; this process can be controlled and is less prone to error.

❑ **Unlimited Data**: Because data is stored in records (down the table) as opposed to fields (across the table), the data is not limited to predefined structures. For example, when you want add another product to an invoice, you simply add another record to tblInvoiceDetails, where before in the flat file you would have had to add a third or fourth product column.

It may look like a lot more work to maintain a relational database when you look at Figure 3-3 because of the multiple tables, but you very quickly learn to appreciate the benefits of the relational database despite the extra work needed in the beginning. Next, you'll read about the elements that make up relational databases.

Tables: Where Data is Stored

As mentioned in a note earlier in the chapter, tables are where your data is stored. Tables have specific component: fields, primary keys, and indexes.

Fields

When created, table structures consist of fields that represent pieces of data. Fields have properties that give you control over the data that goes into them. Here are a few of those properties common to different database systems such as Access and SQL Server:

❑ **Name**: Field names are what you will refer to when you want to pull information from the field or assign data to the field. You will want to assign names that are easy to understand. For example, in the tblCustomer table the two fields displayed in Figure 3-3 these would be CustomerID and CustomerName.

❑ **Data Types**: Data types tell the database system how to handle the data placed in the field. Which types of data types there are will depend on the specific database system. Microsoft Access calls text data under 255 characters the Text datatype; in SQL Server this would be nvarchar(255).

❑ **Other Properties**: There are a number of other properties that help control data going into the fields, and those properties will again depend on which database system you are using. Some properties, such as Default Value, are used by most systems, but then some, such as the Caption property, are used by Access but not SQL Server.

You can see an example of the table structure for tblCustomers listed in Figure 3-3 with the Customer field highlighted. The table structure is displayed in Microsoft Access.

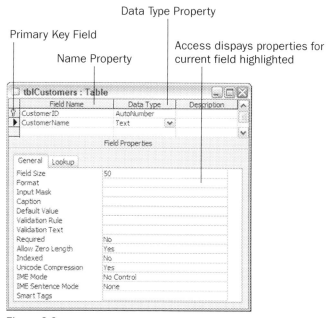

Figure 3-3

Primary and Foreign Key Fields

Notice the callout for the Primary Key field in Figure 3-4. Each table should have a primary key. In the case of tblCustomers, the primary key is the field CustomerID. The primary key makes sure that each record in a table is unique, and it provides the ability to always find a specific record. How primary keys are specified will again depend on the database system you are using.

Foreign key fields are fields in a table that point to primary key fields in other tables. For example, you will see CustomerID in tblInvoice, which is used to match the primary key field CustomerID in tblCustomers. Primary and foreign key fields are especially important in the use of relations.

It's All about Relations

Relationships are how you tie (relate) data together using separate tables. Figure 3-4 is a repeat of 3-2 because it actually shows the relationships window in Access, displaying the relationships for `Coffee.mdb`.

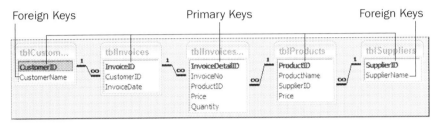

Figure 3-4

There are three types of relationships found in relational databases. Because `coffee.mdb` mainly uses one type of relationship, other examples are listed outside that database:

❑ **One-to-One Relationship**: Used when you want to have records in one table match up with individual records in another table based on the same primary key in each table. An example of this in a banking database is a table that stores private information that would match up directly with a table that stores information that can be viewed by anyone. This is probably the least used type of relationship, because the use of queries (Access) and views (SQL Server) can limit the data you can access in tables.

❑ **One-to-Many Relationship**: This type of relation is used to relate a table such as tblCustomer (a customer) with one such as tblInvoices (the customer's invoices). The way you look at it is that one customer can have many invoices. Note that the primary key is in tblCustomer, and the foreign key in tblInvoices.

❑ **Many-to-Many Relationship**: This is a pair of one-to-many relationships used with three tables. An example of this could be used in an insurance database. Insurance companies can have multiple customers, and customers can have multiple insurance companies.

Which type of relationship you use will depend on the need being met. You can use all three in the same database or just use one type of relationship throughout the database. It really comes down to the data.

Referential Integrity

One of the important aspects of relational databases is maintaining the referential integrity of the data. An example of maintaining referential integrity in the coffee database is that a record in the tblInvoices table can't be created without a related record existing in tblCustomers. Another example would be that a record in the tblProducts table could not be added if a record were already in the tblSuppliers table.

Depending on the database system, you can set referential integrity up to also help maintain data once it is in the database. For example, you can specify that a record can't be deleted in one table, such as tblCustomers, if there are records in tblInvoices related to it.

Another use for referential integrity with current data is to have records deleted in related tables, such as tblInvoices, when a record is deleted in the table that contains the primary key, in this case, tblCustomers.

Normalizing Your Data

Normalizing data is the steps taken to take non-normalized data (a flat file) and shape it into what is called *normal* (relational) form. Refer again to Figure 3-1.

Here are the steps and the tasks you take for each step:

First normal form (1NF):

1. Remove duplicate columns from the table.
2. Create separate tables for each group of related data, identifying each row with a unique column or set of columns. This unique column or set of columns would be the primary key.

In the case of the table displayed in Figure 3-1, the Product1, Product2, and product-specific information is removed from the main table and broken out into separate rows.

Second normal form (2NF):

1. Remove subsets of data that apply to multiple rows of a table and place them in separate tables.
2. Create relationships between these new tables and their predecessors through the use of foreign keys.

In this case, you would remove the customer information and store it into a separate table, then create a relationship between the new customer table and the table containing the invoice information.

Third normal form (3NF):

❏ Remove columns not dependent upon the primary key.

Invoice detail is broken out into separate tables at this point and each item is given its own ID, with a foreign key pointing to the invoice header record. At this point, the tables and relations would look as shown in Figure 3-5.

Fourth normal form (4NF):

❏ A relation is in 4NF if it has no multivalued dependencies.

There are additional forms possible, depending on how far you want to take the normalization. The majority of databases are in used in third or fourth normal form.

Working with Various Databases

You've read about flat file and relational databases and now know the differences. There is some additional information you need to know about the available relational databases and their platforms. Before talking about Microsoft Access and SQL Server specifically, there is some terminology you need to get comfortable with.

File Server versus Client Server

File server databases are those where the database is stored in a folder on a file server. When you access the database, all the data is brought over the network and locally processed. Microsoft Access is a file-server-based database system.

Client/server databases are stored on a server, but when it comes time to process the data, the processing is performed on the server, and just the necessary data is brought over the network. Microsoft SQL Server is a client/server product.

With most development environments, how you develop against the two types of database platforms will vary. With InfoPath, you use the same methods for both platforms.

Front and Backends

When working with database applications, you have front- and backends. The database containing the data is the *backend*. The application created to control the input and output of the data is called the *frontend*. The application contains forms, reports, and other programming elements. When connecting to a database, the data source, such as Microsoft Access or SQL Server, is the backend and the InfoPath form is the frontend.

The next sections describe the two databases that Microsoft InfoPath connects to directly: Microsoft Access and Microsoft SQL Server.

Microsoft Access

Perfect for small to medium-sized solutions when used as a backend, Microsoft Access is a popular database system with thousands, if not millions, of installations. Access can also be used as a frontend, but that is a topic for another book. You can see Access with the `Coffee.mdb` open with tblCustomers displayed in Figure 3-5.

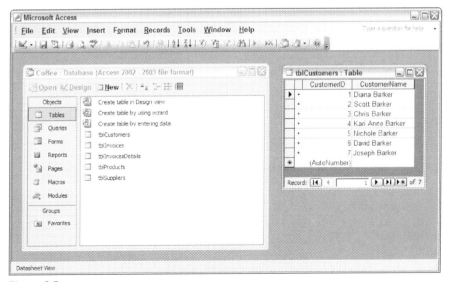

Figure 3-5

Benefits and Issues of Microsoft Access

There are quite a few benefits to using Access as opposed to other database products. Some of the positive aspects of Access are:

❑ **Established Application**: Access has been around for quite a few versions, with Microsoft enhancing the product with each version. The current version is Microsoft Access 2003.

❑ **Powerful Report Writer**: It includes a banded report writer, with bands set up for Report Headers/Footers, Group Headers/Footers, Page Headers/Footers, and Detail. You can embed reports within reports. The Access report writer is commonly used by other products, including Visual Basic and SQL Server, to create reports.

❑ **Can Be Used as a Frontend and/or Backend**: It is almost as common to find Access used as a frontend for a SQL Server database as it is to see it used strictly with Access. It can be used with SQL Server by linking tables in a ＊.mdb or by using an Access ＊.adp, which is a database project specifically set up to be a frontend for a SQL Server database.

❑ **Macro Language for Beginners and VBA for Developers**: Access provides a powerful forms package with the Visual Basic for Applications (VBA) development language behind it, or a macro-type language.

❑ **Easy-to-Transfer Database Files**: Just by using Windows copy and paste, you can move or copy Access databases locally over a network, or you can even store the database in a compressed folder and e-mail the folder.

There are some issues that can arise when using Access for your databases:

❑ **Large Databases Bog Down**: You can run into problems with large databases, if those databases are not carefully created.

❑ **Large Number of Users Bog Down the System**: You need to be very careful when creating an application for a large number of users, as the application can bog down when users are querying and updating data. This is especially true with large databases, as mentioned in the previous bullet.

❑ **Form Designer Can Be Confusing to Use**: As powerful as they both are, the form and report designers in Access can be confusing to use when moving beyond the basics.

❑ **Not Built for Use with the Internet:** Because Access is a file server product and not meant for the truly high volume you get when using database over the Internet, Access is made more for use on a local area network (LAN).

Access works very well with InfoPath as a backend when you have a limited number of people accessing the data. Access is also a great database to prototype applications in, for later use in another development language such as Visual Basic with the data moved to SQL Server. You also can use the Access database from other products without having to have a version of Access installed, which makes Access even more worthwhile to use with InfoPath.

Microsoft Access Objects Used with InfoPath

With InfoPath, you will be using the following objects in Access:

❑ **Tables**: Used to store data

❑ **Queries**: Used to recombine data using Select statements; also provide a means of adding, updating, and deleting data from tables

Microsoft SQL Server

Built for small to enterprise-wide databases, SQL Server is designed for use with other development products and includes no form management tools of its own.

You can see SQL Server's Enterprise Manager with the CoffeeSQL database open in Figure 3-6.

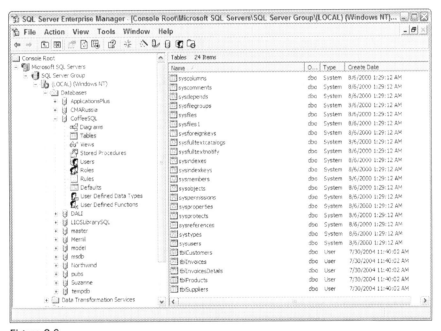

Figure 3-6

Benefits and Issues of Microsoft SQL Server

As with Microsoft Access, there are a number of benefits to using Microsoft SQL Server. Some of those benefits are:

❑ **Established Application**: As with Access, SQL Server has been around for quite a few versions. At the time of the printing of this book, SQL Server 2000 is the current version.

❑ **Robust Set of Client Tools for Data Management**: Headed by Enterprise Manager and Query Analyzer, SQL Server has a number of tools that help you to manage data in your databases.

❑ **Extensive SQL Language for Data Manipulation**: Using Transact SQL you can create stored procedures that can manipulate data in just about any way necessary. Also available is Data Transformation Services (DTS), which enables you to create packages to schedule tasks for working with the information in your database.

❑ **Large Amounts of Data Can Be Handled**: SQL Server is made for large amounts of data. On a server that has been properly set up, you can store many gigabytes of data. In addition to residing on the proper system, the data needs to be normalized and care taken when creating views and stored procedures.

❑ **Works Well with the Internet**: Because SQL Server works well with large databases and a large number of users, it works well as a database for use with the Internet. Of course, you do need to be conscientious when creating the database.

There are some issues that can arise when using SQL Server for your databases:

❑ **Tools Are Not End-User-Friendly**: Where Access's tools are built for end-user use, SQL Server's tools are made for use by system administrators. So while the tools are powerful, they are not very friendly.

❑ **No Form Management Tool**: You will have to use other products as frontends to SQL Server databases, because it doesn't have any type of forms management. There is not a reports management tool available.

❑ **Not Convenient for Transferring Databases**: While it can be done, you need to use the tools available for the system administrators for detaching/attaching databases to SQL Server, or use code. You also can back up and restore databases, again using a tool or code. Once these procedures are done, you can then copy and paste the files using Windows commands.

SQL Server works well using InfoPath for the frontend, and is easy to connect to databases for data sources.

Microsoft SQL Server Objects Used with InfoPath

When using SQL Server as a backend to InfoPath, you will be using the following objects in Microsoft SQL Server:

❑ **Tables**: Used to store data. You can see the tblCustomers table displayed using the SQL Server Enterprise Manager in Figure 3-7.

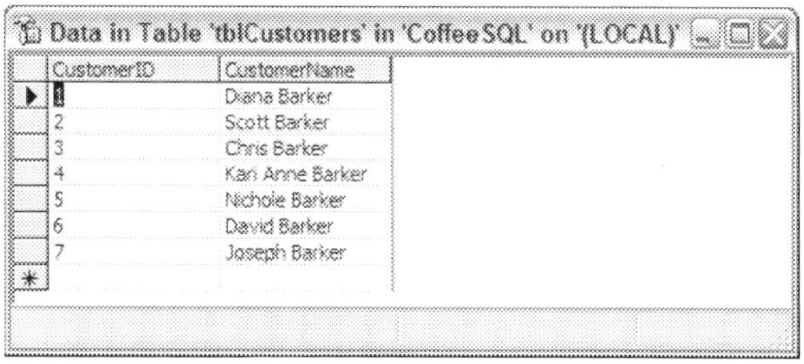

Figure 3-7

❑ **Views**: Used to recombine data using Select statements, views allow you to display data as needed in various ways.

❑ **Stored Procedures and Functions**: Provide means for adding, updating, and deleting data from tables.

There is a version of Microsoft SQL Server called the MSDE, which stands for Microsoft SQL Server Desktop Edition. This version of SQL Server comes with various products such as Visual Studio .NET, and can be redistributed for use with systems that don't have the full version of SQL Server installed.

Other Databases

When developing InfoPath forms and wanting to work with other databases such as Oracle, Informix, and others, you have to use Web services to connect to them. You can read a brief introduction on Web services in the section called "Introduction to Web Services," found later in this chapter. Developing Web services is discussed in Chapter 15, "Creating and Working with Web Services."

Looking Briefly at XML

One of the exciting things about InfoPath is that under the covers it all comes down to XML (Extensible Markup Language). As mentioned, XML has fast become the de facto standard for transferring and storing data on and off the Web, as well as between various business systems. XML itself is not a terribly confusing file structure, because it is just a bunch of tags.

To quickly examine XML, take a look at a small example called `Customers.XML`, shown here:

```xml
<?xml version="1.0" encoding="UTF-8"?>
<dataroot xmlns:od="urn:schemas-microsoft-com:officedata"
xmlns:xsi="http://www.w3.org/2001/XMLSchema-instance"
xsi:noNamespaceSchemaLocation="Customers.xsd" generated="2004-07-30T12:11:47">
<tblCustomers>
<CustomerID>1</CustomerID>
<CustomerName>Diana Barker</CustomerName>
</tblCustomers>
<tblCustomers>
<CustomerID>2</CustomerID>
<CustomerName>Scott Barker</CustomerName>
</tblCustomers>
<tblCustomers>
<CustomerID>3</CustomerID>
<CustomerName>Chris Barker</CustomerName>
</tblCustomers>
<tblCustomers>
<CustomerID>4</CustomerID>
<CustomerName>Kari Anne Barker</CustomerName>
</tblCustomers>
<tblCustomers>
<CustomerID>5</CustomerID>
<CustomerName>Nichole Barker</CustomerName>
</tblCustomers>
<tblCustomers>
<CustomerID>6</CustomerID>
<CustomerName>David Barker</CustomerName>
</tblCustomers>
<tblCustomers>
<CustomerID>7</CustomerID>
```

```
<CustomerName>Joseph Barker</CustomerName>
</tblCustomers>
</dataroot>
```

You may have heard of a language used for Web page design called HTML (Hypertext Markup Language). HTML is a language that uses tags to specify how to create a presentation in a Web browser. XML uses tags to specify how to work with data.

You can see from the XML file just displayed that it refers to another file called `Customers.xsd`. `.xsd` files are called schema files and hold information about fields such as the type of data they are.

```
<?xml version="1.0" encoding="UTF-8"?>
<xsd:schema xmlns:xsd="http://www.w3.org/2001/XMLSchema" xmlns:od="urn:schemas-
microsoft-com:officedata">
<xsd:element name="dataroot">
<xsd:complexType>
<xsd:sequence>
<xsd:element ref="tblCustomers" minOccurs="0" maxOccurs="unbounded"/>
</xsd:sequence>
<xsd:attribute name="generated" type="xsd:dateTime"/>
</xsd:complexType>
</xsd:element>
<xsd:element name="tblCustomers">
<xsd:annotation>
<xsd:appinfo>
<od:index index-name="PrimaryKey" index-key="CustomerID " primary="yes"
unique="yes" clustered="no"/>
<od:index index-name="CustomerID" index-key="CustomerID " primary="no" unique="no"
clustered="no"/>
</xsd:appinfo>
</xsd:annotation>
<xsd:complexType>
<xsd:sequence>
<xsd:element name="CustomerID" minOccurs="1" od:jetType="autonumber"
od:sqlSType="int" od:autoUnique="yes" od:nonNullable="yes" type="xsd:int"/>
<xsd:element name="CustomerName" minOccurs="0" od:jetType="text"
od:sqlSType="nvarchar">
<xsd:simpleType>
<xsd:restriction base="xsd:string">
<xsd:maxLength value="50"/>
</xsd:restriction>
</xsd:simpleType>
</xsd:element>
</xsd:sequence>
</xsd:complexType>
</xsd:element>
</xsd:schema>
```

The good news is that you don't have to deal with the XML files directly to work with InfoPath. If you create a standalone InfoPath form that uses XML for storage, then InfoPath will build the schema for you.

Try It Out   Examining an XML Document

1. Download Customer.xml.

2. In Windows Explorer, right-click on the file, and choose Edit. The file will be displayed in Notepad as shown in Figure 3-8.

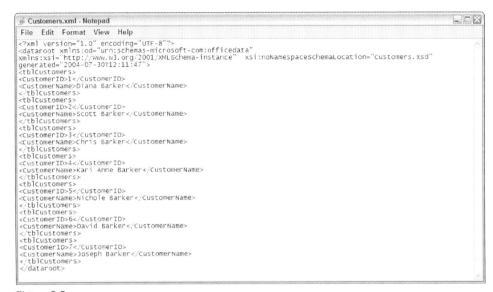

Figure 3-8

3. Repeat the steps for Customers.xsd, which is the schema document.

Introduction to Web Services

You have read thus far in this chapter about two ways of using data with Access: databases and XML documents. The third way is to connect to a Web service. Web services, also called XML Web services, provide the ability to expose your information in a controlled manner to any number of clients over the Internet or an intranet.

Web Services Overview

Web services act as wrappers around your data, allowing you to provide it to users using methods and properties that you want to specify.

Web services are based on SOAP (Simple Object Application Protocol). As with a lot of other new Web development environments, there are tools that generate the SOAP for you so you just have to use common development languages such as ASP.NET, C#, and Visual Basic .NET. Creating your own Web service is discussed in Chapter 15 .

Even better news is that you don't even have to use these tools to connect to Web services. An example of a Web service is one that provides the current weather information for whatever airport code you submit to the Web service. You can see the Web site for this Web service in Figure 3-9.

So if the Airport Weather Web service method `getSummary()` is called with SEATAC as a parameter, it will return the weather for Seattle Tacoma International Airport.

You can use Web services to both retrieve and update information, depending on how the methods of the Web services are set up. There are a number of ways to invoke a Web service, using various development languages, such as Visual Basic, or in InfoPath using a wizard.

Using Web Services with InfoPath

When using Web services with InfoPath, you will be using them as data sources for your InfoPath form. You can connect to the Web service as either the primary data source for querying and updating the main sources of information or as a secondary data source such as populating a drop-down list box with values.

You will read more about connecting to a Web service as a data source in the next chapter.

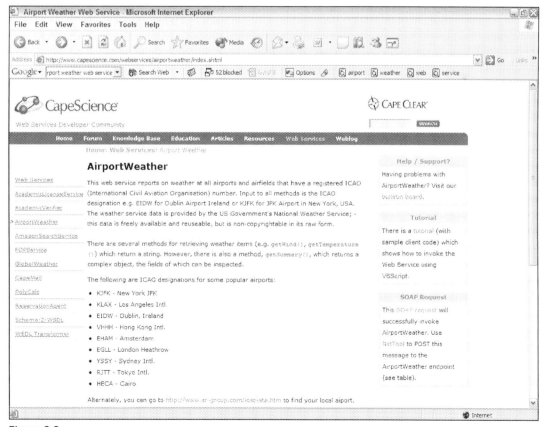

Figure 3-9

Summary

InfoPath is a powerful tool. But it is only as powerful as the information you can use with it. In the chapter, you saw how databases are used in real life every day and how those databases can be visualized using the computer.

There are a number of database models that can be used, but one in particular is very popular: the relational database model. There are a number steps needed to come up with good relational model for your database, but when set up correctly, it can be very intuitive to retrieve and update data.

There are two database solutions that Microsoft offers: Microsoft Access and Microsoft SQL Server. Both connect directly to InfoPath and are relational, but they are made for different scenarios. Two other alternatives for using data with InfoPath are XML documents and Web services.

Exercises

1. Name the two types of databases discussed in this chapter.
2. What are the names of the two Microsoft relational databases that InfoPath connects to directly?
3. What types of fields do you use to create a one-to-many relationship between two tables?
4. What are the steps called when taking a flat file and turning it into relational database?
5. Name two of the file extensions used for XML documents.

Creating an InfoPath Form from an Existing Data Source

Up until this point in the book you have read about the various types of data you can connect to with InfoPath. You have actually seen the native database applications such as Access and SQL Server and have discussed Web services briefly. InfoPath forms have also been created from scratch, to give you a taste of how to use the InfoPath Designer.

Now comes time to combine what you have learned so far to create InfoPath forms based on data located in either databases or Web services. In this chapter you will:

❑ Connect to a database as a data source.

❑ Examine features of the form created.

❑ Add fields from your data source onto an InfoPath form for querying data.

❑ Add fields for updating data.

❑ Update a data source.

Starting the Form Based on a Data Source

When creating forms based on data, the data that is to be used with the form needs to be specified. This does not mean merely which database you want to use, but also the tables or queries, and even the fields. While the InfoPath team has been kind enough to give us a wizard to connect to data sources, there are specifics you need to understand to have the correct data available for use on your InfoPath form.

Specifying the Right Data for the Right Job

When using more than one table for a form, all the tables necessary must be chosen. For example, if you wanted to list customers and their invoices with details, you would choose tblCustomers, tblInvoices, and tblInvoiceDetails. For this chapter, you will be use a Microsoft Access table from the `Chapter 4.mdb` titled tblCustomers. You can see some data from this table displayed in Figure 4-1.

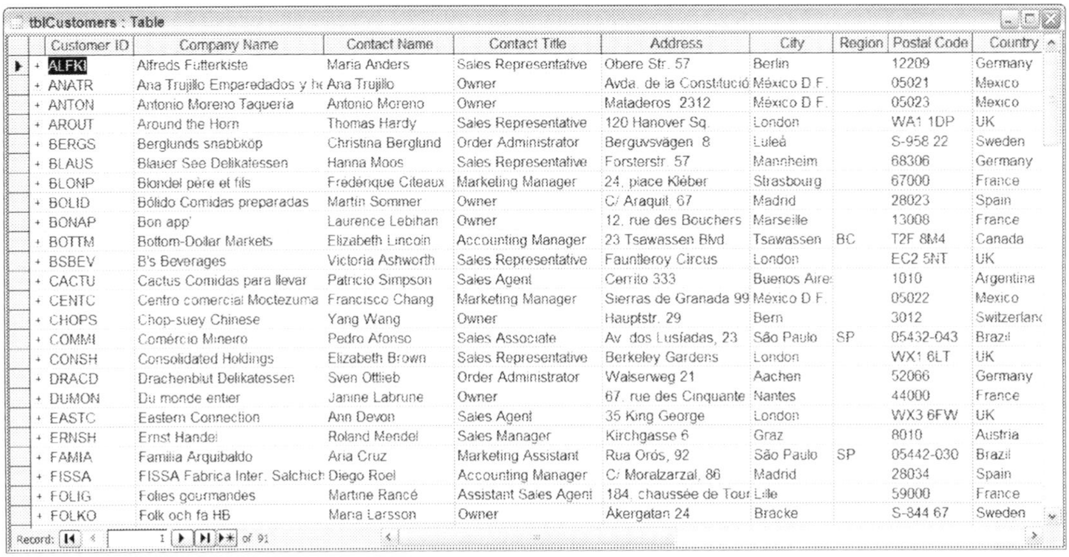
tblCustomers : Table

Customer ID	Company Name	Contact Name	Contact Title	Address	City	Region	Postal Code	Country
ALFKI	Alfreds Futterkiste	Maria Anders	Sales Representative	Obere Str. 57	Berlin		12209	Germany
ANATR	Ana Trujillo Emparedados y he	Ana Trujillo	Owner	Avda. de la Constitució	México D.F.		05021	Mexico
ANTON	Antonio Moreno Taquería	Antonio Moreno	Owner	Mataderos 2312	México D.F.		05023	Mexico
AROUT	Around the Horn	Thomas Hardy	Sales Representative	120 Hanover Sq.	London		WA1 1DP	UK
BERGS	Berglunds snabbköp	Christina Berglund	Order Administrator	Berguvsvägen 8	Luleå		S-958 22	Sweden
BLAUS	Blauer See Delikatessen	Hanna Moos	Sales Representative	Forsterstr. 57	Mannheim		68306	Germany
BLONP	Blondel père et fils	Frédérique Citeaux	Marketing Manager	24, place Kléber	Strasbourg		67000	France
BOLID	Bólido Comidas preparadas	Martín Sommer	Owner	C/ Araquil, 67	Madrid		28023	Spain
BONAP	Bon app'	Laurence Lebihan	Owner	12, rue des Bouchers	Marseille		13008	France
BOTTM	Bottom-Dollar Markets	Elizabeth Lincoln	Accounting Manager	23 Tsawassen Blvd.	Tsawassen	BC	T2F 8M4	Canada
BSBEV	B's Beverages	Victoria Ashworth	Sales Representative	Fauntleroy Circus	London		EC2 5NT	UK
CACTU	Cactus Comidas para llevar	Patricio Simpson	Sales Agent	Cerrito 333	Buenos Aire:		1010	Argentina
CENTC	Centro comercial Moctezuma	Francisco Chang	Marketing Manager	Sierras de Granada 99	México D.F.		05022	Mexico
CHOPS	Chop-suey Chinese	Yang Wang	Owner	Hauptstr. 29	Bern		3012	Switzerlanc
COMMI	Comércio Mineiro	Pedro Afonso	Sales Associate	Av. dos Lusíadas, 23	São Paulo	SP	05432-043	Brazil
CONSH	Consolidated Holdings	Elizabeth Brown	Sales Representative	Berkeley Gardens	London		WX1 6LT	UK
DRACD	Drachenblut Delikatessen	Sven Ottlieb	Order Administrator	Walserweg 21	Aachen		52066	Germany
DUMON	Du monde entier	Janine Labrune	Owner	67, rue des Cinquante	Nantes		44000	France
EASTC	Eastern Connection	Ann Devon	Sales Agent	35 King George	London		WX3 6FW	UK
ERNSH	Ernst Handel	Roland Mendel	Sales Manager	Kirchgasse 6	Graz		8010	Austria
FAMIA	Familia Arquibaldo	Aria Cruz	Marketing Assistant	Rua Orós, 92	São Paulo	SP	05442-030	Brazil
FISSA	FISSA Fabrica Inter. Salchich	Diego Roel	Accounting Manager	C/ Moralzarzal, 86	Madrid		28034	Spain
FOLIG	Folies gourmandes	Martine Rancé	Assistant Sales Agent	184, chaussée de Tour	Lille		59000	France
FOLKO	Folk och fä HB	Maria Larsson	Owner	Åkergatan 24	Bräcke		S-844 67	Sweden

Record: 1 of 91

Figure 4-1

To make it simpler all the data from this table will be used. If using only a few fields from a table, then only those fields should be specified. The Data Connection Wizard guides you in making these choices.

Working with the Data Connection Wizard

The Data Connection Wizard steps you through accomplishing the following tasks:

- **Pick a Database**: Besides picking the type of database (for example, Access, SQL Server, or Web service), the actual database can be specified.
- **Choose Tables and/or Queries**: As mentioned in Chapter 3, "Understanding Data," tables contain the actual data, and queries provide views of the data, letting you combine and limit data as needed. These tables and queries are generally set up ahead of time by the developer or system administrator of the database.
- **Verify and Create Relationships**: Usually created ahead of time by the database creator, the Data Connection Wizard lets you create or modify relationships for use with your InfoPath form when you specify more than one table or query.

❑ **Choose Fields to Use**: Although you can have InfoPath bring all the fields in tables or queries into your form for possible use, performance is enhanced when you only use fields that you will be using. This is especially true when you use SQL Server or Web services based on other client/server products, because only that data specified in the wizard will come down over the wires (network or Internet).

❑ **Edit the SQL Created**: If you happen to be comfortable with writing SQL statements, the wizard provides the ability to modify the SQL created by InfoPath for the data connection. This is especially useful if you want to create more extensive statements with subqueries or even just add an Order By clause on the SQL to specify a sort order.

When picking the data for the initial form, don't worry about picking the data sources for all your controls such as value lists for drop-down list boxes that are going to be on your form. Only the data that is going to be used for inputting or modifying your data on the main form will be chosen using the initial Data Connection Wizard. The other data sources are called *secondary data sources* and can be chosen later in the form design.

Try It Out   Creating the Form and Specifying the Data Source

1. Open InfoPath by choosing All Program ➪ Microsoft Office ➪ Microsoft InfoPath 2003 from the Start menu. The Fill Out a Form dialog box is opened.

2. Click the Design a Form task. You will then see the Design a Form task pane, with a blank design layout.

3. Click New from Data Connection . . . The Data Connection Wizard starts, as shown in Figure 4-2.

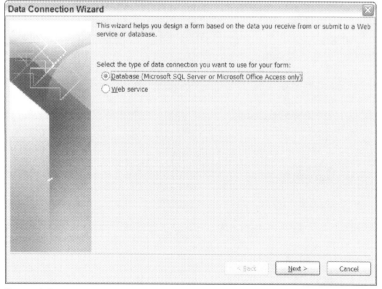

Figure 4-2

4. Because you are going to use an Access database, click the Next button. The next page displays selected tables and queries. Currently it is disabled, except for a button that reads Select Database.

5. Click the Select Database button. The Select Data Source dialog box opens. This dialog box is used by applications that are selecting data sources. Besides selecting Access .mdb files, you also can specify ODBC connections and SQL Server connections. You can see these options in the Select Database dialog box shown in Figure 4-3.

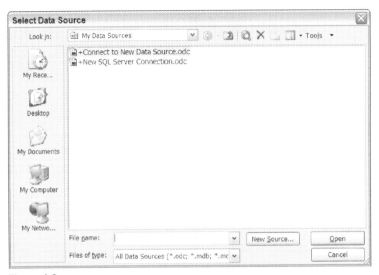

Figure 4-3

6. For this example locate the database for Chapter 4 (Chapter 4.mdb). You can see this file selected in Figure 4-4.

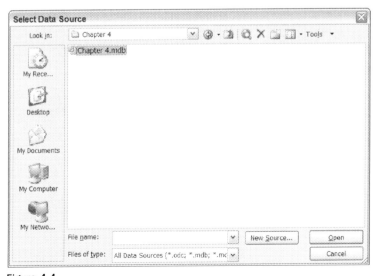

Figure 4-4

7. Click Open. You are now taken back to the Data Connection Wizard and shown a display of the tables and queries in the database you choose.

8. Highlight tblCustomers in the Select Table dialog box, as shown in Figure 4-5.

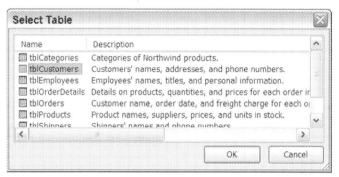

Figure 4-5

9. Click OK. As you can see here in Figure 4-6, the Data Connection tables and queries page with tblCustomers and its fields specified is now displayed.

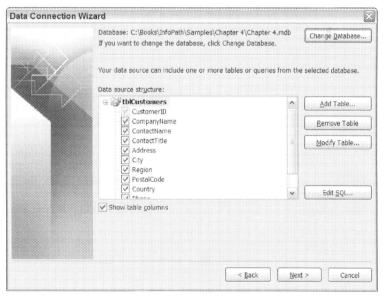

Figure 4-6

In addition to tblCustomers and its fields being displayed, there are also a number of command buttons, a tree view, and a check box that accomplish the following:

Command Label	Description
Data source structure	Lists the tables or queries used in the connection. Columns can be specified by checking or unchecking the check boxes next to the column name.
Change Database	Used to connect to a completely different database.
Add Table	Displays the Add a Table or Query dialog box.
Remove Table	Removes the table highlighted in the data source structure.
Modify Table.	Enables you to modify the sort order of a table or query used with the InfoPath form.
Edit SQL . . .	Used to modify the native SQL statement created by the Data Connection Wizard.
Show Table Columns	Toggles the visibility of the field (column) names in the data source structure.

> If a mistake is made and data not specified correctly, the wizard can be rerun to correct the changes. Modifying the data source, including using the Add Table, Modify Table, and Edit SQL . . . options will be discussed later in this chapter in the section "Updating a Form's Data Source."

10. Click Next because the tblCustomers table and all its fields are utilized for this example. The Summary page of the Data Connection Wizard is displayed, as shown in Figure 4-7.

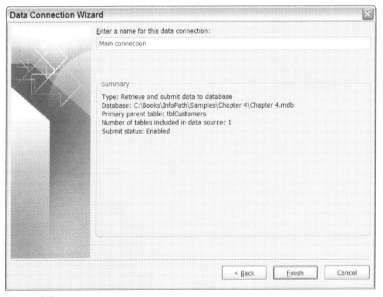

Figure 4-7

You also have the opportunity to specify the data connection name for the InfoPath form, with Main connection being the default.

11. Click Finish, leaving the default connection name. Once you have completed the Data Connection Wizard, InfoPath creates a form, with a number of controls already on it, as shown in Figure 4-8.

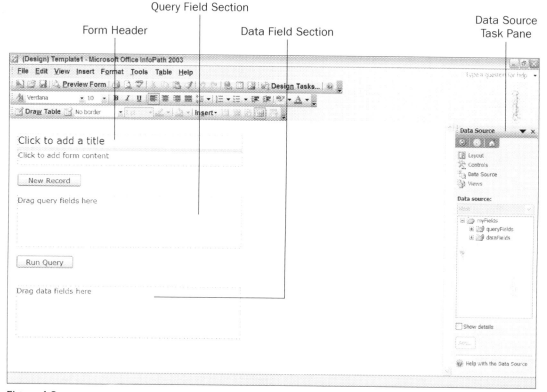

Figure 4-8

Working with the Created InfoPath Form

Before continuing with completing the InfoPath form, it is worthwhile to take a look at the various features created by default on the form and in the designer.

A Look at the Features of the New Form

Working with the callouts in Figure 4-8, the following list details different features of the new form created:

❑ **Form Header**: This section is a layout table with the type of Table with Title. It is used as the header for the form.

❑ **Data Source Task Pane**: This task pane displays the main data source for the InfoPath form. It includes fields used for both the query and data sections of the form.

❑ **Query Field Section**: To limit the data brought down over the network, be it local area network or Internet, fields can be assigned for querying data. When fields are assigned to the Query Field section, they may or may not be used for querying, and the records returned from the query supplied to the form used for display or modification.

❑ **Query Field Section**: To limit the data brought down over the network, be it local area network or Internet, fields can be assigned for querying data. When fields are assigned to the Query Field section, they may or may not be supplied, and records displayed in the form for modifications if specified.

❑ **Data Field Section:** This section contains the data fields used on the form. Data fields are used to display, modify, or append data.

Once data has been updated or added to the Data Field section, the user will click the Submit toolbar button. An alternative is to choose Submit from the File menu. The data is then submitted into the database.

❑ **New Record Command Button**: Once this button is clicked, blank fields are displayed ready for adding new data. Click submit to append the record to the database.

❑ **Run Query Command Button**: After query fields are filled in and this button clicked, a query is sent to the connected database, and data is returned matching the query for use in the InfoPath form.

The remaining sections of this chapter cover each of the features displayed in the prior list. Before moving on to the more interesting features, complete the following Try It Out, specifying the header for the form.

Try It Out   **Filling in the Form Header Information**

Using the form created in the last Try It Out:

1.   Click in the Header section, in the area labeled Click to add a title.

2.   Type **Customer Information**. The header will look as it does in Figure 4-9.

Figure 4-9

The bottom half of the section will not be used for this example.

Data Source Task Pane

The Data Source task pane contains the data sources specified using the Data Connection Wizard. In the initial form as created in the last Try It Out, data sources (tables, queries, and fields) are displayed for queryFields and dataFields using a tree view style display.

Clicking a node in the tree view displayed in the data sources task pane expands the next level of the data source.

Try It Out   Displaying the Fields in the Data Source

Continuing with the form used in the last Try It Out:

1. Click the plus (+) symbol by the queryFields description. The tree node with the label q:tblCustomers is displayed.

2. Click the plus (+) symbol by the q:tblCustomers tree node. The fields you designated to be included from the table are displayed.

3. Perform Steps 1 and 2 for the dataFields node in the tree view to display the fields used in the Data Fields section of the form. The tree view then looks as it does in Figure 4-10.

Figure 4-10

There are a number of other features within the Data Source task pane that you will use throughout the rest of this book. The Data Source task pane and its elements are now set up for use with the rest of the chapter, starting in the next section.

As you drag any of the fields onto the form, InfoPath will create a control for you, based on the type of the data. For example, if you drag a field onto the form that is a Date data type, then InfoPath creates a Date Picker type control for you, bound to the field in the data source. Controls also can be placed upon the form and then bound to a field in the data source.

The default control type created is Text Box. This includes controls dragged into the Query Field section.

Query Field Section

The Query Field section is used to specify fields that can be used to query data in the connected database. An example of this is adding the City field onto the Query Field section. When the form is opened, the user can supply a city such as Seattle and InfoPath returns the records where the data in the City field matches Seattle.

Adding the fields

To add a query field a field is highlighted in the queryFields node of the data source tree. Holding down the left mouse button, the field is dragged over onto the Query Field section of the form. Besides a text box control being created, a label with the field's Caption property is created.

Try It Out   **Adding Fields to the Query Field Section**

Using the form created in this chapter, as displayed in the last Try It Out:

1. Click on the Region field located in the queryFields ⇨ q:tblCustomers node of the data source tree view control.

2. Drag and drop the Region field into the Query Fields section of the form. The section then look as shown in Figure 4-11, with the Run Query button included.

Figure 4-11

You need to supply the fields in the Data Field section before you can see any of the records returned from the database.

Be sure to pull the fields from queryFields tree nodes for the Query Field section. Otherwise, if you use dataFields for the Query Field section an error will be displayed stating "The action will delete all information in the current form." The dataFields fields used in the Data section will display the query data.

Using More Than One Query Field

When using more than one field in the Query Field section, InfoPath will "And" the fields when querying the database. What this means is that if you have both City and Country in the Query Field section and both fields are filled in, then records where both fields are equal will be returned. For instance:

❑   If you have specified Seattle for the city and Canada for the country, then no records will be returned.

❑   If you have specified Vancouver for the city and Canada for the country, then one or more records will be returned.

Data Field Section

Where the Query Field section is for querying the database, the Data Field section is for displaying, updating, and adding the actual data. More choices are necessary when adding the fields to the Data Field section. You can add fields one at a time or add a whole section.

Adding Fields One at a Time

When adding fields individually you have more control over how you want to have the fields displayed as you are adding them. Tables can be added to the form for additional formatting of the form. If you are adding fields one at a time, click the field in the dataFields branch of the data source tree view, dragging it to the location where you want it on the form, much as you did with the queryFields. A repeating section is added when you add the first field onto the form. More information about repeating sections is discussed in the next section.

To add the tables when needed, switch to the Layout task pane, and choose the layout table desired, as shown in Chapter 2, "Getting Started Designing with InfoPath."

Adding Repeating Sections of Fields to the Form

Another way to add fields is to add complete repeating sections to the form. Repeating sections are analogous to tables or queries, in that you will drag them onto the form to create the section that will display one or more records. When you click the table tblCustomers, you will see the menu displayed in Figure 4-12.

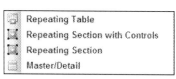

Figure 4-12

The following list discusses the available items:

❏ **Repeating Table**: Displays data in a tabular view similar to a datasheet view in Access, or a spreadsheet in Excel. This is a good choice when you expect to have many records returned from the query.

❏ **Repeating Section with Controls**: Creates a repeating section with the fields going down the page rather than across it like the prior choice. A repeating section with controls is recommended when you are only expecting single records to be returned.

❏ **Repeating Section**: The section created from this choice is bound to the section, but contains no controls initially. This is the option to use when you are planning to add the fields singularly.

❏ **Master/Detail**: These sections are used for two related tables, showing a master record such as invoice information, and one-to-many detail records such as the detail records for an invoice.

Remember that whichever choice you use you can modify the sections to match the vision you have in your mind for the form you're creating.

Try It Out   Adding Fields to the Data Field Section

This Try It Out continues with the form created earlier in this chapter:

1. Highlight the d:tblCustomers table in the data source tree view, holding down the left mouse button.

2. Drag and drop the d:tblCustomers into the Data Fields section. The menu for type of repeating section is displayed.

3. Click the Repeating Table option.

4. Adjust the width of the table and fields to show more of the City field, as shown in Figure 4-13.

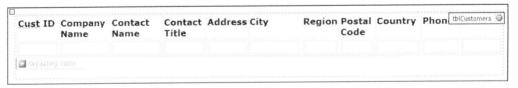

Figure 4-13

The form is now ready for prime time, or at least for you to preview. Before previewing the form, read the following section about the two command buttons created by default on the form.

New Record and Run Query Command Buttons

The two command buttons added to the form include two of the four built-in commands you can assign to command buttons. To check out the actions of command buttons, right-click and pick Properties. You then see the button properties, as shown in Figure 4-14.

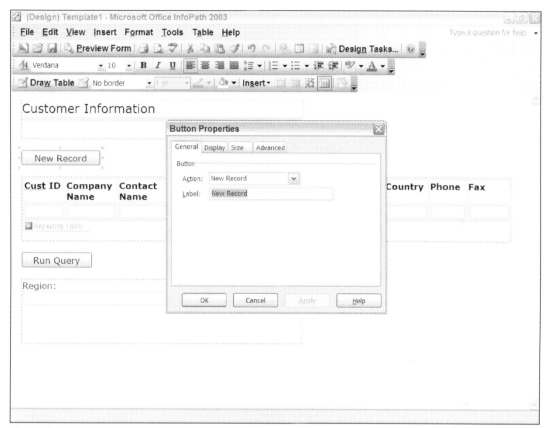

Figure 4-14

The four built-in commands are pretty self-explanatory. Run Query, Submit, New Record, and Delete & Submit are all commands that are performed using the current view against the database. Rules and Custom Code enable the developer to create rules or custom code using scripts (or C#) to accomplish custom tasks.

Try It Out   Examining to Run Query Command Button Action

Continuing with the form created in this chapter:

1. Right-click the command button labeled Run Query.

2. Choose Properties. The Button Properties dialog box opens.

You will see the Run Query action displayed for the action of the command button. More on creating your own command buttons can be found in Chapter 6, "Working with Controls in General."

Previewing the Form

Now that all the work has been done to create the form, it is time to test the work that you have done. It's a good idea to preview a form before you publish the form for other users. To accomplish this, click the Preview Form toolbar button or choose File ⇨ Preview Form.

 Preview Form

> When creating larger forms, test the form as you create major sections. Make sure that the form is looking as you want it when it is to be used in production.

Note that when you make changes to data in Preview mode and submit the data, the data is actually submitted to the database as if you had published the form or opened the form for filling. The reason it is referred to as previewing is because you are viewing it from Design mode rather than from Fill mode.

Try It Out   Querying a Customer Record by Region

The first thing to test when previewing the form is to make sure that the query field is working correctly. To test this feature using the form created in the chapter:

1. Click the Preview Form toolbar button.
2. If necessary, scroll down to the Query Fields section.
3. Type **WA** in the Region query field.
4. Click Run Query. The record of the customer who is located in WA is displayed, as shown in Figure 4-15.

How It Works

When the Region field was added from the queryFields branch in the data source tree view to the Query Field section, InfoPath then knows that you are intending to use that field to query the database. When you supply a value in the Region field and click the Run Query button, InfoPath creates a select query similar to:

```
Select tblCustomers.CustomerID, tblCustomers.Company,... From tblCustomers Where
Region = "BC"
```

The query is then submitted to the connected database. XML is generated in the form of records matching the criteria that are then populated into the fields and displayed in the form. If no records match, a message box is displayed notifying you of the fact that there are no records.

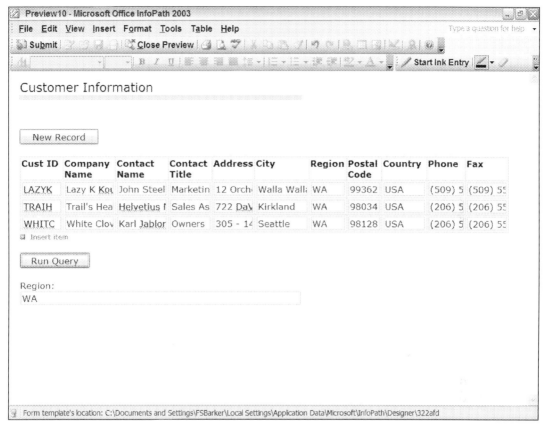

Figure 4-15

Try It Out   **Modify a Customer's Record**

Using the customer record that was retrieved in the last Try It Out:

1.   Modify one of the fields in the record.

2.   Choose File ⇨ Submit, or click on the Submit toolbar button. The data is then updated to the database.

How It Works

When the Submit button is clicked after the information in the field has been updated, an UPDATE SQL statement is generated, with the data updated back in tables in the database specified in the data connection.

Try It Out   **Adding a New Customer**

With the form used in the last Try It Out:

1. Click the New Record button. The fields are then cleared in the form, as shown in Figure 4-16. Notice that the query field has not been cleared.

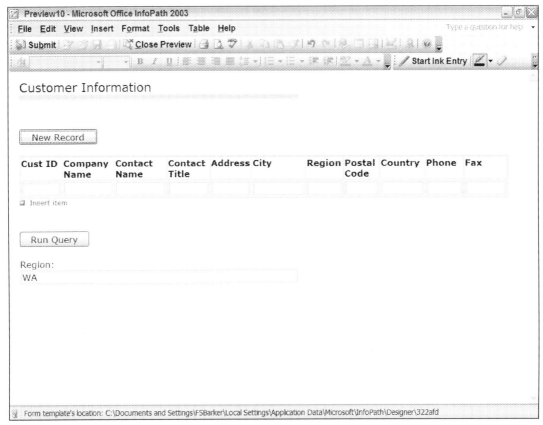

Figure 4-16

2. Add the desired data into the fields.

3. Click the Submit button. The data is then updated in the database.

Notice the arrow below the table displayed in Figure 4-16 with the label Insert Item. This is another way to add a new record to the database, provided by InfoPath, with no additional work to perform on your part.

How It Works

After you have adding the information into the fields and clicked the Submit button, an INSERT INTO SQL statement is generated and the information inserted into the tables in the database that was specified by the data connection.

Updating a Form's Data Source

No matter how well you plan out your forms and the data you base the forms on, there will be many times when you need to modify the data source for a form. Hopefully, you will only be adding a couple of fields to the form that already exists in the database. If you need to modify objects in the database itself, you need to open the database, in Access for example, and modify them there, and then modify the data source in InfoPath.

When you need to modify the data source for a form in InfoPath, use Tools ➪ Data Connections. A dialog box listing the current connections used by the form will displayed, as shown in Figure 4-17.

Figure 4-17

After highlighting the connection you want to use and clicking Modify, the Data Connection Wizard will be opened again. At that point, you can make your modifications that you want to make. There are a number of ways you can make modifications to the data source. For example, if you want to add a sort order to a table you can use the Edit SQL . . . command or choose the Modify Table command, both on the Data Connection Wizard.

Which command you use will depend on if you are comfortable with working with SQL statements directly or not. If so, then use the Edit SQL . . . command. If you are just adding a sort order to a table, then the best method would be to use the Modify Table command, which opens a fairly user-friendly dialog box.

Try It Out — Adding a Sort Order to tblCustomers

Working with the form you have been using for this chapter:

1. Choose Tools ⇨ Data Connections . . . . The Data Connections dialog box will open.

2. Highlight main connection, and click Modify . . . . The Data Connection Wizard starts.

3. Click Modify Table. The Sort Order dialog box opens.

4. Select City. The dialog box will now look like Figure 4-18.

Figure 4-18

5. Click Finish. The Sort Order dialog box is closed.

6. Click Next and then Finish to close the Data Connection Wizard.

Now preview the form, type **WA** for the Region, and click Run Query. You will now see the records in alphabetical order by City, as shown here in Figure 4-19.

You can compare this with Figure 4-15, and you can see that the sort order has been updated as specified.

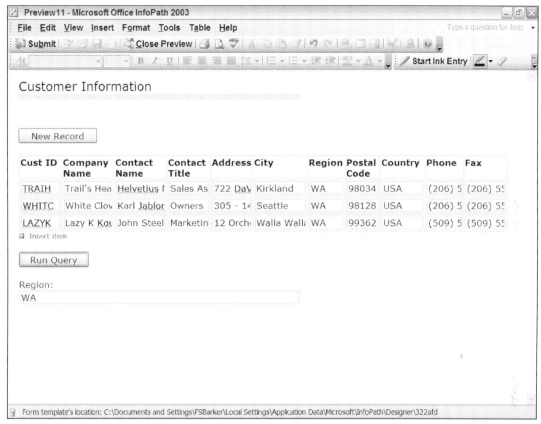

Figure 4-19.

Summary

So, you now know how to create an InfoPath form based on a database. InfoPath performs quite a bit of the work for you, one part of which is supplying the Data Connection Wizard.

The Data Connection Wizard walks you through locating the database you want to use, as well as the tables, queries, and fields necessary. If desired, more than one table or query can be used, and the wizard will help to create or modify relationships if necessary. Once the data source is specified, and the Finish button clicked, InfoPath creates a form that contains a header section, data section, and query section for you.

In this chapter, you also saw and experienced how easy it was to drag and drop the fields onto the form, and choose what kind of repeating sections you want to use. You then saw how to preview a form, query a database, and modify data from the database. Finally, you saw how to modify a data source.

Exercises

1. What is the default control created for a form for fields in a data source?

2. Name the types of sections created when you drop a table onto the form.

3. Name the four built-in actions for command buttons.

4. What are the two ways in the Data Connection Wizard to modify tables?

Utilizing XML and Web Service Data Sources

XML is quickly becoming the standard file format when working with data not only transferred between multiple business systems, but also used within single business systems. Nothing points this out more than Microsoft InfoPath, where besides some of the main data file formats being used (XML schemas and Web services), the physical structures of the forms themselves being maintained use Extensible Markup Language (XML) technology.

Once you have worked with XML schemas for a bit they lose a lot of their mystery, but you gain respect for their simplicity. This chapter lifts the veil of some of the mysteries and has you:

- ❑ Look at some of the file structures used for XML technology.
- ❑ Create an InfoPath form based on an existing XML schema.
- ❑ Use XML data for a data source of an InfoPath form.
- ❑ Take a quick look at the XML files that make up an InfoPath form.

XML Overview

As a power user or developer, chances are you have at least heard of XML. XML is to data what Hypertext Markup Language (HTML) is to displaying Web pages in a browser. While XML describes the data to be used, HTML describes how information is to be presented on a page. Another big difference between the two is that although HTML is primarily for the Web, XML can be used anywhere data is to be utilized. This includes single systems on a desktop, multiple business systems, or utilizing data over the Internet.

The World Wide Web Consortium (W3C), creator of HTML, first met in 1996. It is also the W3C who sets the standards for XML.

What Is XML?

XML is a data file standard. Where the format is agreed upon, the actual commands (tags) used will depend on the technology, system, or development language utilizing the data. There are technologies commonly used by applications that take advantage of XML, a common one being XML documents. An XML document can consist of a single table or an entire database. A good example of various systems that use XML documents are the Office applications. The majority of them can both import and export XML, including Word. You can see an example of exporting XML in this chapter in the next section.

As with the HTML, various XML files use tags. However, that is all you specify in XML, what the data is. You are not specifying how the data looks. One difference between HTML and XML is that XML has much stricter requirements for creating tags. There are certain rules that you must follow. If you have followed those rules in the initial creation of your document, then you are said to have created a well-formed document.

XML Documents

While the information and specific commands included in XML differ based on the technology using them, XML documents are said to be well formed if they conform to the following basic rules of XML:

- ❑ Each XML document must have a unique root element (an element encompassing the entire document).

- ❑ The document has matching start and end tags.

- ❑ The elements do not overlap.

- ❑ Certain reserve characters are part of the XML syntax and will not be interpreted as the characters themselves if used in the data portion of an element.

Besides the *.xml file created, additional files are created when you work with an XML document. XML describes what the data is and is separate from how the data is actually presented. You can use the same data and present it differently based on separate specification files.

Standard XML Files

XML documents can be made up of a single file if necessary. When only one file is used, however, it is up to the systems reading the data to figure out the type of data they're dealing with. When using more than one document to specify the data, you can specify properties such as data types and other attributes.

Here are some of the extensions and types of files used for XML documents:

Extension	Description
*.xml	The XML data document. This is a static snapshot of data itself.
*.xsd	The schema file. This schema was based off the persisted table or query and is in the W3C XSD standard.

Extension	Description
*.xsl	Presentation document. The XSL document specifies how the data in the XML is to be displayed, transforming the data for presentation purposes. A *.XSL is also used for XSLT documents, which use a subset of commands from XSL. One big difference is that XSLT also performs the transformation permanently, and in fact can create other types of files such as HTML from the XML.
*.htm	Final Package. This ties the *.xml (data) and *.xsl (presentation) together to be used on the Web.

*There are ways to embed the definition information inside the *.XML, and thereby not have to include the *.xsd file, however, this is not the recommended practice. The reason for not embedding the definition is that the business systems need to be able to read the embedded definitions. Another reason is that it is generally accepted that, just as you want to keep the presentation of the data separate from the data itself, it is a good idea to keep the definition separate as well.*

If you are passing the data to another business application, then you will probably just send the *.xml and *.xsd files. In the case of InfoPath, if you are going to create a form based off the structure of existing XML data, you have only to specify the *xsd. You will see more on this in the section titled "Creating an InfoPath Form Using an Existing XML Document" later in this chapter.

One of the best ways to understand XML files is to see what they actually look like. For the purposes of this section, you will see the XML files created by exporting the tblCustomers table to XML. You can see the original table structure in Figure 5-1.

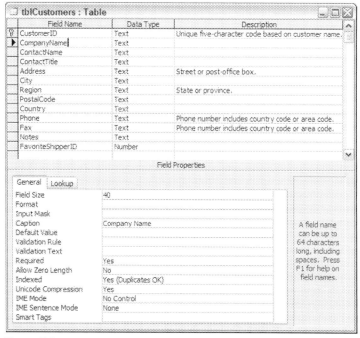

Figure 5-1

Although this isn't an Access book, if you open `Chapter 5.mdb` in the samples folder, you can right-click the tblCustomers table in the Table tab of the database window, and choose Export . . . from the menu. In the Export table dialog box, set XML (`*.xml`) as the type of document to export to and click Export. You are then presented with the XML Export dialog box displayed in Figure 5-2.

Figure 5-2

In Figure 5-2, you can see three of the basic types of files created. For the purposes of using the file structure to base an InfoPath form on, you only need the XSD. But to get a good look at what the XML looks like both the data and the schema were exported.

The XML Data Document (*.xml)

The XML data document is just that, data. So, the tblCustomers table would look like this:

```
<?xml version="1.0" encoding="UTF-8"?>
<dataroot xmlns:od="urn:schemas-microsoft-com:officedata"
xmlns:xsi="http://www.w3.org/2001/XMLSchema-instance"
xsi:noNamespaceSchemaLocation="tblCustomers.xsd" generated="2004-09-20T16:04:16">
    <tblCustomers>
        <CustomerID>ALFKI</CustomerID>
        <CompanyName>Alfreds Futterkiste</CompanyName>
        <ContactName>Maria Anders</ContactName>
        <ContactTitle>Sales Representative</ContactTitle>
    <Address>Obere Str. 57</Address>
     <City>Berlin</City>
      <PostalCode>12209</PostalCode>
       <Country>Germany</Country>
       <Phone>030-0074321</Phone>
       <Fax>030-0076545</Fax>
    </tblCustomers>
    <tblCustomers>
        <CustomerID>ANATR</CustomerID>
        <CompanyName>Ana Trujillo Emparedados y helados</CompanyName>
        <ContactName>Ana Trujillo</ContactName>
        <ContactTitle>Owner</ContactTitle>
        <Address>Avda. de la Constitución 2222</Address>
        <City>México D.F.</City>
        <PostalCode>05021</PostalCode>
        <Country>Mexico</Country>
        <Phone>(5) 555-4729</Phone>
        <Fax>(5) 555-3745</Fax>
    </tblCustomers>
 ...
```

```
<tblCustomers>
    <CustomerID>WOLZA</CustomerID>
    <CompanyName>Wolski  Zajazd</CompanyName>
    <ContactName>Zbyszek Piestrzeniewicz</ContactName>
    <ContactTitle>Owner</ContactTitle>
    <Address>ul. Filtrowa 68</Address>
    <City>Warszawa</City>
    <PostalCode>01-012</PostalCode>
    <Country>Poland</Country>
    <Phone>(26) 642-7012</Phone>
    <Fax>(26) 642-7012</Fax>
</tblCustomers>
</dataroot>
```

The first line of code, `<?xml version="1.0" encoding="UTF-8" ?>`, specifies the version of the XML and encoding format being used.

The `<dataroot>` tag line specifies other information about the whole XML file itself, such as the schema file being used and when it was generated.

The next tag, `<tblCustomers>`, describes the table. If there were multiple tables included, this tag would be repeated for a different table after the field tags for the tblCustomers were specified. After listing the various fields in a record, the end tag of `</tblCustomers>` is used.

> *There are additional customer records included in* `tblCustomers.xml`, *but they are represented with an ellipsis so as not to waste space.*

Finally, the end tag for the dataroot is displayed: `</dataroot>`. You can see from the preceding listing that no information about the structure of the data was included other than the names for the table and fields. The other information was specified in the `*.xsd` file. Field tags in the `*.xml` document match up directly with field tags in the schema document.

The Schema File (*.xsd)

The schema file specifies not only the definitions for the individual fields, but for the whole XML file itself. The `<xsd:element>` tags in the following listing are used to specify each element in the `*.xml` file used for tblCustomers. Other tags are used to specify different attributes matching the properties set for the table and fields in Access.

```
<?xml version="1.0" encoding="UTF-8"?>
<xsd:schema xmlns:xsd="http://www.w3.org/2001/XMLSchema" xmlns:od="urn:schemas-
microsoft-com:officedata">
<xsd:element name="dataroot">
<xsd:complexType>
<xsd:sequence>
<xsd:element ref="tblCustomers" minOccurs="0" maxOccurs="unbounded"/>
</xsd:sequence>
<xsd:attribute name="generated" type="xsd:dateTime"/>
</xsd:complexType>
</xsd:element>
<xsd:element name="tblCustomers">
<xsd:annotation>
```

```
<xsd:appinfo>
<od:index index-name="PrimaryKey" index-key="CustomerID " primary="yes"
unique="yes" clustered="no"/>
<od:index index-name="City" index-key="City " primary="no" unique="no"
clustered="no"/>
<od:index index-name="CompanyName" index-key="CompanyName " primary="no"
unique="no" clustered="no"/>
<od:index index-name="FavoriteShipperID" index-key="FavoriteShipperID "
primary="no" unique="no" clustered="no"/>
<od:index index-name="PostalCode" index-key="PostalCode " primary="no" unique="no"
clustered="no"/>
<od:index index-name="Region" index-key="Region " primary="no" unique="no"
clustered="no"/>
</xsd:appinfo>
</xsd:annotation>
<xsd:complexType>
<xsd:sequence>
<xsd:element name="CustomerID" minOccurs="0" od:jetType="text"
od:sqlSType="nvarchar">
<xsd:simpleType>
<xsd:restriction base="xsd:string">
<xsd:maxLength value="5"/>
</xsd:restriction>
</xsd:simpleType>
</xsd:element>
<xsd:element name="CompanyName" minOccurs="1" od:jetType="text"
od:sqlSType="nvarchar" od:nonNullable="yes">
<xsd:simpleType>
<xsd:restriction base="xsd:string">
<xsd:maxLength value="40"/>
</xsd:restriction>
</xsd:simpleType>
</xsd:element>
...
<xsd:element name="FavoriteShipperID" minOccurs="0" od:jetType="longinteger"
od:sqlSType="int" type="xsd:int"/>
</xsd:sequence>
</xsd:complexType>
</xsd:element>
</xsd:schema>
```

When you are passing data from one business system to another, as long as the system can read XML, the two file types discussed here are all you need to hand off. If you want to specify how the presentation is handled, use the `*.xsl` file. For our purposes the first two files do the job.

> *As with the `tblCustomers.xml` file, there are additional elements included in the `tblCustomers.xsd` file, but they are represented by an ellipsis so as not to waste space.*

Try It Out   Exporting tblShippers from Access to XML

To give you more exposure to working with XML files and transferring them between systems, using Access you will work with the `Chapter 5.mdb` database to export the tblShippers table. You will also utilize the `*.xsd` file you create in a section later in this chapter:

1. Open the `Chapter 5.mdb` database in Access.

2. Click on the Tables tab.

3. Right-click the tblShippers table, and choose Export . . . from the menu. The Export table dialog box opens.

4. Select XML (`*.xml`) for the Save as type. The dialog then looks like Figure 5-3.

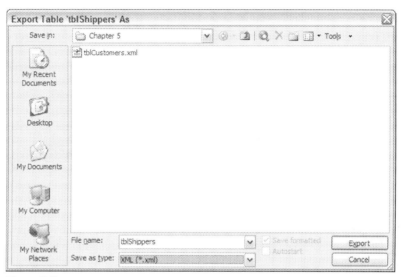

Figure 5-3

5. Click Export. The XML Export dialog box then appears. For this example you once again use the default of creating the `*.xml` and `*.xsd` files.

6. Click OK to create the files.

To test the files you can go to the folders they were created in, and open them in NotePad, WordPad, or some other XML editors.

Now that you have created an XML file, read on to see how to use these files for InfoPath forms.

Utilizing XML Data in InfoPath

Why Use an XML Data Source?

Because you can hook forms up to databases such as Access and SQL Server, you may wonder why you would need to use XML as a data source. Two of the main reasons are portability and collaboration. Because InfoPath gives customers a choice of e-mailing forms, using them on laptops offline, and collaborating with them using Windows SharePoint Services (WSS). WSS is discussed in Chapter 17, "Working with InfoPath and Windows SharePoint Services."

Creating an InfoPath Form Using an Existing XML Document

You created an InfoPath form based on an Access database in Chapter 4, "Creating an InfoPath Form from an Existing Data Source." Creating one based on an XML data source is not much different. However, in contrast to using the database, you have a choice of basing the InfoPath form on just the structure of the database rather than also having to use the data itself. For the purposes of this section you do just that. Use the task *New from XML Document or Schema* . . . from the Design a Form task pane. Once you have clicked the task, you are taken to the Data Source Wizard, introduced in Chapter 4. The information requested is different because you will specify which XML document you want to use instead of database specifics.

Try It Out   Specifying a XML Data Source

1. Open Microsoft InfoPath.

2. Click Design a Form in the Design a Form task pane.

3. Choose New from XML Document or Schema . . . in the Design a New Form task pane. The Data Source Wizard opens, prompting you to enter the location of the XML schema to use. You also can use the Browse button.

4. Locate the XML schema, as displayed in Figure 5-4. Remember that you only want the schema for this Try It Out and not the data.

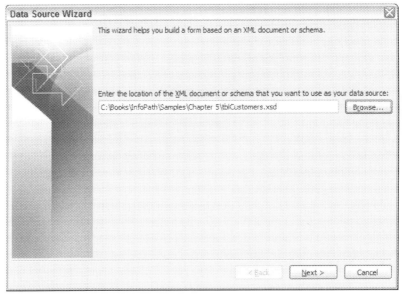

Figure 5-4

5. Click the Next button. You are then asked if you would like to add another XML schema or XML document. The default is no.

6. Click Finish. You now see the blank form displayed. In the Data Source Pane, the tblCustomers are listed. Expand the tblCustomers node, and you then see the fields in the table, as shown in Figure 5-5.

Figure 5-5

Unlike using the database, when you create the form from the data source, the data goes with the InfoPath form. Now it's time to create the form itself. You will follow the same steps you used when you created a form based on the information in the database.

Notice that when InfoPath creates this form, the form is blank; it does not contain query and data sections, only a single area. This is because the only data going in is for this particular form. There is no reason for a query area.

Try It Out **Adding the Fields**

Using the form you just created:

1. Click the tblCustomers node, and drag it onto the form. You are then presented with the options for adding a section to the form, as shown in Figure 5-6.

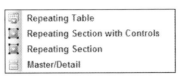

Figure 5-6

2. Select Repeating Section with Controls. The form is then created, and can be seen in Figure 5-7.

Figure 5-7

Utilizing Data with an XML Data Source

In the last section, you saw how to set a data source to an XML schema file. This helps create the structure of the data to be used with the form, but it includes no data. There are times when you want to include the data with the structure. Here are some of the reasons to include the data with the schema:

❏ **To Utilize Data from Another Business System**: When using data from another system by using the XML document, the data can be viewed in the InfoPath form. You also can create code to update the data and return it to the system or recreate an XML document from the updated data.

❏ **To Supply Prototype Data for a New System**: By seeding the InfoPath form, you can suggest the type of data to be entered into the form. When creating an InfoPath form that will be used against a database or Web service (backends), it may take a while for the IT group or whoever is in charge of the backend to have the backend ready for use. Until the backend is ready, you can have the people creating the backend generate an XML document to work with until the backend is complete. You may have to make some modifications to match changes that occur.

❏ **To Add Data for Lookup Purposes**: Even when entering data into individual forms, there are cases when you want to supply some data to the form, even if the main form's data source is created using just an XML schema.

For the purposes of this section, you will be adding a data source using the last scenario, in the Try It Out.

Try It Out   Adding a Data Source Using an XML Document

To show this technique, you will be using the XML document you created when you exported the tblShippers table from Access to `tblShippers.xlm` and the InfoPath form you created in the last couple of Try It Outs. You can see `tblShippers.xml` displayed in Figure 5-8.

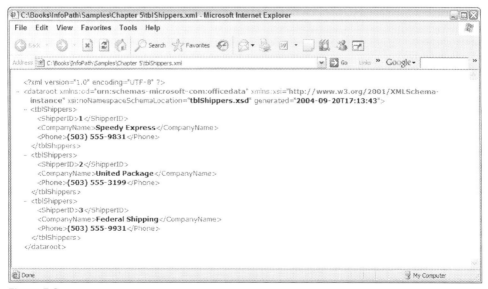

Figure 5-8

The last field displayed in the new form is FavoriteShipperID. The first task is to convert this field from a text field to a list box. Then you will be specifying the XML document as the data source for the list to display for the list box.

1. Open the form created in the last couple of Try It Outs in design view.

2. Right-click the text box bound to the FavoriteShipperID field. The context menu appears.

3. Choose Change To from the menu, and then highlight List Box from the list of controls available, as shown in Figure 5-9.

    Once chosen, the text box bound to the FavoriteShipperID is changed to a list box control.

4. Right-click the new list box control, and choose List Box Properties . . . from the menu displayed. The List Box Property dialog box is displayed.

5. In the List Entries options, click the last one, labeled Look up values in a data connection to a database, Web service, file, or SharePoint library or list, as shown in Figure 5-10. You will be selecting a file.

6. Click Add. The Data Connection Wizard is then displayed. You will be using the default choice, XML document, as displayed in Figure 5-11.

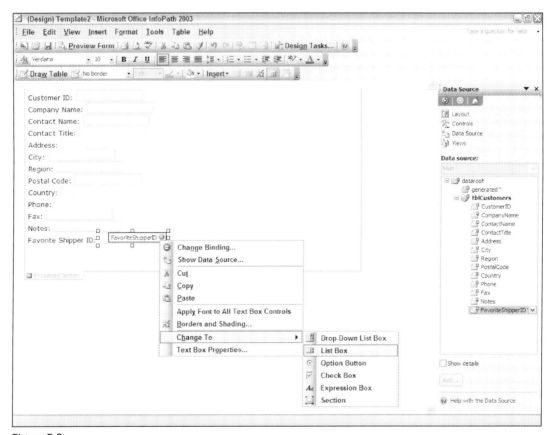

Figure 5-9

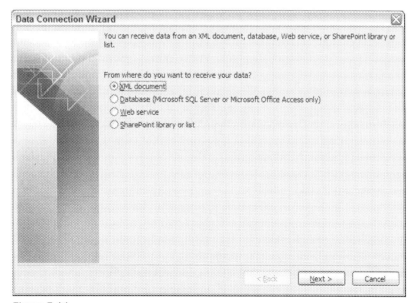

Figure 5-10

Figure 5-11

7. Click Next. The next page of the Data Connection Wizard enables you to choose the actual XML document you want to use. You can either type the path and name of the file or use the Browse button, located to the right of the file text box. You can see the file in Figure 5-12.

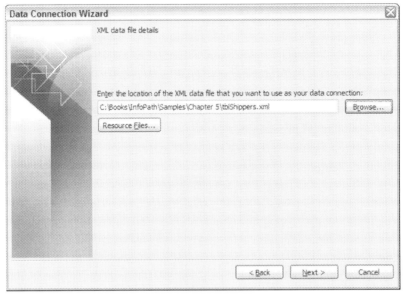

Figure 5-12

8. Click Next to see the last page of the Data Connection Wizard. This summary page lets you specify what you would like to call the connection and also note whether you would like to have the data loaded when the form is opened. Leave the defaults as you can see them in Figure 5-13.

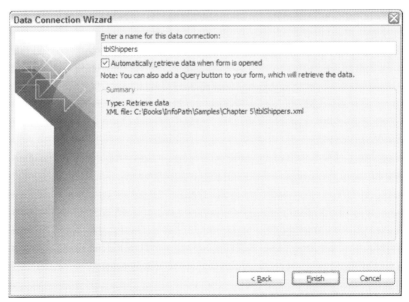

Figure 5-13

9. Click Finish. You will then see a message box displayed informing you that the data is not part of the form. It gives you the choice of adding the file to the form. You can see this dialog box in Figure 5-14.

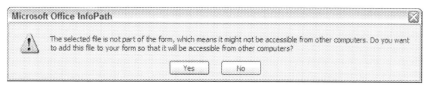

Figure 5-14

10. Click Yes. The name of the new data connection is then listed in the Data Connection property of the property sheet.

11. Click the Select XPath button, next to the Entries text box on the List Box Properties dialog box.

12. Select tblShippers, and click OK. The tblShippers XPath is then added to the Entries text box, and the ShipperID is filled in the Value and Display name properties.

13. Click the Select XPath button next to the Display name text box.

14. Select the CompanyName from the treeview of nodes, and click OK. All the properties are now filled out as they should be for displaying shippers, and can be seen in Figure 5-15.

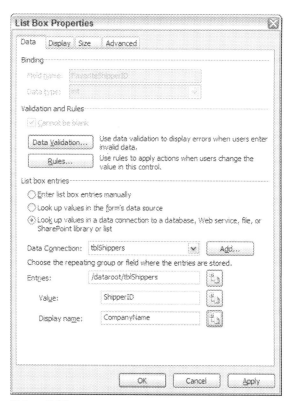

Figure 5-15

15. Click OK to accept the properties.

16. Click Preview Form to view the InfoPath form.

After typing in some values and picking a Shipper, your form should look something like the one in Figure 5-16.

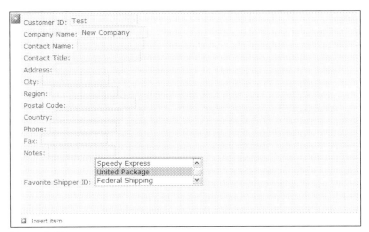

Figure 5-16

A Brief Look at the XML Used for InfoPath Forms

Before finishing up this chapter, it is worth examining more closely the fact that InfoPath forms are created using XML. There is a very cool and easy way to accomplish this. Taking the InfoPath form that has been used throughout the chapter, you can choose File ➪ Extract Form Files . . . while the form is in design view. You can then specify the folder you want to extract, and the files are then extracted. You can see the files displayed in the new folder in Figure 5-17.

Try It Out   **Examining the Files**

You can see from the extension of each file and their descriptions what the purpose of each file is. The manifest.xsf is the file that ties all the others together.

1. Double-click each of the files and take a look at what is displayed.

2. Open manifest.xsf in Notepad, and read through it.

If you double-click manifest.xsf, *it will open the form for filling. However, the form won't open quite right. So, just open the form for viewing.*

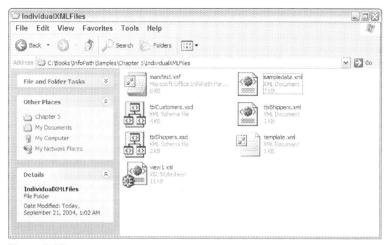

Figure 5-17

You can actually create an InfoPath form programmatically or manually by creating the necessary XML. If you find this a necessity, a great book for seeing how to accomplish this is *Professional InfoPath 2003* also published by Wrox.

Summary

XML has been the standard for sharing data not only over the Internet between business systems, but also within single systems. Just as HTML is used for displaying information, XML is used for describing and working with data. InfoPath goes a step further by utilizing XML not only for data storage, but also for describing InfoPath forms themselves.

XML can be made up of a single file or multiple files, depending on the purpose. Each of the Office applications can import and export data to and from XML files.

As shown, you can bind InfoPath forms not only to databases, but also to XML documents and schemas. When binding an InfoPath form, you can specify whether or not to include the existing data located in the XML or just the schema.

Exercises

1. What does W3C stand for?

2. What are two of the W3C's major contributions?

3. What is the extension for the XML file that contains the schema for the data?

4. What are the two types of XML files that you can use as a data source for an InfoPath form?

Working with Controls in General

As you saw in the last chapter InfoPath provides a powerful designer for creating your forms. When you add the data source and drag fields onto a form, InfoPath adds controls that allow you to view and manage your information. So far we have only scratched the surface of what you can do with the controls provided by InfoPath.

The controls provide so much that two chapters are devoted just to them alone. In the next chapter, you will see how to take advantage of some of the more advanced controls provided. But before that, you will need to see just what you can do with all the controls that come in the control task pane. In this chapter you will:

❑   See what controls are provided, and the purpose of each.

❑   Learn how to take advantage of the Property sheet and some important properties.

❑   Provide data validation on the form.

❑   Work with rules and figure out when to use them.

❑   Use conditional formatting on controls.

❑   Create controls that use formulas.

Using the Right Control for the Right Job

InfoPath has default controls it puts on forms based on the type of data the field is for. It does a good job, but it can only do so much. For instance, if you add a date field to the form, the Date Picker control is created for you. However, if you have a data field that is based on a lookup field, InfoPath doesn't automatically create a drop-down list box to look up the values; you have to know how to do that.

To get comfortable with the different controls, the following table displays the names of the controls in the Controls task pane along with what time of data you would use it with.

Control Name	Type	Description
Text Box	Text Input	Default control for input, accepts plain text, no special characters.
Rich Text Box	Text Input	Accepts both plain text and rich text, allowing formatted text just as would be entered using Word with fonts, colors, and so on.
Drop-Down List Box	List Input	Displays specified values in a drop-down list, initially displaying the selected value.
List Box	List Input	Displays specified values in a list, initially displaying however many values you decide by dropping the control on the form.
Date Picker	Calendar	A calendar is displayed, and values chosen by clicking on a date.
Check Box	Yes/No	Used for specifying a true or false (yes or no) value. A checkmark is displayed in the box when true.
Option Box	Multiple Choice	Also called radio buttons, you can use option boxes to either pick multiple choices or single choices in a group.
Button	Command	Created to trigger actions to automate tasks on the form.
Section	Section	Base control for managing blocks of data such as tables on the form, or simply to break up a form for display purposes.
Optional Section	Section	Creates a section that starts with no records displayed on the form.
Repeating Section	Section	Displays multiple rows from a table in a data source on a form. Displays data in a vertical manner.
Repeating Table	Section	Displays multiple rows from a table displaying the data across the form as an Excel worksheet or Access datasheet would.
Master/Detail	Section	A method for tying together master/detail records such as customers and orders on a form.
Bulleted List	List Display	Displays data in a bulleted list on a form.
Numbered List	List Display	Displays data in a numbered list on a form.
Plain List	List Display	Displays a list of data on a form without bullets or numbers.

There are also additional controls for more advanced features such as file attachments and ink controls. For the complete list scroll through the Controls task pane.

As you are working through the chapters in this book, you will be working with the various types of controls. Each of the various controls share a few things in common, called properties. While the properties may vary depending on the type of control you are using, all controls have them.

Looking at the Starting Form for the Chapter

For this chapter a form was created using the tblCustomers, tblOrders, and tblOrderDetails tables, as seen in the prior chapters . To help you learn the most concepts in this chapter, the form is set up so that you can continue modifying the form in its current state. The form is called Chapter 6 Starting.xsn. You can see the form in Figure 6-1, displayed in design view.

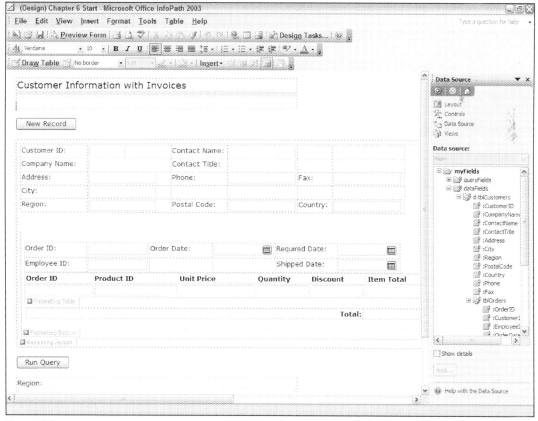

Figure 6-1

Open the Sample Form

As mentioned, you will want to open the `Chapter 6 Starting.xsn` form. To accomplish this, after downloading the sample forms from the WroxWeb site to the Chapter 6 folder:

1. Open Microsoft InfoPath.

2. Click on Design a Form.

3. Click on On My Computer....

4. Locate the `Chapter 6 Starting.xsn` form using the Open in Design Mode dialog box.

5. Highlight the form, and click Open.

How It Works

The form that you are starting consists of three sections, one for each table. The two outer sections are repeating sections (tblCustomers and tblOrders, and the last a repeating table type section, displaying the data from tblOrderDetails. The fields have been arranged on the form using various tables with the default control types used to accept data.

Two labels have been added: Item Total and Total. These labels will be associated with controls that are added in later sections in the chapter. Other controls that are on the form also are used to highlight various features.

The way to take advantage of various control features is to utilize various properties of the controls. As with other applications the way to work with properties is by use of the property sheet.

Working with the Property Sheet

The property sheet can be opened by right-clicking a control and choosing *ControlType* Properties..., with *ControlType* being the type of control you are using. Another way to open the property sheet for a control is to double-click the left mouse button on the control. Which properties exist for a control will depend on what type of control it is.

The property sheet is broken up in to tabbed pages, based on categories of properties. Some examples of properties are Data, Display, Size, and Advanced. You will see an example of the property for a text box on the next section when you are shown how to set the default value of a control.

Setting the Default Value of a Control

When a control is based on a field from a data source, there are some cases when you want to have a value put in the control automatically when new records are added. This value is called the *default value*. In a perfect world the default value of a field is specified for the field in the table, located in the database. However, there will be times when it is overlooked, or you want to override the default value set at the database level.

Which type of data you will use as a default value will depend on the data type of the field. The following table displays some example of default values that could be used with the form used in this chapter:

Field	Default Value	Description
Region	"WA"	Places the abbreviation for the state of WA in the Region field.
Order Date	today()	Use the today() formula to assign today's date.
Quantity	1	Setting a numeric value to 1 or 0; this helps to keep users from leaving values blank.

When set at the form level, default values are just like other values you enter into forms in that you need to click the Submit button to have them saved in the database.

Using Literal Values

The way to specify default values is to use the property sheet of the control. There are several ways to specify default values. The first way is enter the value you want into the Value entry in the Default Value area on the data tab of the property sheet.

Try It Out   **Adding a Default Value to Quantity**

Using the Chapter 6 Starting.xsn form:

1. Right-click the Quantity field, located under the label displaying Quantity in bold.

2. Choose Text Box Properties... The property sheet for the Quantity text box opens.

3. Type 1 into the Value property. The property sheet will then look as it does in Figure 6-2.

4. Click OK. The default value for the Quantity field is now set to 1. It is time to test it.

Figure 6-2

5. Click Preview Form. Even at this point, when the form is showing a blank form, you can see 1 displayed in the Quantity field, as shown in Figure 6-3.

While Figure 6-3 shows a the use of default value, a few more steps will show the default value even better when a new order detail record is inserted into existing records.

Figure 6-3

6. In the query portion of the form, type in BC for the region, then click Run Query. A record appears displaying entries for the Bottom-Dollar Markets company.

7. Click the Insert Item choice, under the existing order detail entries. A new record will appear, and once again the number 1 will be displayed in the Quantity field. You can see this in Figure 6-4.

You should now have a good idea what the default value property accomplishes for you when you type a literal value such as 1 in the property. There also is another way to specify default values, and that is by using a formula, also called an *expression*.

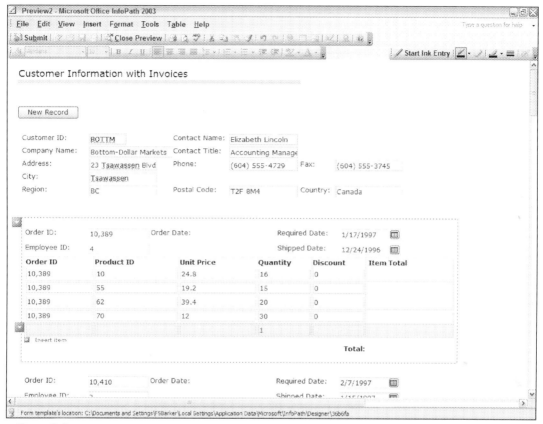

Figure 6-4

Using Formulas

You can use formulas for various purposes on your InfoPath form. Just as with formulas used in Excel, they can be expressions such as the values of two fields being added together or an aggregate function such as Sum(). Formulas can consist of:

❑ Fields and other formula controls being added together

❑ Functions

❑ Combination of functions and fields.

When setting default values, where formulas are concerned you will use functions, because when a default value is utilized, other fields are not yet supplied.

Whatever type of information you want to use, there are two methods you can utilize to create the formulas. For the default values, you can type the formulas directly into the Value field of the Default Value area in the Data tab of the Properties dialog box. The other alternative is to click the Formula command button, located beside the Value field.

If you choose to use the Formula command button, the Insert Formula dialog box will open as seen in Figure 6-5.

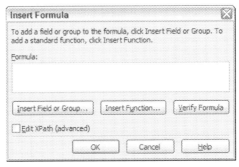

Figure 6-5

The three command buttons accomplish the following:

❑ **Insert Field or Group**: This button enables you to specify an individual field or a group of fields to use. You also can utilize filters to narrow down the data displayed. In the next chapter, you will read about using fields and groups of fields in formulas to display information.

❑ **Insert Function**: This button displays the Insert Function dialog box, where you can pick functions to use from Date and Time, Field, Math, and Text categories. Functions will return a value when given a parameter or parameters, or just when called by itself, depending on the requirements of the functions.

❑ **Verify Formula**: As the caption says, this button verifies the syntax of the formula. Note that if your formula has problems other than syntactical ones, the errors won't show up until you preview the form.

❑ **Edit XPath (Advanced)**: XPath, or XML Path Language, is a language used to search information within an XML document. In Microsoft Office InfoPath 2003, these are the same as fields or controls on a form. If you are familiar with Xpath, you can edit the expressions directly by checking this box.

Try It Out   Using a Formula for Order Date Default Value

For the purposes of examining the use of a formula for default value, you must use a call function within your formula. In the form you have been using thus far in the chapter:

1. Right-click the OrderDate field, underneath the label with the caption Order Date, and choose Date Picker Properties... from the menu. The Properties dialog box opens.

2. Click the Formula button, next to the Value field under Default Value. The Insert Formula dialog box opens.

3. Click the Insert Function command button, opening the Insert Function dialog box.

4. Select the Date and Time category in the Categories list box. You will then see the two functions: now and today. The function now will rerturn both the current system time and date, and the function today returns the current system date only.

5. Highlight the today function, as shown in Figure 6-6.

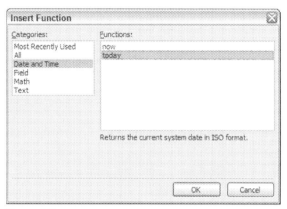

Figure 6-6

6. Click OK to accept the function. The Insert Formula dialog box now displays the today() function as shown in Figure 6-7.

Figure 6-7

7. Click OK to accept the formula. The formula is now displayed in the Value field of Default Property area of the Date Picker Properties dialog box.

8. Click OK to accept the new default value.

Now, when you add a new order for any of the customers, the current date (today) will be set as the Date Ordered default value. You can see this in the form by clicking the Preview Form toolbar button, locating a customer, then clicking the Insert Item button under the Orders section. You also can see it in the default blank record displayed on the form when you first open it, as shown in Figure 6-8.

Figure 6-8

As of this writing, a bug occurs with forms bound to a database where the default value is repeated in all records displayed. This makes this feature currently more useful in forms used with XML.

Working with Rules at the Control Level

While you can specify values as a default value for a control, there are times when you want a control to be updated to a value based on a different control. You can't do that with a default value, because at the time the default value is assigned there are no values, other than default values, in the other fields of the form. If you try to use another field in a default value assignment, you will receive an error. Instead of using the default value, you would specify a rule on the control you want to "trigger" the rule on.

What Are Rules and When Are They Used?

Rules are a combination of conditions and actions that you can use to manipulate values in other controls that are based on the control to which the rules are assigned.

You can have more than one rule per control, and you can specify that those rules either run all the way through or stop when a condition is met. You can also specify the order of the rules, and rearrange them as necessary.

Here are a few examples of utilizing rules:

❑ Assign a default tax on an order based on the city the order was sold in.

❑ Update a contact e-mail field on an order after a customer has been chosen.

❑ Update a ship date field to the order date field plus a couple of days when the order date is specified.

❑ In the current form a good example of a set of rules is assigning various discounts based on the quantity ordered.

We are going to use the last example mentioned to demonstrate creating rules in the next section.

Creating Rules

The way to assign rules is to open the property sheet for the control, in this case the Quantity text box, and click the Rules... command button. After doing so, you will see the Rules dialog box, as shown here in Figure 6-9, minus the two rules.

Figure 6-9

Two rules displayed will be used in this section: The first will be described in detail. The second rule will be created in the Try It Out section.

When you click the Modify command, the Rule dialog box opens, displaying the rule labeled Rule 1, as shown in Figure 6-10.

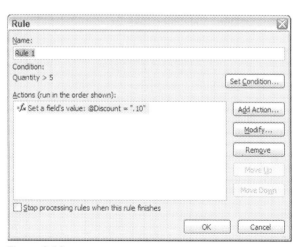

Figure 6-10

The first order of business to create a rule is to set the condition or conditions that you want the rule to perform the action, or actions, on. To accomplish this, you will click on the Set Condition button. The Condition dialog box then opens, and you can set a connection, as shown in Figure 6-11.

Figure 6-11

Note that what is displayed in the second and third drop-down lists is based on what you set the first drop-downlist to. They may also disappear altogether.

The first column contains the field or expression for the comparison, containing the following:

❏ **Fields in the Section**: Each of the fields is listed. When you specify one of the fields, the list of operators is displayed for you to choose from, including the *is greater than* operator displayed in Figure 6-11. You can also choose to fill in the Type a Number text box (which changes with the data type), select a field or group of fields, or specify a formula.

❏ **The Expression**: Enables you to type in an expression directly. Using this option, you can type in your own criteria as the condition. When referring to the current field you are creating the rule in, you can use the period (.). For example, for the condition displayed in Figure 6-10, you would type: . > 5.

❏ **User's Current Role**: With this option, you can customize a form based on the current user, and his or her role. Roles are created in InfoPath and have nothing to do with Windows or SQL Server roles.

❏ **Select Set of Signable Data...**: With digital signatures, you can secure fields, groups of fields, sections, or a whole form. When using this option, you can specify the name of the part of the form to enable digital signitures for, thus adding more security to your form. You can read more on digital signatures in Chapter 16, "Implementing Security."

❏ **Select a Field or Group...**: Picking this option displays all the fields and tables in the data source of the form. Depending on what you pick here, the second drop-down list will display a list of operators. One thing that is different from when you choose a field using the first option, fields in the section, is that in the third drop-down list you can type various data types into the field, instead of the just the data type of the actual field.

Once an option is chosen, the rest of the condition is filled out, varying with the option chosen. When you select a field to use, the operator and value boxes are displayed for you to supply these elements. At this point, additional criteria can be added, creating what is called complex criteria using ANDs and OR. You can see the And button back in Figure 6-11.

Once the condition is completed, click the OK button, and the condition is added to the rule. After the condition is specified, you can assign the actions you want to have performed when the condition you created is met. To create an Action, you will click the Add Action command button. The action for Figure 6-10 can be seen in Figure 6-12.

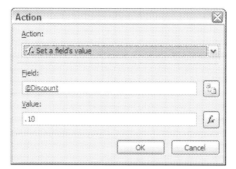

Figure 6-12

The first task to perform when entering the Action dialog box is to assign the Action to be performed. There are a limited number of actions that can be performed, although you can add as many actions to the rule as needed. A list of possible actions appears when you click the Action drop-down list. That list is displayed in Figure 6-13.

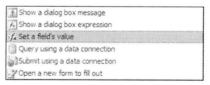

Figure 6-13

The following list explains the actions that can be performed:

❏   **Show a Dialog Box Message**: Displays a literal text string that you specify.

❏   **Show a Dialog Box Expression**: Displays a message that you can create using a combination of literals and formulas, including functions.

❏   **Set a Field's Value**: Assigns the value you specify to field that you also provide. This was the Action used in Figure 6-12.

❏   **Query Using a Data Connection**: Queries the data connection you assign it to, refreshing the data in a form or section.

❏   **Submit Using a Data Connection**: Submits data back to the database using a data connection. This is necessary when you need to update the database when the information has been partially entered.

❏   **Open a New Form to Fill Out**: Opens a form with a blank record.

As with the Condition dialog box, the fields after the Action field will vary depending on the action chosen. After filling in the other field or fields in the Action dialog box, click OK to save the action to the list of actions for the rule. At this point, you can add another action to the rule or accept the rule by clicking OK.

Try It Out   **Adding a Second Rule**

The time has finally come to add your own rule to the list of rules for Quantity. While the first rule establishes that any customer purchasing a quantity greater than 5 receives a 10 percent discount, you want those customers who purchase between 2 and 5 to receive a 5 percent (or .05) discount. To accomplish this, another rule has to be created.

1. Right-click the Quantity field, and pick TextBox Properties.... The property sheet for the quantity text box opens.

2. Click the Rules button. The Rules dialog box is displayed.

3. Click Add... in the Rules dialog box. A new rule is opened in the Rule dialog box.

4. Click the Set Condition button. The Condition dialog box opens.

5. For the first part of the condition, type **Quantity**, **is greater than**, and **1** in the three drop-downs displayed.

6. Click on the And button. A new row will appear in the Condition dialog box.

7. For the next criteria type **Quantity**, **is less than or equal to**, and **5** in the three drop-down lists. The Condition now looks as it does in Figure 6-14.

Figure 6-14

8. Click Ok to accept the condition.

9. Click on Add Action. The Action dialog box opens with a blank action.

10. Choose Set a field's value for the action. The Field and Value fields are displayed.

11. Type @**Discount** for the field, or use the Field locator button, displayed next the Field field.

12. Type **.05** for the Value:. The Action dialog box now looks like Figure 6-15.

Action
Action:
Set a field's value
Field:
@Discount
Value:
.05
OK
Cancel

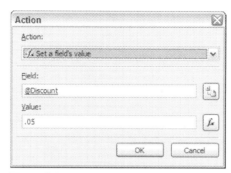

Figure 6-15

13. Click the OK button to accept the action. The Action dialog box closes, and you are back in the Rules dialog box.

14. Click OK twice to close the Rules dialog box and then the property sheet.

15. Click Preview Form to open the form in preview mode.

16. Query the form using BC, then modify the Quantity field to test the rules. Enter in various numbers such as 0, 1, numbers up to 5, and numbers over 5, then view the results. You should see results simular to those shown in Figure 6-16.

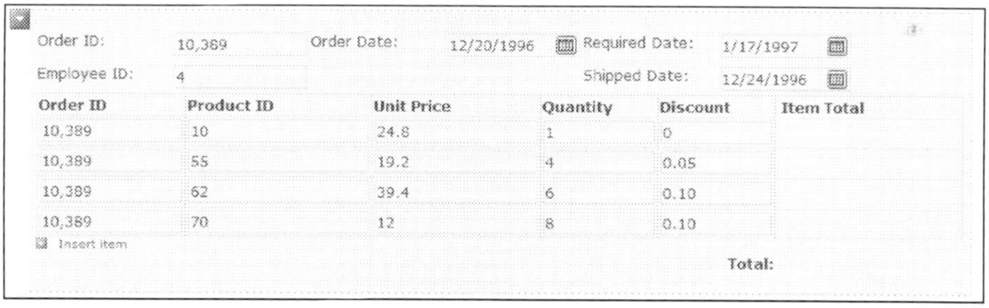

Order ID: 10,389
Order Date: 12/20/1996
Required Date: 1/17/1997
Employee ID: 4
Shipped Date: 12/24/1996
Order ID
Product ID
Unit Price
Quantity
Discount
Item Total
10,389 10 24.8 1 0
10,389 55 19.2 4 0.05
10,389 62 39.4 6 0.10
10,389 70 12 8 0.10
Insert item
Total:

Figure 6-16

As you have just seen, by using the rules as they are, you can accomplish quite a bit in creating a full-featured form that will react as you need it to when users enter data into the various fields. You have control over what happens. In other words you make the rules!

Another way of controlling how your form looks is by setting the formatting of the fields on the form.

Formatting Fields

InfoPath does a good job of looking at the data that you are basing your form on and supplying the control that matches that data. However, there are times when InfoPath can't know how you want the data to actually look. An example of this occurs with the OrderID and UnitPrice fields used in the form for this chapter. Also, it would be nice to display the Quantity field in red if it is a negative number. Looking at the `Chapter 6 Starting.xsn` form, you can see how the fields look, as displayed here in Figure 6-17.

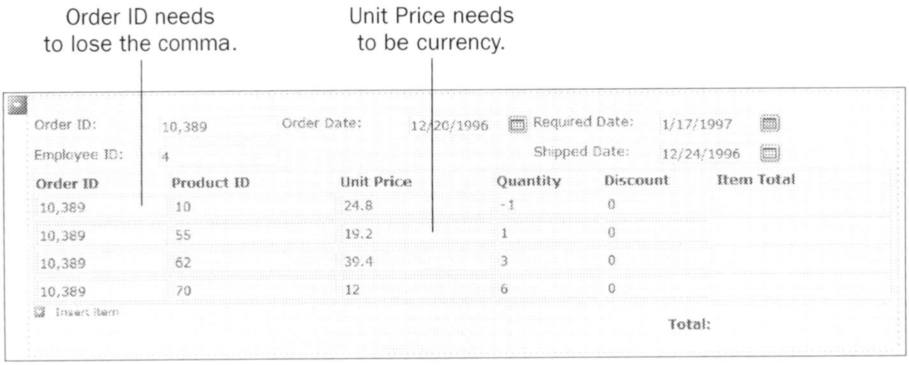

Figure 6-17

Notice that there are two locations where the OrderID field is displayed, in the order header area, and in the detail records. The OrderID field could also be removed from the detail level. Depending on how you want to format your form.

There are two methods of formatting that are used to accomplish what is needed:

❑ **Standard Formatting**: Used to set the format of the field regardless of the value stored in the field.

❑ **Conditional Formatting**: Format the field based on the conditions set in the conditional formatting dialog box. Conditions for formatting are the same as those used for rules.

Using Standard Formatting

To change the formatting of a control, you will once again open the property sheet of the control. Once the property sheet is open, you can choose Format... to open the Format dialog box. InfoPath will provide the formatting choices based on the actual data type of the bound control. For example, if you click the Formatting... button in the property sheet for the OrderID field, then the dialog box displayed is the Integer Format dialog box. The format options are:

❑ **None**: This option displays the raw value provided by the XML.

❑ **Number**: This option displays the designated format for the data type and number size.

❑ **Currency**: This option allows you to specify which currency you want to display the number in, such as U.S. dollars.

Other options are displayed as well, depending on the type of data and size specified. You can see from Figure 6-18 that in order to correct the OrderID, None (display XML value) was selected.

Figure 6-18

Again, by selecting None (display XML value), InfoPath will simply display the value supplied in the field that the control is based on.

Try It Out   Formatting the UnitPrice for Currency

Using the form you have been working in this chapter:

1.   Open the property sheet for the UnitPrice field.

2.   Click on the Formatting... button. In this case, the Decimal Format dialog box opens. You will see that format is set to Number.

3.   Click on the Currency option. The dialog box will now look like Figure 6-19.

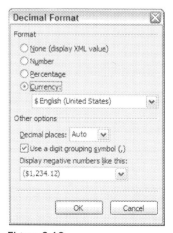

Figure 6-19

4. Click OK. The Formatting dialog box is closed.

5. Click OK to close the property sheet.

6. Click Preview Form to test the form you just modified.

7. Take a look at the UnitPrice field and notice the dollar signs, as shown in Figure 6-20.

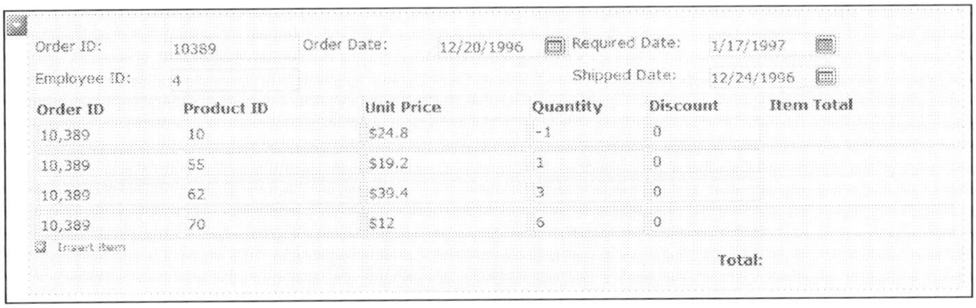

Figure 6-20

Now it's time to take look at the other way of formatting fields.

Conditional Formatting

When you apply conditional formatting, you are basing the formatting of an object on conditions you have specified. You can apply conditional formatting to quite a few controls including buttons.

Formatting Attributes

Almost all the controls, including sections, let you use conditional formatting with them. However, not all the attributes of the conditional formatting dialog box can be used with each control. Attributes of the conditional formatting include things such as Fonts, Bolding, Italicizing, and so on. You can even hide or display a control based on the conditions created.

Display Properties of a Text Box

To apply conditional formatting, click the Display tab of the control that you are working with. It is worthwhile to discuss the Display tab, because you can accomplish so much with it. The Display tab, like other elements of the property sheet, varies with the type of control. In Figure 6-21, you can see the Display tab for the Quantity text box property sheet.

You can see from Figure 6-21 just how much you can do when setting the display properties of the control using this page of the properties sheets. You should take some time to modify some of the properties displayed in the figure and watch what happens.

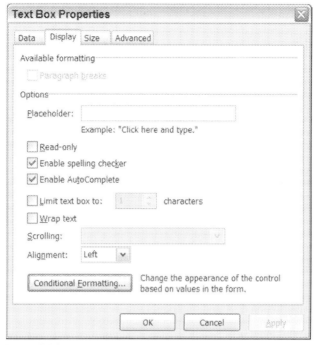

Figure 6-21

Try It Out   Creating Conditional Formatting

It is time to actually create the conditional formatting, by setting up a conditional format for the Quantity field, when values less than 0 are entered. Using the form you have been using for the chapter:

1. Double-click the Quantity text box control to open the property sheet.

2. Click the button with the caption Conditional Formatting.... You will be presented with the conditions that have been specified for formatting. At this point, you can modify or delete any existing conditions, add new ones, and rearrange the conditions, much as in the Rules dialog box.

3. Click Add.... The Conditional Format dialog box is displayed.

4. In the three drop-down lists displayed (the condition), type in **Quantity**, **less then**, and the value **1**. Again, these are just like the entries in the Condition text boxes of the rules you created in the section titled "Working with Rules at the Control Level," earlier in the chapter.

    Just as with the conditions for rules, you can create complex criteria using the And button.

5. Select Red for the font color. Now, the format is set so that when the user enters a quantity less than 0, the Quantity field turns red. You can see this condional format set up in Figure 6-22.

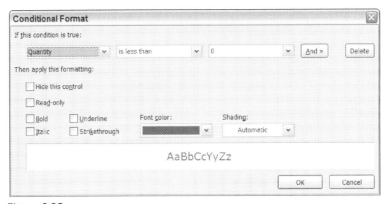

Figure 6-22

6. Test your form by previewing it, querying a record, and entering a value less than 0 for the quantity. The field should turn red.

Again, take a look at some of the other attributes you can set using the Conditional Format dialog box.

Summary

You can have the most powerful and complete database in the world behind your InfoPath form, but if you don't use the right controls for the tasks they were created for, then users won't be able to work with the form intelligently. InfoPath provides controls for controlling how your data is inputted and displayed.

In this chapter, you learned how to control input using controls. The chapter also discussed how default values can be supplied for fields in new records so that you can specify what values those fields start with. Rules also can be created so that actions are performed based on conditions specified at design time. Formatting can be applied to fields and conditional formatting to cause records to be displayed based on values in the record.

Data validation can be added to make sure that good data is entered into your database. Display controls can be created using formulas, and command buttons added to perform tasks on your forms.

Exercises

1. What the two types of default values that can be created?
2. Name the two parts of a rule.
3. How do you create a complex condition?
4. What are the two types of formatting?

Looking at Some Useful Controls and Techniques

The last chapter provided a good overview of what controls InfoPath provides for your forms, as well as some of the properties you can set for those controls using the property sheet. InfoPath supplies controls for all your needs, for both inputting and displaying data. While a number of these controls take more work to set up to use, they are worth the effort.

Besides the two buttons created by default (New Record and Run Query) when a new InfoPath form is created from a data source, InfoPath enables you use buttons for accomplishing whatever tasks you need. Controls such as the drop-down list boxes display data from additional data sources and control entry into fields. In this chapter you see how to use the controls just mentioned. You also see how to:

❑ Use formulas with controls to display data.

❑ Assign actions to buttons for performing tasks.

❑ Utilize drop-down list boxes, binding them to data sources.

❑ Use list boxes with other controls.

Using Expression Boxes with Formulas

Before you jump into the more complicated controls, there is a control that displays formulas on your InfoPath forms. Besides being able to bind text boxes to fields, as is done when you drag fields from the data source, you can display formulas using a control called an *expression box*.

Creating a formula to display in an expression box is the same as creating a formula for a default value except that you can use other fields within the formula. You can use formulas in a number of ways. Following are two of the most common:

❑ Totaling columns: InfoPath supplies built in functions such as sum(), avg(), and others.

❑ Combining the values of multiple fields.

In this section, you get a chance to work with multiple fields.

Once you have added an expression box, you need to specify the formatting of the data being displayed. To do this, you open the property sheet of the expression box control and set the format.

Try It Out   Adding an Expression Box Based on a Formula

Once you open the form called `Chapter 7 Intro.xsn` in Design mode, you can see, as in Figure 7-1, that there is a column with the title of Item Total. The object of this Try It Out is to add an expression box to display a total for each item.

Figure 7-1

1. Place the cursor in the table cell beneath the Item Total label.

2. Click on the Controls task in the Design tools task pane. The Controls task pane is then displayed.

3. Click on the Expression Box control under the Advanced controls. The Insert Expression Box dialog box is opened, as shown in Figure 7-2.

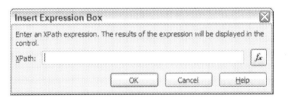

Figure 7-2

4. At this point, you can either fill in the expression if you are comfortable or you can click on the Formula button, as shown in Chapter 6, "Working with Controls in General." If you click on the Formula button, the Insert Formula dialog box opens.

5. Using the steps discussed in Chapter 6, in the section titled "Using Formulas," you can create the following formula in the Insert Formula dialog box displayed here in Figure 7-3.

6. Click Verify Formula to verify the formula.

7. Click OK to accept the formula. The Insert Formula dialog box closes.

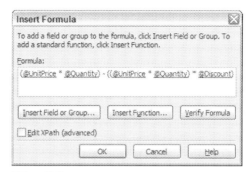

Figure 7-3

8. Click OK to accept the expression box. The expression box is then added to the form. It's time now to set the format of the expression box. In this case, you will be setting the format of the control to the Currency format.

9. Open the property sheet of the new expression box.

10. Select Decimal for the Format as: property.

11. Click the Format button. The Decimal Format dialog box opens.

12. Click the Currency option, as shown in Figure 7-4.

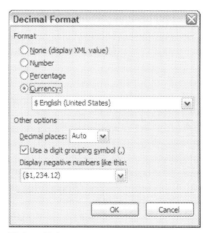

Figure 7-4

13. Click OK twice to accept the formatting. You are now ready to test the form.

14. Click Preview Form, type **BC** for the Region, and click Run Query. You will then see the new expression box on the form, as shown in Figure 7-5.

And there you have it. The Item Total column is displayed with the discount being taken into effect.

Figure 7-5

Utilizing Command Buttons

Command buttons, or buttons for short, are the way you can tell the form to perform various tasks you want to perform. You have already seen a couple of examples of buttons in looking at the Run Query and New Record buttons created by InfoPath.

To add a command button to the form, click on the Controls task in the Design Tasks task pane, and then click a Button, dragging it to the spot you want it located. Once it is on there you can open the property sheet. The first page of the property sheet is a General tab, and on it you can specify the Action you want the button to perform. If you want to have InfoPath perform a task for you from the Action field, you can choose from the following list:

❑ **Run Query**: Queries the database, populating fields specified as data fields.

❑ **Submit**: Saves changes to the database.

❑ **New Record**: Creates a new blank form to be filled out.

❑ **Delete & Submit**: Deletes the current record and saves the change to the data source.

❑ **Rules & Custom Code**: When the four preceding tasks don't do the trick, you can use this task to either create a rule or use custom code to perform your task. This option is discussed in greater detail in Chapter 11, "Working with Code in Your InfoPath Form."

When you specify an Action that includes submitting the form to the database, the Submitting Forms dialog box will appear, enabling you to set up various properties. This dialog box is displayed in Figure 7-6.

The Submitting Forms dialog box is very powerful in that it enables you to submit data not only to the database, as shown in the Submit to field, but also to other entities as well. Following is a complete list of destinations with descriptions:

❑ **Database**: The default, this option submits data to the database using the data connection.

❑ **E-mail**: This option enables you to specify a data connection that e-mails completed form information, including To and Subject lines and the body of the text.

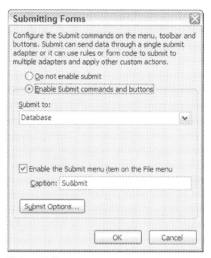

Figure 7-6

❏ **Web service**: A Web service can be set up to accept the data that you specify using methods created on the Web service's side.

❏ **SharePoint form library**: SharePoint is collaborative Web site software, and with InfoPath you can specify a form library where you can store InfoPath forms.

❏ **Web server (HTTP)**: When submitting the form to a Web server, you can submit the XML generated.

❏ **Custom submit using form code**: This option enables you to use either script or manage .NET code to submit the data where specified.

❏ **Custom submit using rules**: Rules are used to control how the data is submitted, specifying actions and conditions.

Try It Out   Adding a Delete Button

When you have InfoPath create a form for you, it gives you a means to add a new record as well as to modify and save an existing record, but no way to delete a record. To add this button, open the form you've been working with for this chapter:

1. Click on the Controls task in the Design Tasks task pane.

2. Click on the Button task, and holding down the left mouse button, drag and drop it onto the form in the location you want.

3. Double-click on the button to open the property sheet.

4. Pick Delete & Submit from the Action list. After you pick this option, the Submitting Forms dialog box will appear, as shown in Figure 7-7.

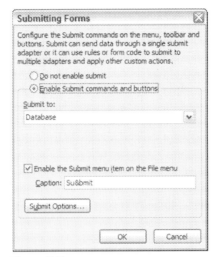

Figure 7-7

This form enables you to specify exactly how you want the submission of the data to be handled. There may some cases in the future where you will want to hold off submitting the data or have the data go to another data connection.

5. Click OK to accept the properties as they are for submitting forms.

6. Type Delete in the Label field. The dialog box will then look as shown in Figure 7-8.

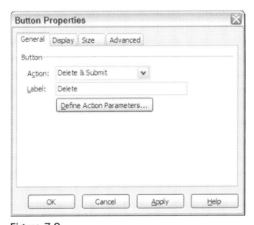

Figure 7-8

7. Click OK to accept the button properties.

8. Click Preview Form.

9. Type **SP** for the Region, and click Run Query.

10. Pick a record and click the Delete button. The record and its related records in other tables will be deleted provided that Cascade Deletes have been turned on for its relationships.

Should you try to delete a record that contains related tables without having Cascade Deletes turned on, an error will be displayed from Access. For more on table relationships reread Chapter 3, "Understanding Data."

Utilizing Drop-Down List Boxes on the Form

Drop-down list boxes are extremely useful for both controlling the data that goes into your form and adding convenience for users by supplying the necessary choices for the field currently being updated.

A few good examples of locations where drop-down list boxes can be useful can be seen right on the form you have been modifying. On the form that is being used for this chapter, Employee ID, Product ID, and Ship Via are currently using text boxes that take a number as a value. The problem with selecting a value is you can't be sure what the value represents unless you have looked at data the values are based on. For instance, instead of displaying the field Employee ID, you could display the names of the employees and have the user choose from that list. See Figure 7-9.

Figure 7-9

Although the Product ID field is hidden under the drop-down list box, you can see the Ship Via field displaying an integer value instead of the various shipping options such as Speedy Express and United Package.

This whole section can be applied to the list box control as well as the drop-down list box. Which you decide to use depends on one main question: How much room is there to display data? The methods for setting properties such as the data source will be the same.

Adding a Drop-Down List Box to a Form

There are two ways to add a drop-down list box to an InfoPath form:

1. Add the control from the data source as a text box, and then change it into a drop-down list box.

2. Add a drop-down list box control from the Controls task pane, setting the binding at that time.

Try It Out — Adding the Field from the Data Source as a Text Box, and then Changing It

Using the form that called `Chapter 7 Intro.xsf`:

1. Click the right mouse button, and highlight Change To.... You can now see the list of the types of controls you can change the control to, as shown in Figure 7-10.

2. Click the Drop-Down List Box. A drop-down list box is displayed in the form.

The new control is now ready to have you specify the data source for the list. You can use the steps just presented to create a drop-down list box from an existing control. However, there will also be times when you simply want to add a control to an existing form. The next Try It Out shows you how to do this.

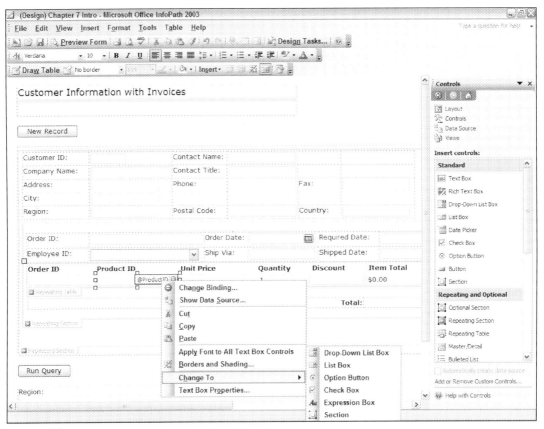

Figure 7-10

Try It Out   Adding a Drop-Down List Box and Binding it to a Field

To add a drop-down list box control right from the Controls task pane, you must first delete the text box used for Ship Via from the form you have been using in this chapter:

1. Click the text box bound to the @ShipVia field, next to the label with the same text.

2. Press the Delete key. The text box is now gone.

3. Click the Controls task in the Design Tasks task pane. The controls will be listed in the Controls task pane.

4. Making sure that the cursor is in the cell of the table where the old text box was located, click the Drop-Down List Box control. The Drop-Down List Box Binding dialog box appears.

5. Locate and highlight the ShipVia field in the tblOrders table. The dialog box then looks as it does in Figure 7-11.

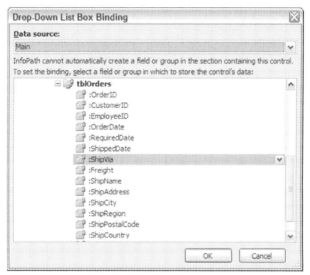

Figure 7-11

Note that the data source you are setting is what the control is bound to, not what is going to be listed in the drop-down list box for the users' choices.

6. Click OK to close the dialog box. The drop-down list box control is added and is bound to the ShipVia field.

7. Delete the text for the label, which reads ShipVia, that has been added for the new control.

As with the last Try It Out, the drop-down list box control has now been added to the InfoPath form, but it still needs to have the data source and properties assigned for the data to be listed.

111

Specifying List Box Data Sources

Once you have added a drop-down list box to your InfoPath form, you need to add data source properties for the list itself using the property sheet of the control. You can see an example of this using the control bound to the EmployeeID field in the InfoPath form you have been using for this chapter. You can see the property sheet in Figure 7-12.

There are threes ways to supply the data that is displayed in a drop-down list box. They are:

❑ **Enter the list box entries manually**: Here you will be specifying both the value to be stored in the field that the control is bound to and the text you want to be displayed for the individual values. This is useful if you have a static list that is fairly short.

❑ **Look up values in the form's data source**: When you want to limit the data to the data source specified for the form, you can use this option, including when you want to use the control as a filter for the form.

❑ **Look up values in a data connection to a database, Web service, file, or SharePoint library or list**: This option enables you to add additional data connections from the various sources. You will get the same dialog box used when specifying the form's main data connection.

Figure 7-12

Which of these options you use depends on what you need to accomplish with the list box.

Working with an Additional Data Source

In the case of the drop-down list box bound to the EmployeeID field, as shown in Figure 7-6, a new data connection is created. Using the tblEmployees table for the data connection, the EmployeeID field is used for the Value property, and an expression called EmployeeName is used for the Display name.

To look at the data connection called Employee Id and Name, choose Tools ⇨ Data Connections.... In the Data Connections dialog box, click Modify... with the Employee Id and Name data connection highlighted. Once you are back in the Data Connection Wizard, click Edit SQL...; you will then see the SQL statement used here:

```
select [EmployeeID],[LastName] & ', ' & [FirstName] as EmployeeName from
[tblEmployees] as [tblEmployees] order by [LastName]
```

You have just read about specifying another data connection for a drop-down list; now it's time to do the same task yourself by completing the next Try It Out.

Try It Out   Specifying an Additional Data Source

When modifying a data source using Tools ⇨ Data Connections..., you can add a new connection right in the control's property sheet. To see how to do this and specify the necessary properties, you will work with a drop-down list box bound to the ProductID field on the form you have been working with:

1. Open the property sheet for the drop-down list box bound to the ProductID.

2. Select the third option in the List box entries option group. A Data Connections drop-down list is displayed, as well as an Add... button.

3. Click the Add... button. The Data Connection Wizard opens.

4. Select Database for the source, and click Next>. You are taken to the main page of the Data Connection Wizard for databases.

5. Click on Select Database....

6. Locate the Chapter 7.mdb database, as shown in Figure 7-13.

7. Click Open. The Select Table dialog box opens.

8. Select tblProducts from the Select Table dialog box, and click OK. You are now taken back to the main page of the Data Connection Wizard, with all the fields displayed in tblProducts.

9. Deselect all the fields except ProductID and ProductName, as shown in Figure 7-14.

10. Click Next. The last page of the Data Connection Wizard is displayed.

11. Click Finish to complete the wizard, accepting the default values on the last page.

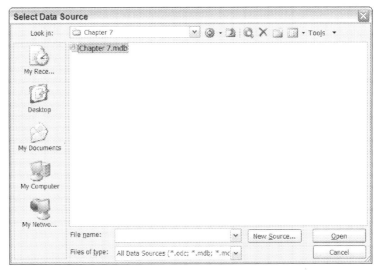

Figure 7-13

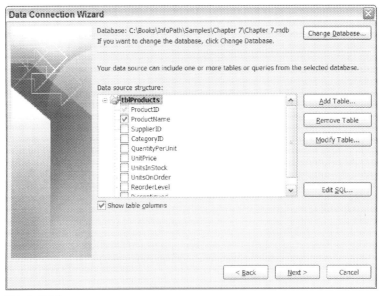

Figure 7-14

The name of the new data connection, tblProducts, is entered into the Data Connection property of the drop-down list box. You're not done yet. Although you have created a new data connection and assigned it to the control as needed, there are some additional properties that need to be assigned.

List Box Data Connection Properties

There are three properties that need to be set, which were briefly mentioned earlier in the section:

❑ **Entries**: The specific table or query within the data connection to be used. The text displayed will be the XML XPath from within the form.

❑ **Value**: The XPath representation of the field to be stored in the bound field of the control when an item is chosen from the list.

❑ **Display name**: Again, an XPath representation, but this time specifying the name of the field to be used for displaying the choices in the list.

You can get a good idea of what values to use by working with the following Try It Out.

Try It Out   Setting a List Box's Data Connection Properties

While still using the drop-down list box control bound to the ProductID field:

1. Click the XPath button next to the Entries properties. The dialog box that enables you to specify what field or group to use for the entry is displayed in Figure 7-15.

Figure 7-15

2. Click d:tblProducts table, and then click OK. The XPath for the group is populated in the Entries property.

3. Click the XPath button next to the Value property. The Select a Field or Group dialog box is once again displayed.

4. Choose ProductID, and then click OK. You can see in Figure 7-16 that @ProductID is filled in for both the Value property and Display name.

The reason both the Value and the Display name boxes are filled in with the field specified in the Value property is that many times you can use the same field for both properties, so InfoPath is saving you some work. In this case, however, you will be also specifying a different field for the Display name.

5. Click the XPath button next to the Display name property. Once again the good old Select a Field or Group dialog box is displayed.

6. Highlight the ProductName field, as shown in Figure 7-17.

Figure 7-16

Figure 7-17

7. Click OK. The Display name field is now populated with the @ProductName XPath name for the desired field. You can see the property sheet one final time in Figure 7-18.

8. Click OK to save the properties as you have set them.

9. Click Preview Form.

10. Supply **BC** for query entry in the Region field, and click Run Query. You will now see the product names displayed in a drop-down list box, as shown in Figure 7-19, rather than just the product IDs.

There you have it. That is all there is to specifying a new data connection and assigning which fields to use in your list box. Practicing a few more times will have you adding list boxes all over the place in your forms.

Remember that you can modify the data connections as described in Chapter 4, "Creating an InfoPath Form from an Existing Data Source." Using the methods described in that chapter, you can specify sort orders for the lists after they have been created.

Entering the List Manually

Sometimes as you are creating your forms you will want to base a drop-down list box on a list that doesn't exist anywhere in a data source or database. This occurs frequently with small static lists. An example of this is that the Ship Via accepts values that represent three different shipping companies: 1 for Speedy Express, 2 for United Package, and 3 for Federal Shipping.

It is recommended that you store this type of information in a table so that more information, such as contact address and phone numbers, could be stored for each shipping company. For the purposes of this example, you type the figures in yourself.

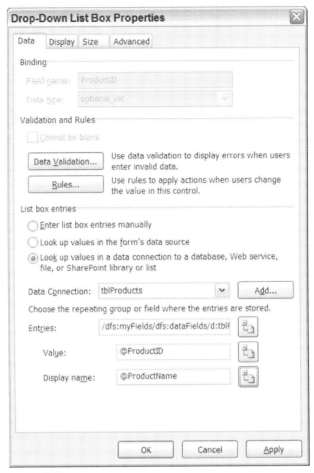

Figure 7-18

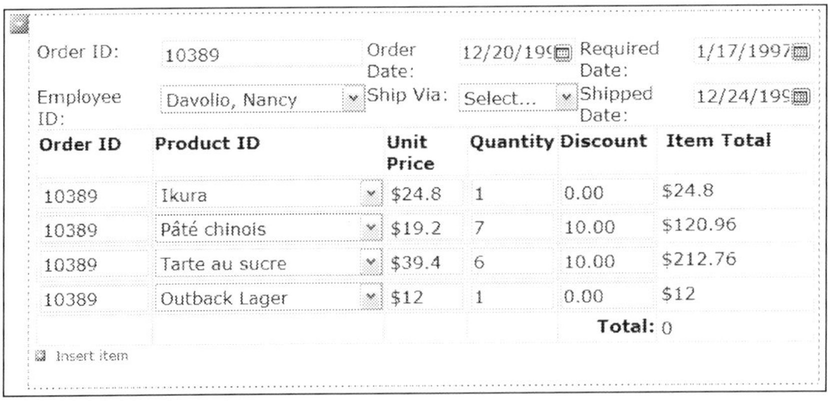

| Order ID: | 10389 | | Order Date: | 12/20/199 | Required Date: | 1/17/1997 |
| Employee ID: | Davolio, Nancy | | Ship Via: | Select... | Shipped Date: | 12/24/199 |

Order ID	Product ID		Unit Price	Quantity	Discount	Item Total
10389	Ikura		$24.8	1	0.00	$24.8
10389	Pâté chinois		$19.2	7	10.00	$120.96
10389	Tarte au sucre		$39.4	6	10.00	$212.76
10389	Outback Lager		$12	1	0.00	$12
					Total:	0

Insert item

Figure 7-19

Another situation in which it makes sense to type the figures in statically is if you are going to be using the InfoPath form without a database behind it, for example, if you are going to e-mail the form to other users and just have the data stay with form, instead of in an Access or SQL Server database. As far as the users are concerned, the input experience will be the same when filling out the form.

Try It Out   Creating the List Manually

Using the drop-down list box control bound to the ShipVia field in the form you have been working with in this chapter:

1. Open the property sheet.

2. Leaving the default of Enter list box entries manually for the list box entries option and click on the Add... button, located next to the list of current entries. The Add Choice dialog box opens.

3. Add the first entry: **1** for Value and **Speedy Express** for the Display name. The dialog box then looks as it does in Figure 7-20.

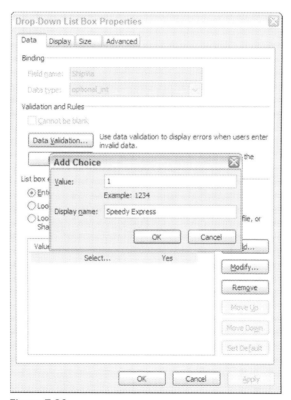

Figure 7-20

4. Click OK to accept the choice.

5. Repeat Steps 3 through 4 for the other two choices (United Package and Federal Shipping) displayed in Figure 7-21.

Figure 7-21

6. Click OK to close the property sheet.

7. Click Preview Form, supply **BC** for the Region, and click Run Query. The form then displays a record with United Package displayed in the Ship Via field. Remember that prior to this, a 1 was displayed in the Ship Via text box control.

8. Click the Ship Via drop-down list box. You then see the possible list entries, as shown in Figure 7-22. Picking another item from the list stores the values specified in the Value property in the database once the Submit button is clicked.

Order ID:	10389		Order Date:	12/20/1996		Required Date:	1/17/1997	
Employee ID:	Davolio, Nancy		Ship Via:	United Packac		Shipped Date:	12/24/1996	
Order ID	**Product ID**		**Unit Price**	Select...		count	**Item Total**	
10389	Ikura		$24.8	Speedy Express		00	$24.8	
10389	Pâté chinois		$19.2	United Package		00	$120.96	
10389	Tarte au sucre		$39.4	Federal Shipping	6	10.00	$212.76	
10389	Outback Lager		$12		1	0.00	$12	
							Total: 0	

⊡ Insert item

Figure 7-22

Summary

Besides using text boxes for inputting and displaying field data, you can use expression box controls for displaying expressions or formulas. InfoPath provides formatting for the expressions as well as the means for inputting the expressions themselves by the entering the formulas directly or by using a wizard.

InfoPath also provides a means for adding your own buttons using either some built-in actions provided or by adding your own code or script.

Drop-down list boxes, as well as other list boxes in InfoPath, enable the developer to control how the data is input into the InfoPath form. This is accomplished by either supplying the entries for the list or by specifying the data connection for the data to be displayed.

Exercises

1. What type of control would you use to display a formula on an InfoPath form?

2. Name the six types of built-in actions you can assign to a button.

3. What are the three ways to specify the data used for a list box?

4. How do you modify a data connection in InfoPath?

Working with Sections

One of the powerful features of InfoPath is the ability to create sections that provide additional control over data for the developer of the form. Using sections with InfoPath forms means much more than this does in other applications such as Word and Access. In those other products, when you talk of sections you are talking about areas of forms or documents where data is entered, but using sections in these applications does not accomplish nearly as much as it does in InfoPath. When you specify a section on a form in InfoPath, you can have a whole section displayed or hidden with the data behind it (bound to it) being affected as well. Data can be repeated, optionally displayed, or tied to specific data in a preceding section, much as the subform controls are used in Access.

The majority of the different types of sections available in InfoPath forms have been touched upon at one time or another in the chapters leading up to this one. Now it is time to see just how powerful sections are, and what you can do with them. In this chapter you will:

❑ See the various types of sections available in InfoPath.

❑ Examine using choice sections.

❑ Work with optional section and repeating sections.

❑ Look at useful section properties.

❑ Filter data in a section.

Overview of Types of Sections in an InfoPath Form

InfoPath provides various types of sections depending on the task you need to accomplish. These sections are added to forms as controls and contain other controls within them. The majority also are bound to groups of data. A group of data is related records in one of the tables included in a data source, usually in a one-to-many relationship.

An example of using a bound section is an optional section. An optional section is a repeating section where data can be entered, but is not required. An example of an optional section is one bound to the tblCustomerNotes table, which is related to tblCustomers on the CustomerID field. As with other data tasks, InfoPath will take care of a lot of the work to handle adding the data in the CustomerID field in the related table, based on how you set up the section.

Setting up some of the types of sections is covered throughout the rest of the chapter, but for now, take a look at the types of sections available on InfoPath forms, and how you would use them. Some of the controls can be found in the Sections task pane of the Controls task pane.

❏ **Choice Section**: These are individual sections that are used in a Choice Group control. This control lets you specify fields to fill in based on a choice the user makes. You can also add a repeating choice group when you want to add more than one entry for the choice.

❏ **List Control**: Though it is technically not a section, it is worth mentioning the List control because it displays data in a section-like manner. There are three flavors of lists: bulleted, numbered, and plain. You can bind list controls to data or let the users create the lists on the fly.

❏ **Master/Detail Section(s)**: Used to represent a one-to-many relationship, these type of sections are created in one of two different ways: manually, by putting a repeating table and repeating section on the same form, or by choosing a Master/Detail control (version 1.1) and filling out the properties.

❏ **Optional Section**: As the name suggests, the data in this section is optional, thus it takes up no room on a form if it is not needed. A notes section for products is a good example of this. Not every product is going to have a note, so why take up the room?

❏ **Repeating Section**: This is probably the most used type of section, whenever groups of data are used. Examples are customers, orders, or products. All of these groups of information can be managed using repeating sections.

❏ **Repeating Recursive Section**: One of the most confusing section controls, this control lets you embed other controls, including itself, so that you can recursively display and enter information. An example of this is a hierarchical employee chart, where employees can be specified at different levels with the same fields being used.

❏ **Scrolling Region**: As with the list control, the scrolling region is not described as a section, but displays data in a section-like format. Other controls can be placed in a scrolling region control so that instead of scrolling down a whole form, users scroll down in a specific area.

Looking at Choice Sections and the Choice Group Control

Choice sections and groups are very useful when you display and store a set of data in a form based on a choice the user makes. There is no need to have fields on the form that don't need to be filled in if the data is not going to be used. In some form packages:

❏ Developers have to programmatically disable or make fields invisible.

❏ Users have to tab over the fields that aren't necessary.

The Choice Group control solves the problem by displaying data in choice sections based on the choices made.

A good example, and one you will deal with in this chapter's Try It Out is what information you want filled out when a user chooses the type of payment he or she wants to make for an order, such as Cash, Check, or Charge. You can see final form with the payment choice of Charge selected in Figure 8-1.

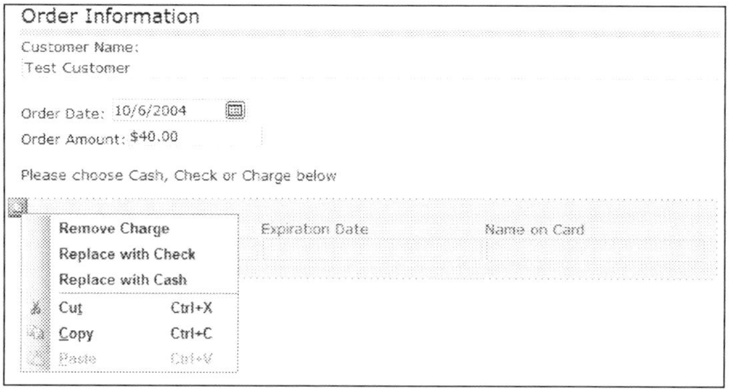

Order Information
Customer Name:
Test Customer

Order Date: 10/6/2004
Order Amount: $40.00

Please choose Cash, Check or Charge below

Remove Charge		Expiration Date	Name on Card
Replace with Check			
Replace with Cash			
Cut	Ctrl+X		
Copy	Ctrl+C		
Paste	Ctrl+V		

Figure 8-1

The credit card number is located under the menu in Figure 8-1. When the payment choice is Check, the form looks as shown in Figure 8-2.

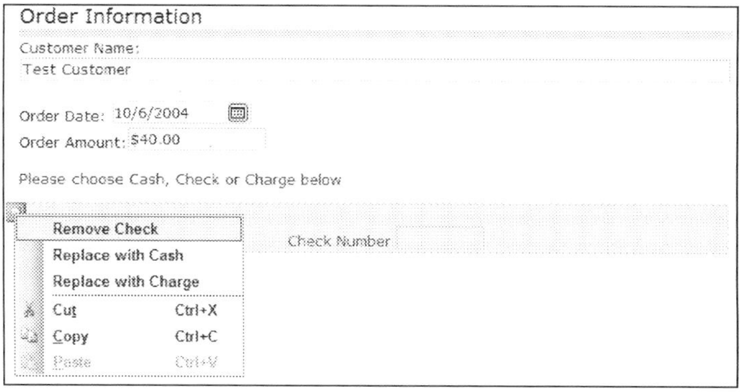

Order Information
Customer Name:
Test Customer

Order Date: 10/6/2004
Order Amount: $40.00

Please choose Cash, Check or Charge below

Remove Check		Check Number
Replace with Cash		
Replace with Charge		
Cut	Ctrl+X	
Copy	Ctrl+C	
Paste	Ctrl+V	

Figure 8-2

When the choice is Cash, then no fields are displayed in the section.

After dragging a Choice Group control onto the form, two Choice Section controls are added by default. You will then add controls to each of the sections, based on the data you want the user to edit in each. To have the menu display the various names of the choices, the field name is filled in using the Choice Section property sheet. To add an additional choice to the Group Choice control, Choice Section is selected from the Advanced section of the Insert Controls task pane. This will all become clearer as you work on the following Try It Out.

Try It Out Adding a Choice Group Control

For the purpose of this Try it Out, you will be creating a new form. When completed it will look as it does in Figure 8-3.

Figure 8-3

1. Open Microsoft InfoPath 2003. The Fill Out a Form dialog box is displayed.

2. Choose Design a Form.

3. Click on New Blank Form from within the Design a Form task pane. A blank form will be displayed.

4. Add a Table with Title from the Layout task pane.

5. Add the controls and text as displayed in Figure 8-4. What the names of the controls are isn't important for this Try It Out.

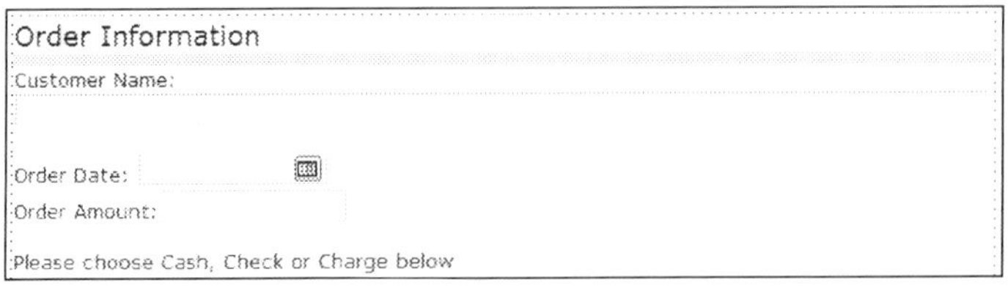

Figure 8-4

6. Drag a Choice Group control from the Advanced section of the Controls task pane. You will see the control displayed on the form as shown in Figure 8-5.

7. Add the desired controls to the first two sections — in this case, nothing in the first section and a 3-column table with a label and text box for the Check Number as shown in Figure 8-3.

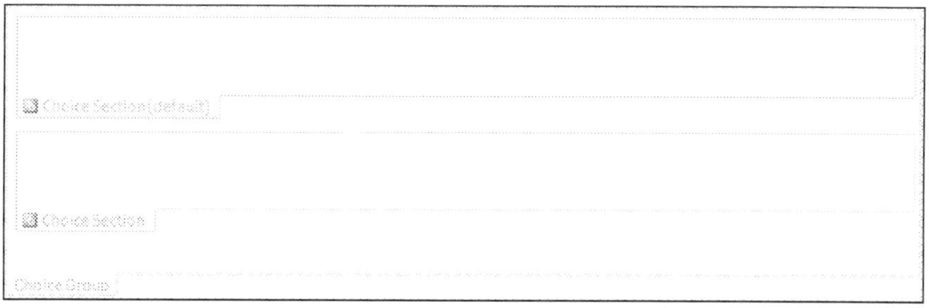

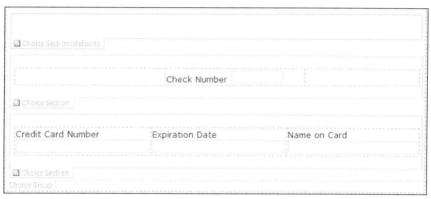

Figure 8-5

8. Drag and drop a Choice Section control from the Advanced section of the Controls task pane into the bottom of Choice Group control.

9. Add a three-column table with the necessary controls, as shown in Figure 8-6.

Figure 8-6

10. Next, to have the choices displayed, click Preview Form, and click the area below the prompt: Please choose Cash, Check, or Charge.

11. Make your selections, and the form will be displayed as shown in Figures 8-1 and 8-2.

One issue with binding the choice group to a database is that you need to have the data structured as it is on the form. Therefore, it is simplest to use the control with a new form, creating the XML schema with the form.

Optional Sections

You have seen optional sections inserted earlier in forms in other parts of the book, but it's time now to take a closer look at them and see how to really take advantage of the different properties of the optional section.

Optional sections are useful when you have data that is not required on the form. Some examples of data that is good in optional sections are notes, activities, appointments, or any information that does not require at least one entry to be included. If you need to include at least one entry, for example, when detail lines in an order need to include at least one item to order, the entries are not optional.

You can include other types of sections, such as repeating sections within optional sections. That way if you might have more then one note, but don't need to include any at all if you don't want to, then a repeating section within an optional section is the way to go.

When working with optional sections, you can specify to:

❏ Include the section on the form by default.

❏ Not to include the section by default.

❏ Whether or not to allow users to insert the section.

❏ Whether to show an insert button and the hint text.

The last choice is also available for other types of sections. You can also set up rules, default values, and custom commands, all of which were discussed in Chapter 6, "Working with Controls in General." The way to specify all of these options is to use the Section Properties dialog box, displayed in Figure 8-7.

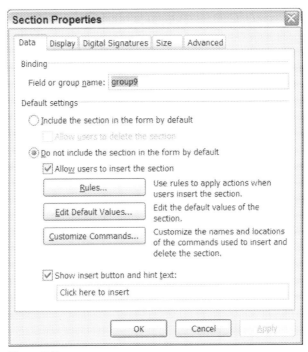

Figure 8-7

Try It Out   Adding an Optional Notes Section and Setting Its Properties

Using the form you created in the last Try It Out:

1. Place the cursor under the Choice Group.

2. Select the Optional Section from the Repeating and Optional section of the Controls task pane. The optional section will then be added to the form.

3. Type **Notes** into the optional section added in Step 2.

4. Add a Text Box control, naming it **Notes**.

5. Open the property sheet for the optional section you added.

6. Type **NotesOptionalSection** in the property labeled: Field or group name.

7. Change the hint text to: **Click here to insert a Note**.

8. Click Apply. The property sheet and form will look as it does in Figure 8-8.

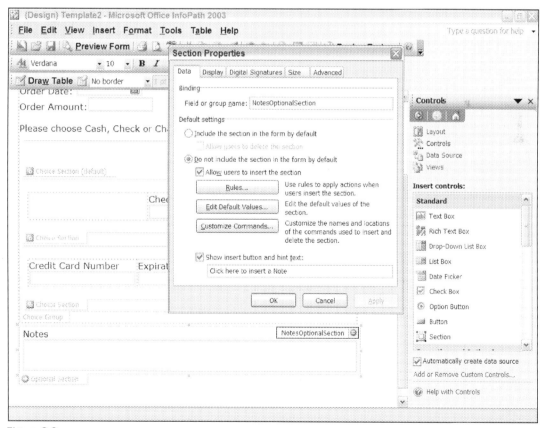

Figure 8-8

9. Click OK.

10. Click Preview Form. The form will open, and at the bottom of the form you will see the prompt added in Step 7, as displayed in Figure 8-9.

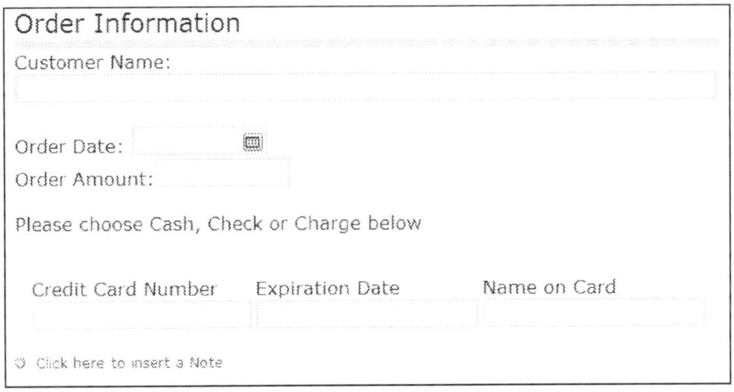

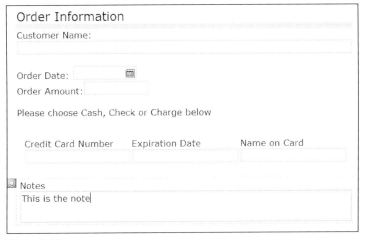

Figure 8-9

11. Click the prompt labeled Click here to insert a Note. The Note text box will then be displayed.

12. Type some text in the text box, as shown in Figure 8-10.

Figure 8-10

Specifying Filters on InfoPath Forms

When working with data located in a Web service or database you can limit the amount of data, or filter, by using the query fields. There are times when it is convenient to limit data when using a standalone form as well. One way to do this is to specify filters, which can be done for a whole form, or individual repeating tables.

The way to accomplish filtering is by setting the Filter Data properties on a repeating table or section, located on the Display table in the property sheet, and pointing them to another control containing the values to filter for, such as a drop-down list box. You can see an example of this in Figures 8-11 and 8-12, where first all records are displayed,

Figure 8-11

Figure 8-12

Try It Out: Filtering a Repeating Table Using a Drop-Down List Box

For this task, you will make a new blank InfoPath form that will create a list of employees with their type.

1. Open InfoPath.

2. Click on Design a Form.

3. Click New Blank Form....

4. Add a Repeating Table control from the Repeating and Optional section of the Controls task pane. The Insert Repeating Table dialog box will open, as shown in Figure 8-13, with the default value of three columns displayed.

Figure 8-13

5. Click OK.

6. Add text and text boxes for Last Name, First Name, and Employee Type, naming the text boxes as the labels are, without the spaces. You can see the EmployeeType field displayed in Figure 8-14.

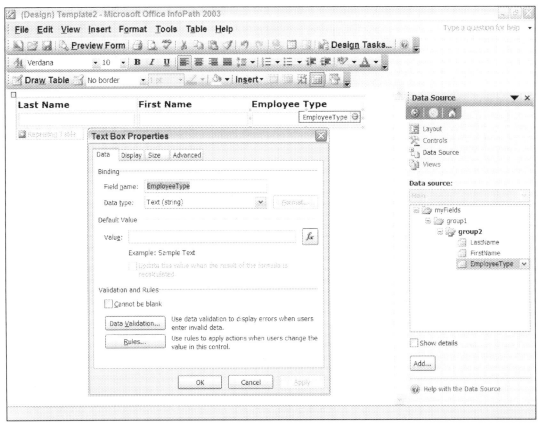

Figure 8-14

7. Click OK to accept the EmployeeType field.

8. Add a Drop-Down List Box control, naming it ddEmployeeTypeFilter.

9. Add the values Display All, Full Time, and Part Time for the list box entries, as displayed in Figure 8-15.

10. Click OK to accept the properties for ddEmployeeTypeFilter.

11. Right-click the label for the repeating table, and choose Repeating Table Properties.

12. Click the Filter Data... button on the Display tab. The Filter Data dialog box opens.

13. Click the Add... button. The Specify Filter Conditions dialog opens.

14. Choose Select a field or group, then ddEmployeeTypeFilter for the first box. Choose Is equal to in the second box

15. Choose Select a field or group and then EmployeeType for the third box.

16. Click the And button to add another condition.

17. Select "or" in the fourth box.

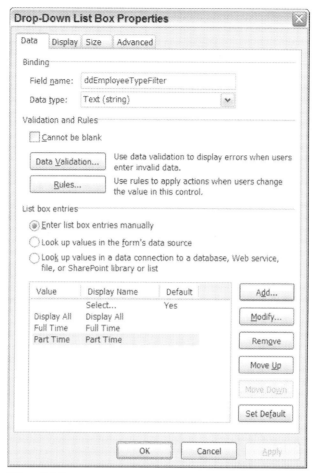

Figure 8-15

18. Choose Select a field or group and then ddEmployeeTypeFilter for the first box in the second row.

19. Type **Display All** without the quotes in the third box. The Specify Filter Conditions dialog box should now look as it does in Figure 8-16.

Figure 8-16

20. Click OK to accept the filter conditions.

Now when you click Preview Form, you can enter data and see it filtered as shown in Figures 8-11 and 8-12.

Master/Detail Sections

When you use Web services and databases as data sources for InfoPath forms, master/detail sections are created automatically when you drag fields from a data source onto your form, such as tblOrders and tblOrderDetails, which have been used in prior chapters.

Master/Detail sections are created by two basic methods:

❑ Dragging and dropping a Master/Detail control onto the form.

❑ Dragging on two or more tables as mentioned in the last paragraph.

Using either of these methods creates a repeating table as the master section and a repeating section for the detail section. When created, a field (or fields) needs to be specified to link the two sections.

Summary

Sections make up a large part of InfoPath forms. Just about any solution to various tasks you may have will most likely require one type of section or another. Sections are added to forms in a number of different ways, including just adding fields from a data source onto the form or creating a repeating table. You can add sections onto a form by also utilizing various section controls, including adding the ability to hide data, or to include data only when specific choices are made using the choice sections.

This chapter also showed you how to filter data using the Filter properties on repeating sections and tables.

Exercises

1. What are the three types of repeating objects?

2. Name the objects used for displaying areas of data based on user selections.

3. Which tabs are the Filter Data properties on, and which type of section and table?

Managing Views

Views in InfoPath provide the ability to organize and present data in your forms. Where other applications use multiple forms for managing information, views accomplish the same tasks in single InfoPath forms. With traditional applications, you generally have a main switchboard and then switch between forms that refer to specific areas of data.

InfoPath provides the ability to switch between views by either using the built-in menus or creating custom task panes. This chapter explains how to work with views. In this chapter you will:

- ❑ See an overview of using views in InfoPath forms.
- ❑ Take a look at the various view properties.
- ❑ Learn about multiple views.
- ❑ Design a print view.
- ❑ Learn about custom task panes.

Views Overview

InfoPath provides views (pages) to help you create forms that are organized in a way that makes sense for users, rather than just putting all the data on a single page.

You can see in Figure 9-1 where views have been created for Customer, Notes, and Order information, tied together with a custom task pane.

For the purpose of this chapter, one InfoPath form will be created from start to finish based on the database called Chapter 9.mdb. *The tables called tblCustomers and tblOrders will be used.*

Besides creating views to break up information, you can also create views based on secondary data sources, or special views made to print information for current views. These are discussed in the last section in this chapter.

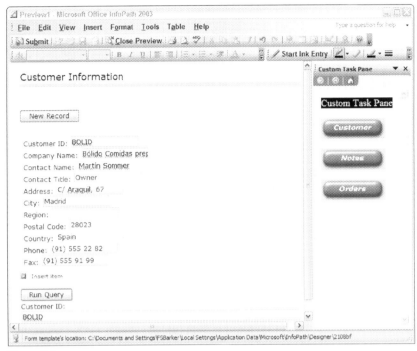

Figure 9-1

Try It Out   Creating the Default View

To get started with managing multiple views, you need to start with one view. To give you a feel for creating more than one view, you will specify the data as you would in real life.

1. Open InfoPath.

2. Click on Design a Form. The Design a Form task pane will appear.

3. Click on New from Data Connection.... The Data Connection Wizard will start, with the first page asking if you would like to use a database or Web service.

4. Click Next, specifying to use a database by default. The next page displays only one button, Select Database.

5. Click the Select Database button. The Select Data Source dialog box will open.

6. Locate and select the desired data source — in this case Chapter 9.mdb, as shown in Figure 9-2.

7. Click Open. The Select Table dialog box will appear.

8. Select tblCustomers, and then click OK. You will be taken back to the Data Connection Wizard.

9. Choose Add Table, and use the Select Table dialog box to choose tblOrders. The Data Connection Wizard will now look as it does in Figure 9-3.

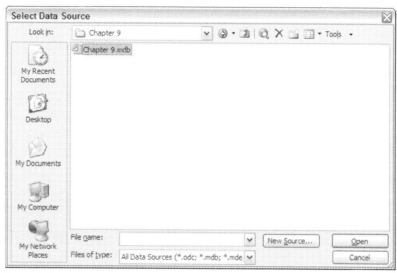

Figure 9-2

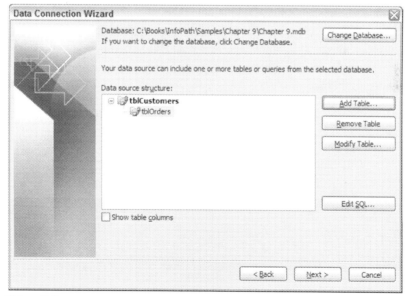

Figure 9-3

10. Click Next. The final page of the Data Connection Wizard is displayed.

11. Click Finish. The initial InfoPath form is created with the query and data areas on the default view of the form.

12. Drag and drop the CustomerID field from the queryFields tree in the Data Source task pane into the area below the button labeled Run Query.

13. Drag and drop the d:tblCustomers group from the dataFields tree in the Data Source task pane into the area below the button labeled New Record. The right-click list (list on the right) will appear displaying the section choices.

14. Choose Repeating Section with Controls from the list displayed. The fields from both the tblCustomers and tblOrders tables are displayed on the form.

15. Click the border of the section for the tblOrder fields, as shown in Figure 9-4.

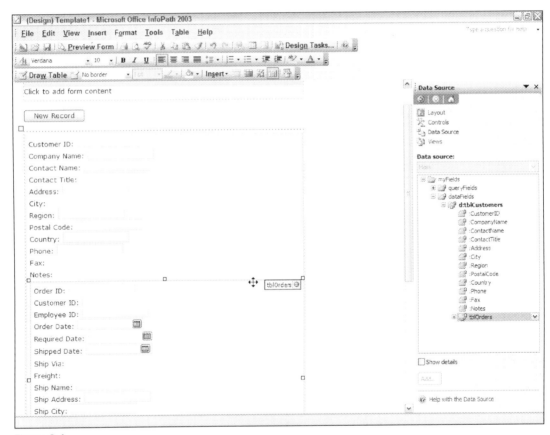

Figure 9-4

16. Press Delete. The tblOrder fields will disappear.

15. Delete the Notes label and field.

17. Add the title **Customer Information** to the top of the form. You form will now look like the one in Figure 9-5.

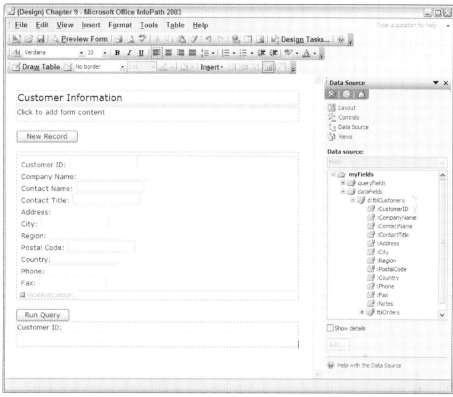

Figure 9-5

You can spruce up your form as you see fit. In Figure 9-5 extra spaces have been removed.

The default view has now been created. The next two views will be created in the section titled "Creating Multiple Views."

Working with View Properties

Another great feature of InfoPath is the ability to set properties at the view level. This means that you can give users visual clues as to which view they are working on by setting the views up with different properties such as background color and size, and even adding a background picture if desired.

Reviewing the Views Task Pane

Before discussing the property sheet itself, take a look at the Views task pane and what the options are for working with views. You can see the views task pane in Figure 9-6.

The first thing you will notice is the list of views. This list displays all the available views, including print views. You will see this list grow as the chapter goes on. Below the list is the View Properties button. This button opens the property sheet for the currently highlighted view. You can also open the property sheet by double-clicking the view.

Figure 9-6

In the Actions tasks, you can see the following choices:

❑ **Add a New View**: Creates a new view in the current form you are in. When clicked, a blank view will be created, based on the main data connection. You can also create views based on secondary data sources.

❑ **Add Print View for Word**: This task takes the data from the InfoPath form view and allows the user to specify an XML transformation file (XSLT) to create the file for printing use Microsoft Word.

❑ **Create Print Version for This View**: With this option you can create a view that can be formatted for printing. This view can combine information from multiple tasks and display it in a single view, which may be more convenient when printing.

The best way to open a view is to click the Views task in the Design Tasks task pane. In the Views task pane you can click the View Properties buttons, located below the list of views.

Getting to the View Properties

Properties for views are broken up into four categories, which you can see in the following series of figures:

❑ **General properties**: This tab, displayed in Figure 9-7, contains three categories of settings. The first is View settings, which is where you will specify the name of the view. When there is more than one view, you can set when you want a particular view to be the default view and whether or not you want to have the view displayed on the View menu. For example, you may not want a view to be displayed on the View menu if you are switching to that view by using a button or after submission instead.

Figure 9-7

Within the General tab there are also Background properties, including color and a picture if desired. Finally, Layout settings enables you to specify a custom width for the form.

❑ **Text Settings**: This tab enables you to set the formatting properties for the various types of controls you have on the current view. By setting the properties at this level, you make all the controls of that type consistent, but different from other views if desired. Note that not all control types use all the properties. You can see the Text Settings for the current view in Figure 9-8.

❑ **Print Settings**: Using this tab, you can set various properties for how you want the view to print. Categories include using a specific view to print with, Orientation as in Portrait or Landscape, Headers and Footers, Number of copies, and number of pages to print. You can see this page in Figure 9-9.

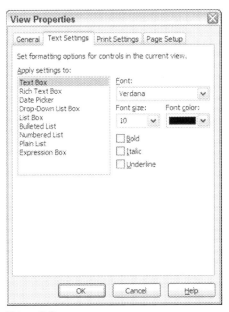

Figure 9-8

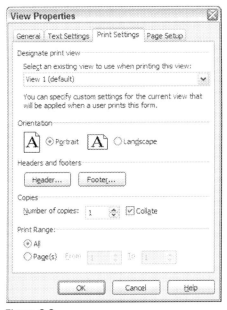

Figure 9-9

❑ **Page Setup**: The last tab contains settings for which printer to use, the type of paper, and the margins for the page. This tab can be seen in Figure 9-10.

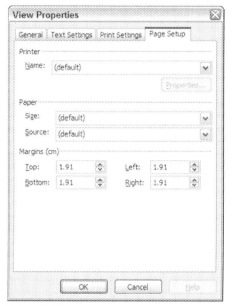

Figure 9-10

Try It Out   Changing the Default View's Properties

For the purposes of this chapter, you will not be changing too many properties. In fact, using the form you created in the last Try It Out, you will be simply changing the name of the view so that you can distinguish it from the other views you are creating in the next Try It Out.

1. Click the Views task in the Design Tasks task pane.

2. Click the View properties button, or double-click the only view in the Views list: View 1. The property sheet for the view will open.

3. Change the name of the view to **Customer Information**, as displayed here in Figure 9-11.

4. Click OK. The property sheet closes, and the new name is reflected in the Views list.

Because the purpose of this chapter is to see how to use multiple views, it's time to get busy.

Figure 9-11

Creating Multiple Views

Creating multiple views is actually quite easy and can greatly enhance the usability of the InfoPath forms. To accomplish creating a new view, press the Add a New View... button. This will create a blank view that you can fill in. Since you will be using the same data source you don't have to worry about that step. Once the view is created you can then modify the view properties for display in the menu and customize as needed.

Try It Out   Adding the Notes and Orders Views

It's time now to create a couple of more views for your form. You will be using the Notes field for one view and the tblOrders table for the other. Using the same form you have been working on in this chapter:

1. Click the Views task in the Design Tasks task pane.

2. Click the Add a New View... link. The Add View dialog box will be displayed.

3. Type **Notes** in the New view name text box, as shown in Figure 9-12.

Figure 9-12

4. Click OK. A blank view will be created and displayed.
5. Click the Data Source task in the Design Tasks task pane.
6. Drag and drop the Notes field from the tblCustomers table in the dataFields branch of the data source. A repeating section will be created with Notes field included.
7. Arrange the Notes label and field on the view as shown in Figure 9-13.

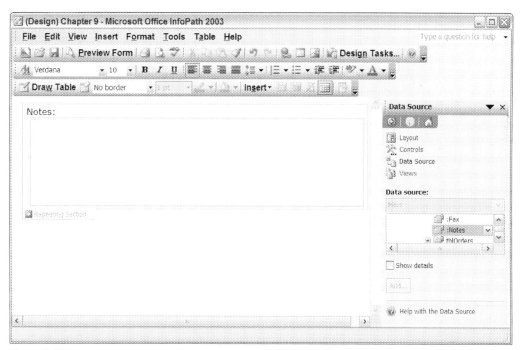

Figure 9-13

8. Click the Views task in the Data Source task pane.

9. Click the Add a New View link once again. The Add View dialog box appears.

10. Type **Orders** for the new view name, and click OK. A new blank view will be displayed.

11. Click the Data Source task.

12. Drag and drop the tblOrders table onto the view. Then a menu with types of sections will appear on the right.

13. Choose Repeating Section with Controls. The new view is then created as shown in Figure 9-14.

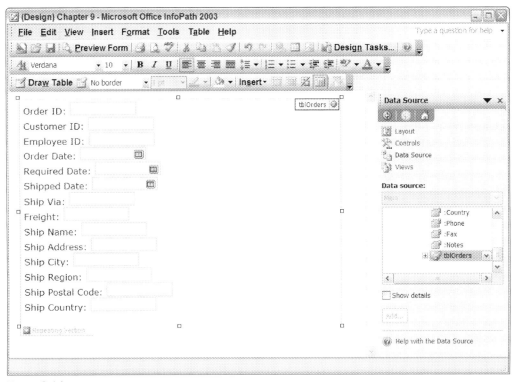

Figure 9-14

Try It Out   Switching between Multiple Views

The new views have now been created. It's time now to test the new views.

1.   Click Preview Form. The InfoPath form opens.

2.   Type in **BOLID** for the Customer ID field under the Run Query button.

3.   Click Run Query. The customer information is displayed.

4.   Click the View menu, you will see the three views displayed, as shown in Figure 9-15.

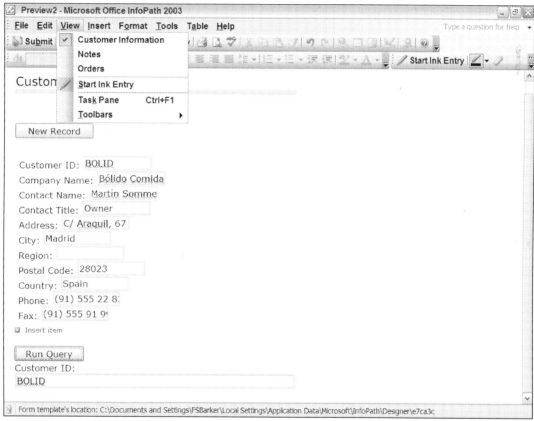

Figure 9-15

5. Select View ➪ Notes. The Notes view becomes visible, as shown in Figure 9-16. You may modify the text of the note and click the Submit button.

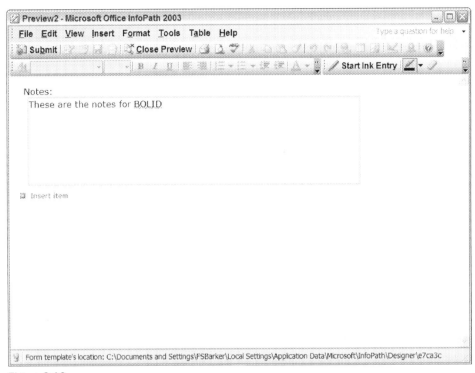

Figure 9-16

6. Select View ➪ Orders. The Orders view is now displayed, as shown in Figure 9-17.

It is great to be able to switch between views without any work using the built-in menus. However, it is nice to give users a custom task pane that displays the views that are available. The next chapter covers just this.

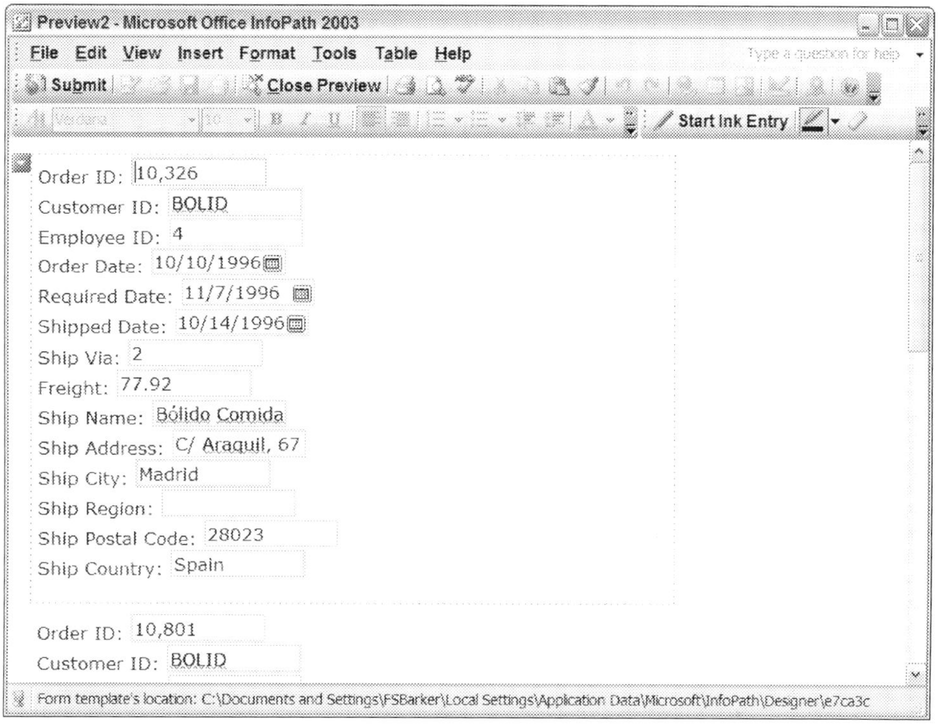

Figure 9-17

Custom Task Panes

Besides switching views, you can create custom task panes for various purposes such as displaying context-sensitive help, as discussed in Chapter 14, "Real-World Tasks and Coding Examples." A custom task pane consists of a Hypertext Markup Language (HTML) Web page using links or code that switches the current view. You also can include button images, as shown in Figure 9-18.

Once you have created the HTML page that contains the necessary code, you can set form options to tell InfoPath which files (resources) make up the Web page, and that you want the InfoPath to include a custom task pane.

The logical place to start in using a custom task pane is to outline what goes into creating the HTML Web page.

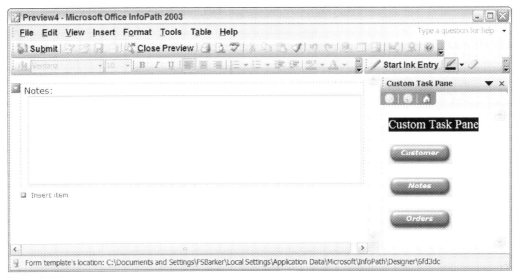

Figure 9-18

HTML Web Page Used for Custom Task Pane

While the HTML Web page created for the custom task pane is pretty straightforward as far as Web pages go, it does involve some Java Script coding and using the InfoPath object model. Normally, this would be covered in a later chapter such as Chapter 12, "Getting Starting Using Script," which will cover the topics discussed here in greater detail. However, because the code is minimal and the topic so useful, it is logical to include this custom task pane in this chapter.

In the HTML Web page you will have the standard tags for <html>, <head>, and <body>. You will also use the images in the Web page as well. The biggest change is the use of <script> in the code, and a function that is created. The function is called SwitchView() and is used to switch views.

```
<script>
        function SwitchView(view)
        {
                gobjXDocument = window.external.Window.XDocument;
                gobjXDocument.View.SwitchView(view);
        }
</script>
```

This code uses the XDocument object, which is the primary InfoPath object for programming the InfoPath object model. Using the syntax:

```
window.external.Window.XDocument
```

the code specifies the XDocument object of the window that the Web page is residing in, which will be the InfoPath task pane area. Within the XDocument object is the View object. When the following line of code is called:

```
gobjXDocument.View.SwitchView(view);
```

the SwitchView method of that object is called, being passed the name of the view to switch to. An example of assigning the call to the custom function within the HTML is:

```
<p><img border="0" src="Notes.png" width="123" height="38"
        onclick="SwitchView('Notes')"></p>
```

You also will have to create the image files, in this case Notes.png, to use as the buttons.

Try It Out   Creating the Task Pane in HTML

You can find all the objects created in this and the next Try It Out in the Chapter 9 folder for this book on the Wrox Web site. As mentioned, the image files will have to be created using a image editor. For the purposes of this Try It Out, three image files: Customer.png, Notes.png, and Orders.png, were created.

1. Open NotePad.exe.

2. Type in the following text:

```
<html>
  <head>
        <title>Custom Task Pane</title>
        <script>
                function SwitchView(view)
                {
                        gobjXDocument = window.external.Window.XDocument;
                        gobjXDocument.View.SwitchView(view);
                }
        </script>
  </head>
  <body>
        <p><font color="#ffffff" size="4"><span
        style="BACKGROUND-COLOR: #000000">Custom Task Pane</span></font></p>
        <p><img border="0" src="Customer.png" width="123" height="38"
            onclick="SwitchView('Customer Information')"></p>
        <p><img border="0" src="Notes.png" width="123" height="38"
            onclick="SwitchView('Notes')"></p>
        <p><img border="0" src="Orders.png" width="123" height="38"
            onclick="SwitchView('Orders')"></p>
  </body>
</html>
```

3. Save the text as `index.htm` in the Chapter 9 folder on the Wrox Web site.

4. Copy the image files into the Chapter 9 folder.

That's all there is to it. Now you are ready to specify the task pane information in InfoPath.

InfoPath Custom Task Pane Properties

InfoPath lets you easily specify which custom task pane files to use on the Form Options dialog box. Using the dialog you will specify the following properties:

- ❑ **Enable custom task pane**: When checked the next custom task pane properties and options are enabled.

- ❑ **Task pane name**: This is used to specify the name for the task pane.

- ❑ **Task pane location**: This property points to the main task pane HTML file you have created. The file will need to added using the Resource File dialog box.

- ❑ **Resource Files button**: This opens the Resource File dialog box, which enables developers to specify the files used for the custom task pane, including the HTML and image files.

When you specify the resource files, when you publish the file, then the files are included in the `.xsn` created. You can export the files from the form using the Resource Files dialog box.

Try It Out   **Specify Task Pane Files in Your InfoPath Form**

Using the InfoPath form you have created throughout the chapter and the HTML file and images mentioned in the last Try It Out.

1. Open InfoPath.

2. Open the form in design view.

3. Choose Tools ➪ Form Options from the menu. The Form Options dialog box will open.

4. Click on the Advanced tab.

5. Type **Custom Task Pane** in the Task pane name field, as shown in Figure 9-19.

6. Click the Resource Files... button. The Resource Files dialog box opens.

7. Click the Add... button. The Add File dialog box opens.

Figure 9-19

8. Locate and select the four files that make up the custom task pane including: index.htm, Customer.png, Notes.png, and Orders.png.

When the last file is selected, the Resource Files dialog box will look as it does in Figure 9-20.

9. Click OK. The dialog box closes.

10. Select index.htm for the Task pane location drop-down dialog box, as shown in Figure 9-21.

Figure 9-20

Figure 9-21

11. Click OK to accept and close the Form Options dialog box.

12. Click the Preview Form button to display the new form. The form is now displayed with the custom task pane on the right side, as shown in Figure 9-22.

13. Click the various choices in the task pane to test the new form.

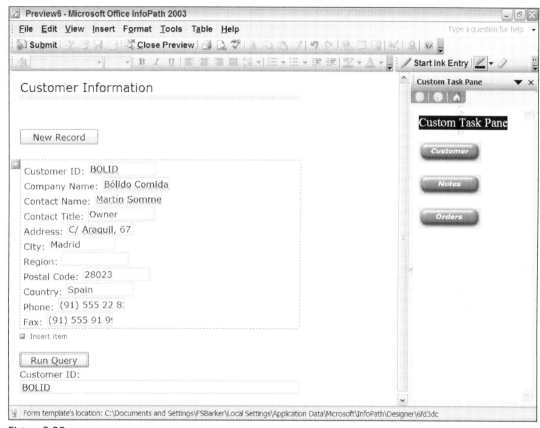

Figure 9-22

Print Views

The last topic to cover with views is the use of print views, which enable developers to organize the data that users are modifying in a way that makes it easier to handle, and also print additional information if desired.

Print views can either be displayed or not on the View menu. Creating print views is as easy as creating any other view. After selecting the view to create the print view for, you will design the new view just as you would other views, by dragging and dropping objects on to the form. Then, to use the new print view, you will choose File ➪ Print just as you would for other applications, but InfoPath will use the print view for the information printed.

Try It Out   **Creating Print Views**

Using the InfoPath form created during this chapter:

1. Click the Views task.

2. Click the Customer Information view in the Views task pane.

3. Click Create Print View for This View... link. The Create Print View dialog box will appear, displaying the suggested name in the New view field, as shown in Figure 9-23.

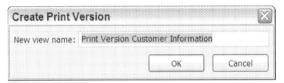

Figure 9-23

4. Click OK to accept the default name. A blank view will be displayed.

5. Click Data Source.

6. Design the print view as you desire, showing the data in the form you want. In Figure 9-24, you can see that the tblCustomers fields are displayed in a section with controls, and the tblOrders field in a repeating table format.

7. Select Views Properties... from the Views task pane. The View Properties dialog box opens.

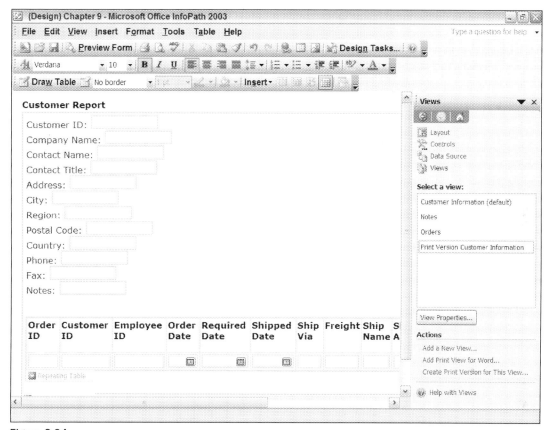

Figure 9-24

8. Unselect the check box next to the label Show on the View menu when filling out the form. The dialog box then looks as it does here in Figure 9-25.

This will cause the view name to not show up on the View menu with the other view choices. Of course, if you are supplying a custom task pane, then you also can leave the choice off the task pane as desired.

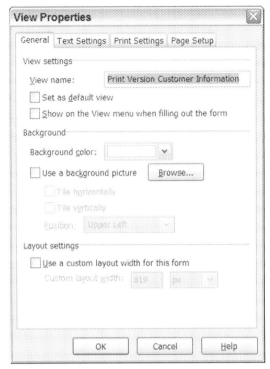

Figure 9-25

9. Click OK.

10. Click Preview Form. The form is displayed.

11. Type **BOLID** in the Customer ID field under the Run Query button.

12. Click the Run Query button. The customer information for BOLID is displayed.

13. Choose File ➪ Print Preview..... The print preview for InfoPath is displayed using the new view, as shown in Figure 9-26.

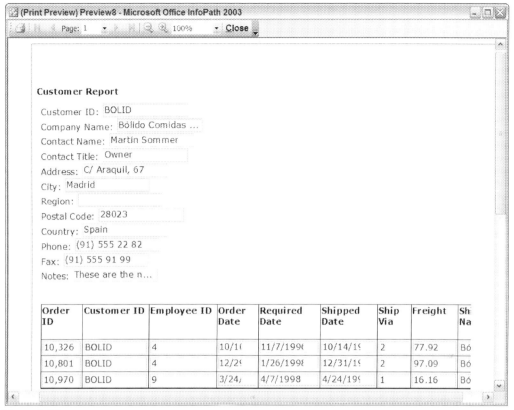

Figure 9-26

Summary

InfoPath lets you manage how you have users input information into your InfoPath forms by giving you the ability to organize your data using views. This makes entering data into the forms simpler from the user's standpoint and also gives you, the developer, more control. Creating multiple views is as simple as creating a single view using the Views task pane.

Using HTML you can create custom task panes, giving your form a more professional and custom look. Print views enable you to print more information than is displayed on the current view, and can be set to not show up in the View menu.

Exercises

1. How do you create more than one view?

2. What do you have to do to get the view to show up on the View menu?

3. Where are the properties for specifying a custom task pane?

Publishing InfoPath Forms

With many other programs such as Access or development languages such as Visual Basic, when you create applications with forms you need to distribute the applications onto either a shared network or using a setup program. When Web applications are created and are ready for production, the HTML files are published to a Web server for user access. InfoPath enables you to use some of the ways just mentioned to distribute forms, but also introduces new ways as well.

Thus far in the book you have primarily seen how to design and preview forms. This is great, but if you don't know how to publish them for other people's use, or for your own use beyond your computer, they don't do much good. This chapter discusses how to publish your form. In this chapter you will:

❑ See the various ways to publish InfoPath forms.

❑ Publish an InfoPath form to a shared location on the local network.

❑ E-mail a form to a user for them to fill out.

❑ Publish an InfoPath form to a Web Server.

❑ Merge data from multiple forms.

What It Means to Publish an InfoPath Form

As mentioned previously InfoPath forms are made up of multiple XML-type files, creating the form templates you design. When you publish a form, you are going to place the template in a shared location that can be:

❑ **In a shared local area network folder**

❑ **On a Web server**

❑ **In a SharePoint library**: Windows SharePoint Services is software created by Microsoft to enable companies to create collaborative Web sites. These Web sites include areas for: document libraries, events, various lists, tasks, and much more. The additional areas and publishing to SharePoint are discussed in detail in Chapter 17, "Working with InfoPath and Windows SharePoint Services."

Differentiating Forms to Fill from Their Templates

When the user fills out a form based off a template, that form is then saved separately. But it is still based on the original form template. One of the really cool things about this is that when the template is modified, the forms based on that template are updated as well. This makes it extremely easy to modify and update published forms.

Ways to Distribute InfoPath Forms

Once the template has been placed where it is accessible to users, there are different ways that users can fill out the forms. The ways to fill out InfoPath forms depend on where you published the forms, because a form must have access to the template it was based on. So, you can have users access the form:

❑ On a shared network drive

❑ Using a Web server

❑ In a SharePoint library

❑ By e-mailing users forms to fill out

All the methods just mentioned require that the user have access to the form template and a copy of Microsoft InfoPath installed on their local system.

Finally, you can also distribute a filled out form either in e-mail, or as a static Web page.

Publishing to a File Server

This method of publishing forms is probably the most straightforward. All you need is the UNC (Universal Naming Convention) path of the folder you want to publish the form to and to be connected to that folder. Utilizing the UNC path is discussed in the following Try It Out.

Besides running the Publishing Wizard as outlined in the next Try It Out, you need to make sure that users have access and write permissions for the folder in which you are going to publish the InfoPath form.

Try It Out   **Publishing a Form on a File Server**

To illustrate publishing a form on a file server, you will use a sample form provided by InfoPath:

1. Open InfoPath. The Fill Out a Form dialog box opens.

2. Click Design a Form task. Microsoft InfoPath opens with the Design a Form task pane displayed.

3. Click Customize a Sample.... The Customize a Sample dialog box is opened, listing all the sample forms.

4. Highlight the Absence Request form, and click OK. The form opens in Design mode.

5. Choose File ⇨ Publish.... The Publishing Wizard begins, displaying the introduction page shown in Figure 10-1.

Figure 10-1

6. Click Next. The next page gives the options for publishing the form: to a shared folder on the local area network, network, SharePoint form library, or Web server, as shown in Figure 10-2. For this first Try It Out you will use the first choice.

7. Click Next. This page is where you will specify the folder on the network share and name of the form.

8. Click Browse to locate the folder.

9. Click OK. You will see the file path and name of the form, as shown in Figure 10-3.

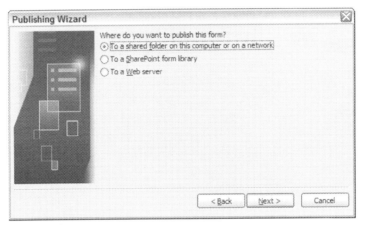

Figure 10-2

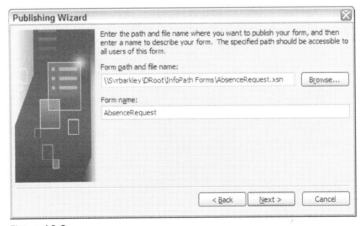

Figure 10-3

10. Click Next. The next page displays the file path and name of the form you specified. It is used to verify the choice made on the last page. It asks you to make sure that others have access to the form and lets you specify an alternate route to the form, as shown in Figure 10-4.

Note that if there had been problems accessing the form itself an error message would have been displayed.

11. Click Finish to accept the form as it is. The last page of the Publishing Wizard is displayed, giving you two options: notify users via e-mail and open the form (to fill) from the new location, as shown in Figure 10-5.

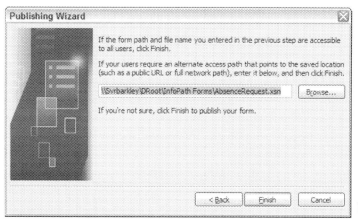

Figure 10-4

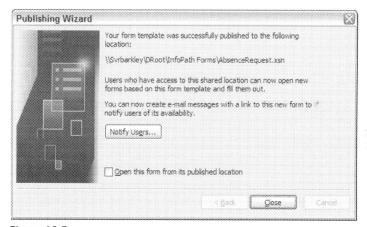

Figure 10-5

12. Click Notify Users.... Outlook, or whatever your e-mail program is, will open and information will be displayed regarding the newly published form. This will include a hyperlink to the form, as shown in Figure 10-6.

13. Close the e-mail.

14. Click the checkmark next to the label: Open this form from its published location.

15. Click Close. The form will now open, as shown in Figure 10-7.

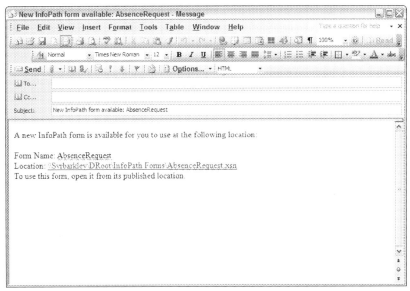

Figure 10-6

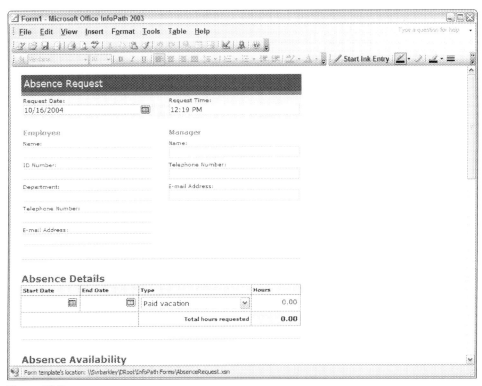

Figure 10-7

Notice that the path in the status bar at the bottom of the form reflects the new form template location. When you save the form, you will be asked where to save it, because the form is separate from the template.

Publishing to a Web Server

The steps for specifying a Web server are very similar to those for publishing an InfoPath form on a file server. Instead of using a UNC path, you will use a URL (Uniform Resource Locator) to designate where to publish the form.

Along with knowing the URL you want to publish to, you also want to make sure the users will have access and write permissions for the folder. You also will want to make sure that the Web server you are going to be publishing to has Microsoft WebDAV enabled. Microsoft WebDAV is an extension to the Hypertext Transfer Protocol (HTTP). Microsoft WebDAV allows developers to perform remote authoring and manages Web content. If the Web server doesn't have WebDAV enabled, then you will need to use the shared folder method to publish the InfoPath form.

Try It Out   Publishing an InfoPath Form to a Web Server

For the purpose of this Try It Out you will once again use the Absence Request form. Instead of publishing to a shared folder you will be specifying a Web server.

1. Open InfoPath.

2. Click Design a Form. InfoPath opens, and the Design a Form task pane is displayed.

3. Click Customize a Sample.... The Customize a Sample dialog box opens.

4. Select Absence Request, and then click OK. The form is now displayed in design mode.

5. Select File ➪ Publish.... The first page of the Publishing Wizard is displayed. This page is merely an introductory page.

6. Click Next. The next page displays the various choices for publishing the form.

7. Select the option: To a Web server, as shown in Figure 10-8.

8. Click Next. The next page is where you specify the URL to which to publish the InfoPath form. In this case `http://www.AppsPlus.com` and `AbsenceRequest.xsn` is the form. You can see this in Figure 10-9.

9. Click Next.

   At this point, you may be asked to enter a login name and password for the Web server.

   As with the last Try It Out, this page verifies the address you specified for the published template, as shown in Figure 10-10. If required you could enter an alternate access path. Depending on the set up for the Web server, you may or may not require login information from the users.

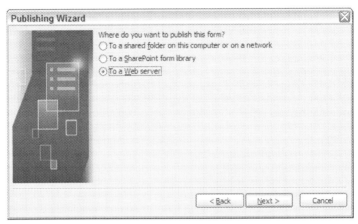

Figure 10-8

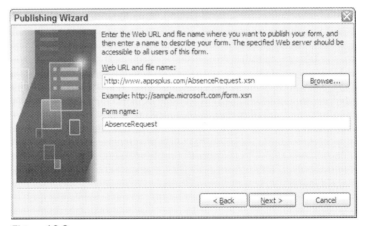

Figure 10-9

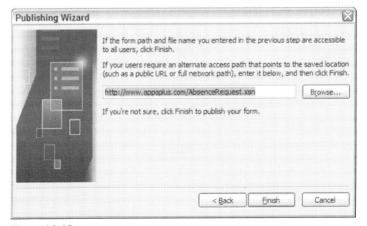

Figure 10-10

10. Click Finish. The last page, displaying the final location where the form template has been published is displayed, as shown in Figure 10-11. As with publishing to the file server, you can notify users that a form has been published.

Figure 10-11

11. Click the option Open this form from its published location.

12. Click Close. InfoPath will then attempt to open the form from the Web server. You may then receive the message box displayed in Figure 10-12, which is common when opening files from the Web. This will depend on the level of Internet security. Also, if the form is digitally signed you can have this form open without this dialog box. Internet and InfoPath security, including digitally signing forms, is covered in Chapter 16, "Implementing Security."

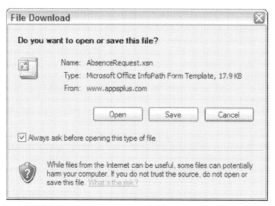

Figure 10-12

13. Click Open. The form is then opened with the template location displayed in the status bar of the form, as shown in Figure 10-13.

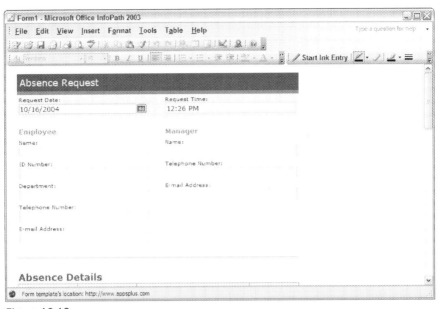

Figure 10-13

You have now seen how to publish InfoPath template forms on both a file server (on a network) and on Web servers. You also have opened the form template in both locations for filling out the data. Another way of enabling users to fill out is using e-mail. You can send a form just for viewing as well.

E-mailing InfoPath Forms

If the e-mail program you are using is Outlook, you can e-mail InfoPath forms for either data input or viewing by opening forms the following ways:

❑   For filling out a form from the location where you published the template, picking File ➪ Send to Mail Recipient.

❑   In Design mode, select Send Form as Attachment....

Both of these methods require that the template form be in a shared location.

Another thing to remember is that depending on what the template form is using as a data source will determine how much work the user has to do when filling out the form. If the data source (connection) is a Web service or database such as Access or SQL Server, then the data is put in the data source when the form is submitted. If you are using an XML document for the data, then the user needs to e-mail the XML document back to you so that you have access to the data.

While users will be able to see the data already in the form that was sent for them to update and return, they need to open the XML file attached to the e-mail. They will then choose File ➪ Send to Mail Recipient after filling in the information in the form.

Try It Out   E-mailing an InfoPath Form When Filling

After publishing as shown in the last few Try It Outs and then opening the form for filling in, you want to send it to someone via e-mail:

1. Choose File ➪ Send to Mail Recipient. An e-mail message will be created, with the form displayed in the body of the e-mail. Along with your standard fields of To, CC, and Subject there is also another field with the label of Introduction. This field lets you introduce the form and provides instructions about how you want the user to fill out the form and send it back to you.

2. Fill in the Introduction. You can see the form with the introduction field displayed in Figure 10-14.

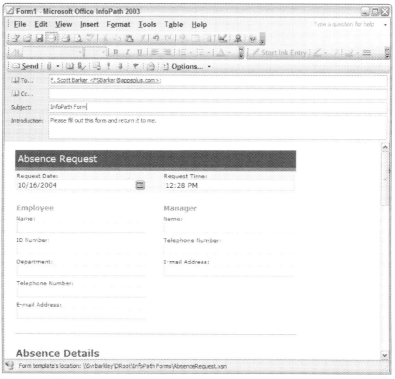

Figure 10-14

3. Click Send. The user will then receive the form as shown in Figure 10-15. Notice the Attachment with the name of form1.xml. As mentioned, while users can read the form in the e-mail body itself, to fill out the form they need to double-click the Attachment.

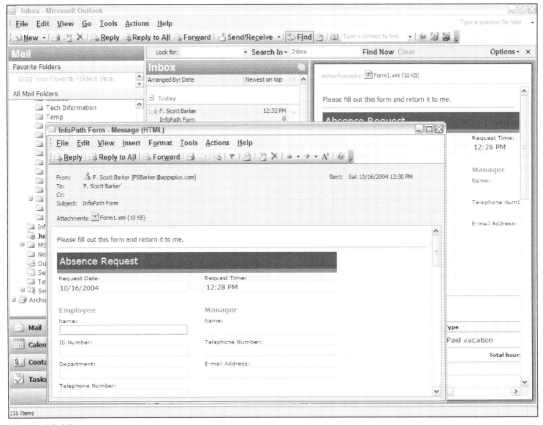

Figure 10-15

4. Double-click the attachment Form1.xml. The form opens, and you can fill out the information, as shown in Figure 10-16.

5. Choose File ➪ Send to Mail Recipient to e-mail the changes in data back to the person who first sent the form.

Remember that if the form uses a Web service or a database as the data source, you don't have to mail the information back to the sender.

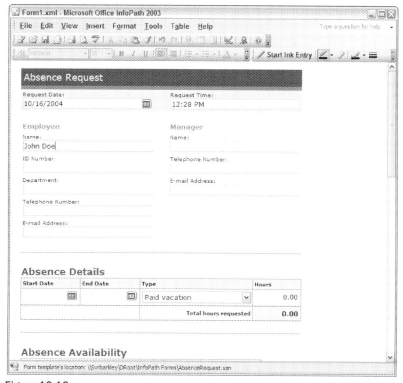

Figure 10-16

Exporting to a Web Page

There are times when you want to display the InfoPath form and data, but don't want to necessarily have the information updated. The way that InfoPath enables you to accomplish this is by allowing you to export your forms. The forms are then exported to a file that includes both the HTML and XML needed to display the form and data together.

When exporting a form, you have the choice of exporting it to either a Web page or an Excel spreadsheet. For the purpose of the next Try It Out, you will be exporting it to a Web page.

Try It Out   Exporting an InfoPath Form

To export a form such as the Absence Request form used throughout the chapter:

1. Choose File ➪ Export To ➪ The Web..., and the Microsoft Excel menu is then displayed as shown in Figure 10-17.

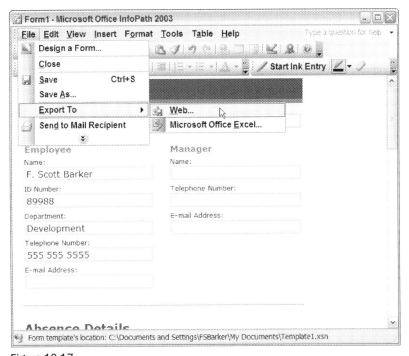

Figure 10-17

2. Click Web.... The Export to Web dialog box is then displayed. This dialog box enables you to put the Web page created in the location where you want it to be. You can then name it as you see fit. For the purposes of this Try It Out, the default name was used, as was the default location. You can see the Export to Web dialog box in Figure 10-18.

3. Click Export. The file is then created in the location specified. To take a look at the Web page, you will want to locate the new file, and double-click it. The page will look just as it does in Figure 10-19.

And that's all there is to it.

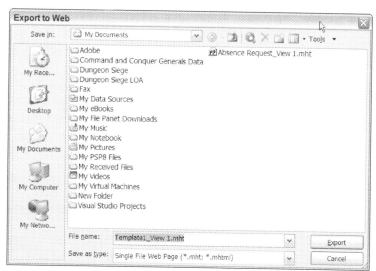

Figure 10-18

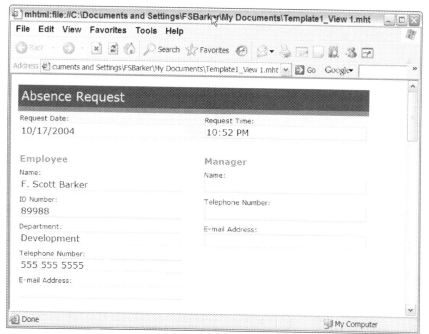

Figure 10-19

Merging Data from Separate Forms

The last task to talk about is the ability to merge data from multiple forms. This is extremely useful when you have data that you want to accumulate into one form such as expense sheets, sales figures, and in the case of this chapter, the aggregated absence requests. To accomplish this, you will need to have published the form.

Next, you need to choose Tools ⇨ Form Options... when in design mode. On the General page, you will see the choice of Enable Form Merging. You need to check that choice, as displayed in Figure 10-20.

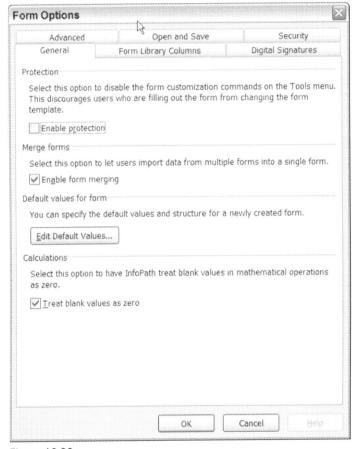

Figure 10-20

Now you are ready to merge forms.

Merging Data from Separate InfoPath Forms

To merge data from separate InfoPath forms, you must first fill out the forms with separate data:

1. Fill out the form first using John Doe as the employee.

2. Fill in the Start Date, End Date, Type of Absence, and finally the number of hours absent.

3. Save your form. In this case, the first form has been saved as `JohnDoe.xml`, as shown in Figure 10-21.

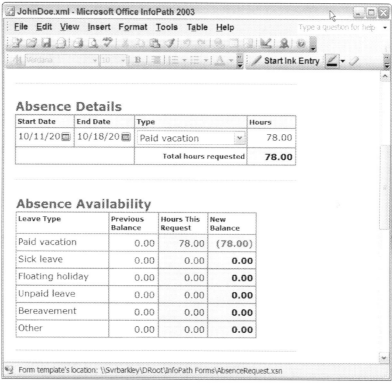

Figure 10-21

4. Close the form.

5. Open the second form by double-clicking the template once again.

6. Fill out the form for Jane Doe this time.

7. Fill in the Start Date, End Date, Type of Absence, and finally the number of hours absent.

8. Save your form. In this case the first form has been saved as `JaneDoe.xml`, as shown in Figure 10-22.

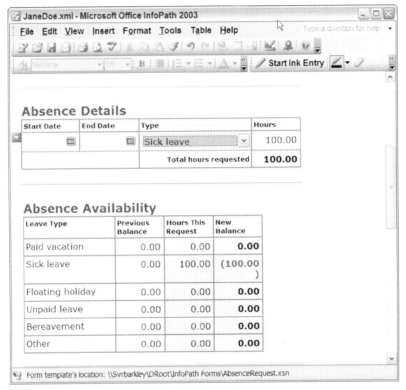

Figure 10-22

9. Double-click the form template you are using one more time.

10. Pick File ⇨ Merge Forms.... The Merge Form dialog box will open.

11. Locate the forms you want to merge the data for. In this case, it is `JohnDoe.xml` and `JaneDoe.xml`, as shown in Figure 10-23.

12. Click Merge. The data in each of the forms will now be merged into the currently opened form, as shown in Figure 10-24.

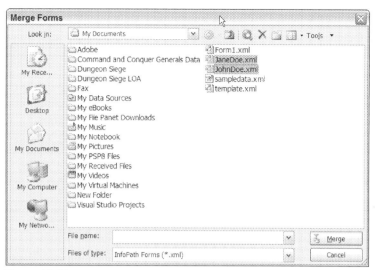

Figure 10-23

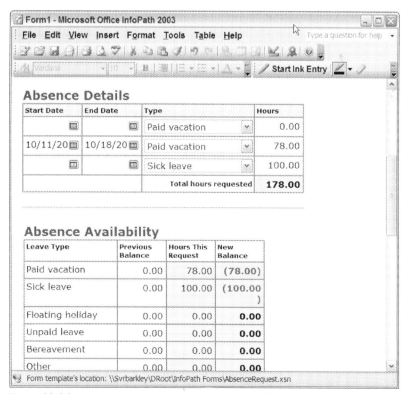

Figure 10-24

Summary

InfoPath has a number of ways to publish forms using form templates, which when shared allow users to open forms on their local machines. You can publish forms using network shared folders or Web servers, and finally SharePoint form libraries. Once published the form can be opened from users' machines as well as e-mailed to users for data import. E-mail can be used for data that needs to be added or for sending data. You can also export InfoPath forms to be a standalone Web page.

In this chapter, you also saw how to combine data from multiple forms by merging them into a single form.

Exercises

1.   What are three locations you can publish your form template to?

2.   What kind of access permissions do users need to have to access folders containing form templates?

3.   What is the technology used to enable remote authoring of Web sites and content management?

4.   Export an InfoPath form to Excel using the File ⇨ Export To... menu option.

Working with Code in Your InfoPath Form

You have been able to create quite a few InfoPath forms throughout the book that have been very useful with a stitch of code. However, as with other development products, the more you use InfoPath, the more extensive your needs are likely to become. As you start to look at working with other products such as BizTalk and adding functionality such as e-mailing users from forms, the need for more power than you get just by using the InfoPath editor and main form templates becomes more apparent.

Microsoft InfoPath originally gave you the ability to automate using your choice of VBscript or JScript and editing with the Microsoft Script Editor. With the Microsoft Office Service Pack 2 the ability to utilize managed code such as C# or Visual Basic .NET has been added. In either environment, an object model and events have been provided to let you accomplish just about anything you need to do.

The next few chapters go into greater detail about what technologies you can use to develop code, including giving some real-world examples. Because of the choices you have, this chapter gives an overview of what capabilities are being developed in code. In this chapter you will:

- ❑ Look at the two different development environments.
- ❑ Get started working in each environment.
- ❑ Learn about creating code with .NET.
- ❑ Work with the InfoPath event model.

When Is Code Necessary?

The majority of those working with Microsoft InfoPath forms will be able to use forms as they are "out of the box." By using the form designer they can create most forms that will cover their tasks.

However, as larger needs arise, requiring more extensive development, InfoPath gives you a number of choices to take care of those needs.

Before getting into detail about what Microsoft provides, it's good to take a look at some of the situations that may require coding. Some of those situations may be:

❑ **Adding Security through the User Interface**: There are times when you may want to add additional security, or create your own. For example, you may want to toggle the visibility of certain sections of a form based on the user working with the form.

❑ **Interacting with Other Enterprise-Wide Applications**: These situations may involve anything from sending data on to various databases not connected directly to the form to working with Microsoft Biztalk, enterprise server application software used for managing information workflows. There is more information on using InfoPath forms with BizTalk in Chapter 17, "Working with InfoPath and Biztalk."

❑ **Extending Forms Functionality**: This is probably the most used reason for coding behind InfoPath. It also covers a number of different tasks, including adding additional validation to forms, e-mailing users, and data manipulation such as working with dates. The last two of these examples are cover in Chapter 14, "Real-World Tasks and Coding Examples."

Again, these are just a few possible situations. The possibilities are endless.

Choose Your Flavor of Code: Script or Managed Code (.NET)

Version 1.0 of Microsoft InfoPath originally shipped with Microsoft Script Editing technologies, giving the user the choice of using either Microsoft JScript, which is the default scripting language for a form, or Microsoft Visual Basic Scripting Edition (VBScript). Other Microsoft Office products ship with Visual Basic for Applications (VBA), except for Outlook, which also uses scripting to program with Outlook forms.

JScript or VBScript?

The choice of which of the scripting languages you depend on may come down to which one you have had experience with. If you have used Java in the past, you may want to use Jscript; if you have used one of the Visual Basic development languages, then VBScript may be the way to go.

If you're just starting out in developing, you will probably want to use the default scripting language, which is JScript. If you decide to go with VBScript, then you change the default script language by selecting it on the Advanced tab of the Form Options dialog box.

If you want to change the default programming language behind an InfoPath form, you have to do it before the form has any code behind it.

Try It Out: Setting the Default Script Editor

Using a new form:

1. Open InfoPath.

2. Create a new blank form.

3. Choose Tools ⇨ Form Options.

4. Click the Advanced Tab.

5. Click on the Form code language , under the Programming Language section. The drop-down list can be seen in Figure 11-1.

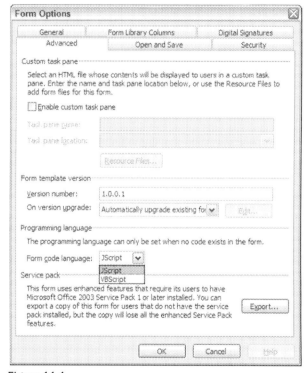

Figure 11-1

6. Select the language of your choice.

7. Click OK.

The language will now be specified, and InfoPath and Microsoft Script Editor will create the necessary commands in a script file.

Managed Code with .NET

With the introduction of InfoPath 2003 Toolkit for Visual Studio .NET, developers have other choices when deciding what programming language to use behind their InfoPath forms. Developers can use managed code in .NET to write code for their forms. .NET managed code languages, such as C# and Visual Basic .NET, are supported for InfoPath.

Besides simply allowing you to create managed code files behind your InfoPath forms, Microsoft also provides support in Visual Studio .NET for InfoPath project files, giving you a development platform in which to create your applications. Assemblies and classes are provided for working with the InfoPath object model, providing access to methods, properties, and events. Events and the InfoPath object model are discussed in the remaining sections of this chapter.

While .NET and creating InfoPath applications in .NET will be covered in detail in Chapter 13, "Working with .NET Managed Code," the first thing you want to do is download and install the InfoPath 2003 Toolkit for Visual Studio .NET.

If you want to use the toolkit mentioned earlier, then you will already need to have Visual Studio .NET installed with the desired language: C# or Visual Basic .NET.

Try It Out   Downloading the InfoPath 2003 Toolkit for Visual Studio .NET

On your development machine that you are using to create your InfoPath forms:

Microsoft may have changed some of the links and Web pages by the time you read this. But you should be able to find the download using these pages.

1. Using your favorite Internet browser, go to the Microsoft Office Online Web site. As of this writing the Web address was:

   ```
   http://office.microsoft.com/en-us/officeupdate/default.aspx
   ```

   You can see the page shown in Figure 11-2.

2. Click Downloads for Office 2003, located under BROWSE DOWNLOADS in the middle of the page. The Downloads for Office 2003 page will be opened.

3. Click the Add-Ins link under InfoPath 2003. The Add-Ins for InfoPath 2003 page will be displayed, listing the InfoPath 2003 Toolkit for Visual Studio .NET.

4. Click the InfoPath 2003 Toolkit for Visual Studio .NET link. The download page will then be displayed.

5. Click Download. If you are in Internet Explorer, a security warning is given.

6. Click Run to download and install the toolkit. You will see the message displayed in Figure 11-3.

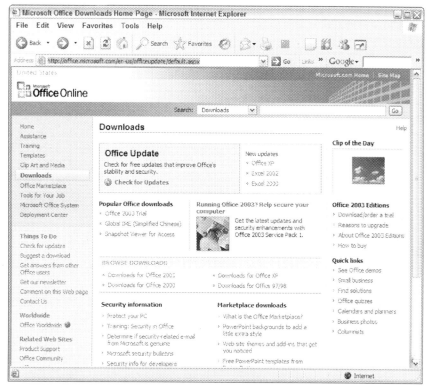

Figure 11-2

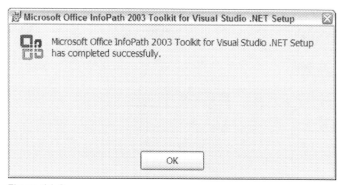

Figure 11-3

After downloading and installing the toolkit, you can open Visual Studio .NET. When you select a new project, additional choices will be displayed, offering C# or Visual Basic .NET projects, as shown in Figure 11-4.

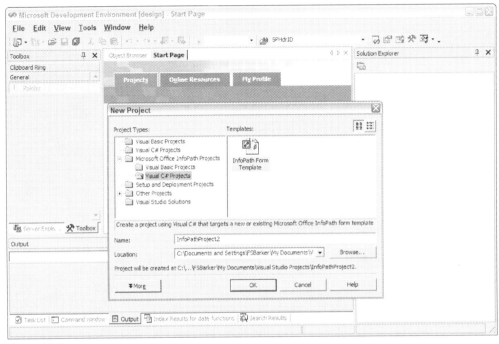

Figure 11-4

Creating a project using managed code will be covered further in Chapter 13. For now, take a look at what it means to develop using event-driven programming.

Looking at Event Programming

Regardless of which language you decide to use, scripting or managed code, you need to understand how event programming works. Most applications created for the Windows platform use event programming to enable developers to capture events that occur and create routines to perform tasks based on those events.

What Is an Event?

In Windows, events occur when a user clicks a button, data is entered in a field, or a key is pressed. Windows applications also have their own set of events that can be programmed against, so that developers can control their applications. The object model of an application will include the available events in a development environment such as InfoPath. Object models will be discussed in the next couple of chapters, but for now take a look at the available events created for your use in InfoPath forms.

InfoPath Events

As with other development environments, InfoPath has some built-in events that can be utilized to perform tasks when triggered. The following table outlines those events.

Event Name	Description of When Event Occurs
OnAfterChange	After you have changed the XML document that is bound to a form.
OnAfterImport	After data has been import or merged into a form.
OnBeforeChange	Before changes are made to the XML document bound to the form.
OnClick	When a command button is clicked on a form.
OnContextChange	When moving from one element on a form to another. An example is moving from one field to another.
OnLoad	When a form is first loaded.
OnMergeRequest	When a merge request is made on a form either made using the UI or programmatically.
OnSaveRequest	When a save request is made on a form using either the UI or programmatically.
OnSign	When data is signed digitally.
OnSubmitRequest	When a submit request is made on a form using either the UI or programmatically.
OnSwitchView	When switching between views on a form.
OnValidate	When validating data on a form.
OnVersionUpgrade	When a form is upgraded from one version to a later one at runtime.

The more common events are listed in the Tools ➪ Programming menu, as shown in Figure 11-5.

Figure 11-5

After you have created events, you can edit the code by selecting one of the events listed, or by selecting the last choice, Microsoft Script Editor.

Try It Out   **Creating Your First Scripted Event**

To create your first scripted event you will create a new blank form:

1. Open InfoPath.

2. Choose Design a Form.

3. Click New Blank Form.

4. Choose On Load Event from the Tools ⇨ Programming menu. The Microsoft Script Editor opens with the OnLoad event defined against the XDocument object. This object will be discussed in greater detail in the next section.

5. Type the following line in between the curly brackets of the OnLoad event:

```
XDocument.UI.Alert("Instructions could be given here for the form.");
```

The code will then look as it does in Figure 11-6.

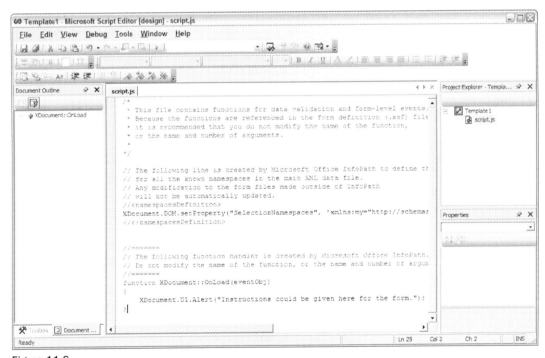

Figure 11-6

6. Choose File ➪ Exit. The Save Changes dialog will be displayed.

7. Click Yes to save the `script.js` file.

8. Click the Preview Form button. The message box displayed in Figure 11-7 appears.

Figure 11-7

There you have it: Your first InfoPath script event. Now take a look at the steps to create the same thing using Visual Studio .NET.

Try It Out   Creating Your First Managed Code Event

If you have installed Visual Studio .NET 2003 and the InfoPath 2003 Toolkit for Visual Studio .NET, you can create an InfoPath form with code behind it:

1. Choose Microsoft Visual Studio .NET 2003 from the Windows Start menu.

2. Click the New Project link. The New Project dialog box will open.

3. Click the Microsoft Office InfoPath Projects node in the Project Types tree. You will then see the two choices of Visual Basic Projects and Visual C# Projects.

4. Click the Visual C# Projects node.

5. Specify the location of the project where you would like to have it stored, as shown in Figure 11-8.

6. Click OK. The Microsoft Office Project Wizard will open, shown in Figure 11-9. The default choice of the type of InfoPath form is to create a new InfoPath template.

7. Click Finish. A new blank InfoPath form will be created, with Visual Studio .NET displaying the InfoPath project in the Solutions Explorer.

8. Choose On Load Event... from the Tools ➪ Programming menu. You will then be taken to the Visual Studio .NET editor, and the new event code will be displayed, as shown here:

```
// The following function handler is created by Microsoft Office InfoPath. Do not
// modify the type or number of arguments.
[InfoPathEventHandler(EventType=InfoPathEventType.OnLoad)]
public void OnLoad(DocReturnEvent e)
{
    // Write your code here.

}
```

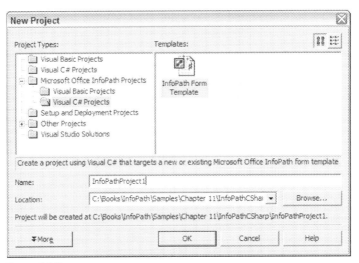

Figure 11-8

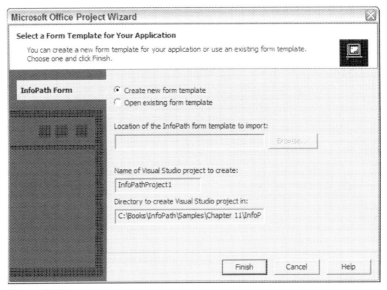

Figure 11-9

9. Add the following line of code in place of the line that reads // Write your code here.

```
thisXDocument.UI.Alert("You can add information here about the form.");
```

The code will look as it does in Figure 11-10.

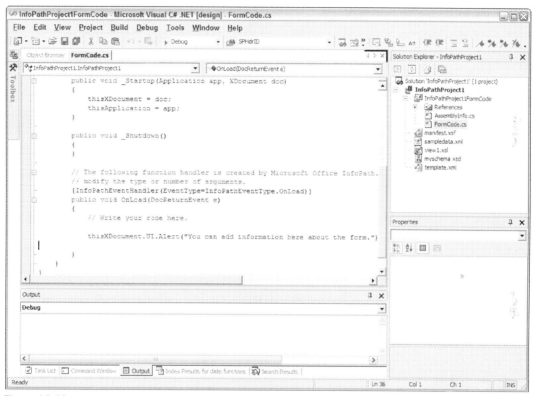

Figure 11-10

10. Choose Debug ➪ Start to test the form. The form will open in preview mode, with the specified dialog box displayed, as shown in Figure 11-11.

Figure 11-11

Summary

As with other development environments, InfoPath offers choices for creating code behind your InfoPath forms. While the majority of the users will probably find their needs met without creating code, some tasks require writing either script or managed code using .NET. As with other Windows applications you can use events to perform tasks when needed.

Microsoft provides editors for whichever development environment you wish to use.

Exercises

1. What are the two development environments used for writing code behind InfoPath forms?
2. Which two Microsoft scripting languages can developers choose?
3. What is the name of the toolkit used for creating managed code?

Getting Started
Using Scripts

As mentioned in the last chapter, 80 percent of the users who work with Microsoft InfoPath do so mainly by creating forms through the user interface with very little code. However, when it comes time to use code, and if you don't own Visual Studio .NET 2003, then you have to use Microsoft Scripting Technologies to automate your forms using code. Once you decide to use script, you need to decide which script language to use, Microsoft JScript or Microsoft VBScript.

Regardless which scripting language you decide to use, the natural editor to use is the Microsoft Script Editor provided by InfoPath for editing your script. This chapter discusses using the editor. In this chapter you will:

❑   Create another scripting routine.

❑   Be introduced to the different elements Microsoft Editor.

❑   Learn about the InfoPath object model in .NET.

Introduction to Microsoft Script Editor

The last chapter introduced you to the Microsoft Scripting Technologies and briefly showed you the Microsoft Script Editor while creating your initial script routine. The Microsoft Script Editor is very straightforward to use, especially if you have used other Microsoft editors such as Visual Studio or even other Office products. The other Office products use the Visual Basic for Applications programming language and have an editor called the IDE, or independent development editor.

The Microsoft Script Editor (MSE) has fewer features than other similar editors. This makes it less powerful but simpler to use. You can see an example of the editor in Figure 12-1.

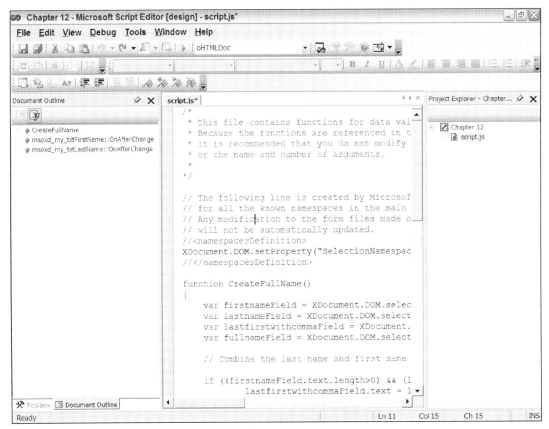

Figure 12-1

The first two panels displayed are ones that you will use the most when editing scripts in the MSE. The Document Outline panel displays the various events and procedures that you have created code for, and it allows you to move between them. The Main Editing panel, displaying the code in script.js in Figure 12-1, is where the code you will be editing is displayed.

As with other Microsoft editors, the MSE has color formatting for various elements of the languages it supports, including JScript. As you type the commands, you will see the code reflected in different colors, such as comments in green and command statements in blue. As with other limited features, you can change various colors by choosing Tools ⌦ Options while in the editor, and then click the Fonts and Colors choice under Environment. You can see the Comments color choice in Figure 12-2.

The best way to introduce the editor is to use it, as you did in the last chapter, with real code. As with other chapters, this one will walk you through the creation of an InfoPath form. This time the chapter takes you through the various steps you would perform if you were creating your own form using scripting. The chapter also takes you through various features of the editor and scripting. To start off, you need to create the form.

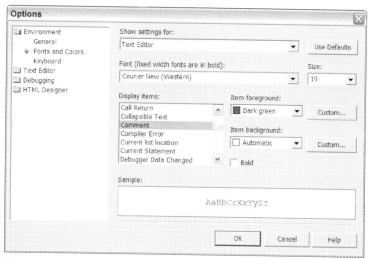

Figure 12-2

Try It Out   **Creating the Initial Form**

To show you the features of the editor and scripting, you will create a form that has the user provide his or her first and last name. The form then displays the name in two different formats: LastName, FirstName and Full Name consisting of First Name and Last Name. You can see an example of the completed form in action in Figure 12-3.

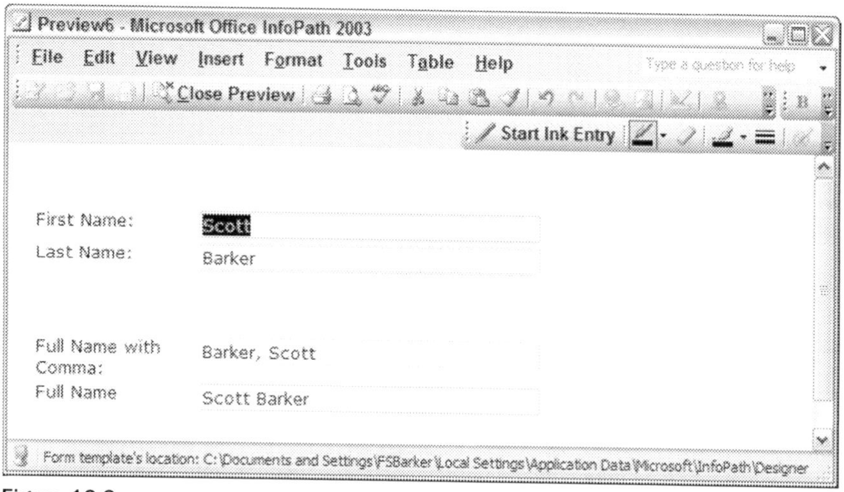

Figure 12-3

1. Open InfoPath.

2. Click Design a Form.

3. Click New Blank Form under the Design a Form.

4. Click on the Layout task.

5. Click on Two-Column Table.

6. Using the methods described throughout the book, add the labels and four fields as shown in Figure 12-4.

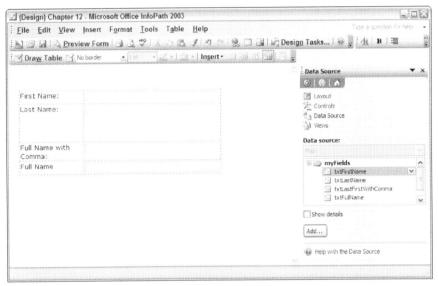

Figure 12-4

7. Name the four fields, as shown in Figure 12-4.

Once you have the form set up as described, you are ready to work with code. In the last chapter, you saw the Load:: function used in conjunction with a form to display a message box. In this chapter, you will use more than just the Load:: function. To prepare you for that, take a look at a few commands available in JScript.

Working with JScript

To cover all the features and commands of JScript would take a whole book, so in this chapter the features used in the sample code will be covered. To start off, it is a good idea to discuss creating your routines.

The order of the JScript discussion will follow the flow in which the sample application will be created, thus providing meaningful examples as the discussion progresses.

Working with Custom Functions

Custom functions are even more straightforward. To create a custom function that doesn't return anything requires the following syntax:

```
function functionname
{

}
```

where *functionname* is the name of the function you specify.

Curley brackets are used to segment pieces of code. Besides using them for functions as described previously, you will use them for loops and branching code such as if statements. You can see more about if statements in the sections following.

Try It Out: **Creating a Custom Function**

For the purpose of the example in this chapter, you will be creating your own function called createFullName. This routine ultimately will take values set in the first name and last name fields (called txtFirstName and txtLastName). To start, open the form you created in the last Try It Out:

1. Choose Microsoft Script Editor from the Tools ➪ Programming... menu selection. The MSE will open, placing you in the script.js file, listing comments, and the following line of code:

```
XDocument.DOM.setProperty("SelectionNamespaces",
'xmlns:my="http://schemas.microsoft.com/office/infopath/2003/myXSD/2004-11-17T07:09
:33"');
```

   The XDocument object will be displayed in the next section.

2. Place the cursor in the bottom line of the editor.

3. Type in the following lines of code:

```
function createFullName()
{
  XDocument.UI.Alert("Filler for now");
}
```

While the names of functions and variables discussed in the next section are case sensitive, how you name them is up to you. You should land on a standard and use it throughout out your programming. Having a standard makes it easier to document and follow your own code when you have to come back and read it at a later date.

The XDocument.UI.Alert method, introduced in the last chapter, is just to help you test that the function is being called until you put more meaningful code in place.

You will be using this function as you progress through the example. When you want to use the function you just created, you type the name of the function, with its parentheses, on a line by itself, and end the line with a semicolon. So the line of code looks like this:

```
createFullName();
```

Try It Out: **Calling a Custom Function**

You will be using the function you just created in the AfterUpdate events of the first and last name fields.

1.   Close the script editor, saving the file.

2.   Double-click the field called txtFirstName on your InfoPath form. The Text Box Properties dialog box will open.

3.   Click the Data Validation button. As introduced in previous chapters, this dialog box enables you to create conditions for validating your data. This is also the place where you can specify script to run for various events.

4.   Click the drop-down list under the Script label. You will see the list of possible events for the txtFirstName text box, as shown in Figure 12-5.

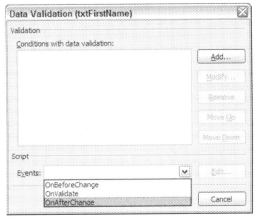

Figure 12-5

5.   Select the OnAfterChange event.

6.   Click the Edit button. The MSE will open, placing you between the opening and closing braces of the new event code created.

7.   In the line just above the closing brace, type the following code:

```
createFullName();
```

The code will then look as follows:

```
function msoxd_my_txtFirstName::OnAfterChange(eventObj)
{
// Write code here to restore the global state.
if (eventObj.IsUndoRedo)
    {
        // An undo or redo operation has occurred and the DOM is read-only.
        return;
    }
    // A field change has occurred and the DOM is writable.
    // Write code here to respond to the changes.
    createFullName();
}
```

The other code, created by InfoPath for you, gives the ability to trap if the redo or undo command has been given, and it enables you to program for that event. However, you don't have to worry about that at this point.

The // denotes comments in the code. These are used for documentation and highly recommended to use. As mentioned earlier in the chapter, they will be displayed in green.

8. Close and save the script file.

9. Click Preview Form. The form is displayed.

10. Type in a name in the txtFirstName field, and then press tab. The message box is displayed (see Figure 12-6).

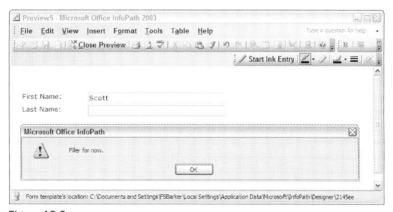

Figure 12-6

11. Repeat Steps 2 through 7 for the txtLastName field on the form.

Now that you have added your custom function to the form and are successfully calling it from events on the form, it is time now to look at some meatier topics that make scripting useful for more than just displaying an alert dialog box. The first thing to talk about is the use of variables to work with the fields on the form.

Using Variables

Just about every programming language uses variables. There are several types of variables in JScript: reference and value variables. Whichever type of variable you use, you must declare the variable, and then assign the value, or reference. You can accomplish this using either two lines of code, or one:

```
var variablename
variablename = value
```

or

```
var variablename = value
```

Reference Variables

The first type of variable is one that points to another object. Any operation that is performed using the variable, such as assigning a value to it, will be reflected in the object that the variable references. An example of this is assigning a variable to a field on a form. When you modify the text of the variable, the value in the field on the form is modified. This is the type of variable that will be used in this example.

Value Variables

When you assign a value to a variable of this type, a copy is made of the data you have assigned to the variable. This means that when you modify the data, it does not reflect back to the original information.

Before using the variables in a Try It Out, because so much of working with variables on InfoPath forms in script involve creating references to fields on the forms, why not start right away, and learn how to accomplish this task. To learn about working with forms in script, you need to learn more about the InfoPath object model.

XDocument Object

When you deal with the InfoPath object model, you will be working with XML object models as well. The main object used in the example in this chapter is the XDocument object. In the code of the last Try It Out, the following line of code was mentioned:

```
XDocument.DOM.setProperty("SelectionNamespaces",
'xmlns:my="http://schemas.microsoft.com/office/infopath/2003/myXSD/2004-11-17T07:09
:33"');
```

The previous line of code, which was added automatically when you specified that you wanted to work in script with your InfoPath form, sets up your code to use the object model used for InfoPath forms. The DOM (Document Object Model) is a standard XML object that provides a number of methods and attributes that let you manipulate an XML document, in this case an InfoPath form.

To assign a reference to an InfoPath field, as mentioned in the last section, you will use a method of the DOM object called `selectSingleNode` and provide the XPath to the object on the form.

```
var firstnameField = XDocument.DOM.selectSingleNode("//my:txtFirstName");
```

Note that to specify the XPath you will use `"//my:"` and then the name of the field you want to use. This line of code enables you to work with the field on the form by manipulating the text property of the `firstnameField` variable.

Try It Out   Adding References to Fields on an InfoPath Form

You will be using the function you created in the last Try It Out.

1.   Position the cursor between the opening and closing curly braces of the `CreateFullName` function.

2.   Type in the following lines of code:

```
var firstnameField =   XDocument.DOM.selectSingleNode("//my:txtFirstName");
var lastnameField = XDocument.DOM.selectSingleNode("//my:txtLastName");
var lastfirstwithcommaField =
       XDocument.DOM.selectSingleNode("//my:txtLastFirstWithComma");
var fullnameField = XDocument.DOM.selectSingleNode("//my:txtFullName");
```

Your editor should now look similar to the one displayed in Figure 12-7.

For the purposes of displaying all the text in the editor, the panels on each side were collapsed. You can accomplish this by clicking the pins in each panel. Then as you need them you just bring the cursor over the tab such as Document Outline. This works the same in all the Microsoft editors.

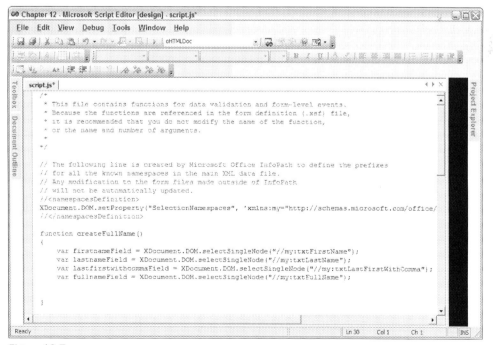

Figure 12-7

At this point, the code merely assigns a reference to the fields on the InfoPath form and is not doing much with them. The next section discusses how to manipulate the fields using the variables.

Performing Operations on Variables

One of the most useful purposes of variables is being able to perform operations with them. This can take the form of performing mathematical calculations in the case of numeric type variables, or performing string manipulations in the case of character data.

In the case of working with fields as specified in the last Try It Out, because you will be working with the data in the fields on the form, you will use the text property of the fields, concatenating them with the + sign. The line of code looks like this:

```
fullnameField.text = firstnameField.text + ' ' + lastnameField.text
```

This line of code concatenates the field referenced to the `firstnameField` variable with a space and the field referenced to the `lastnameField`. The space is treated as a literal value because it is between the single quotation marks.

Try It Out   Updating the txtFullName Field from Code

Using the ongoing example in this chapter, in the InfoPath form:

1. Choose Microsoft Script Editor from Tools ⇨ Programming....

2. Scroll down to the line of code that reads:

```
XDocument.UI.Alert("Filler for now");
```

3. Type in the following line of code:

```
fullnameField.text = firstnameField.text + ' ' + lastnameField.text
```

4. Close and save the script file.

5. Click Preview Form.

6. Type in the first and last names. The Full Name is now displayed, as shown in Figure 12-8.

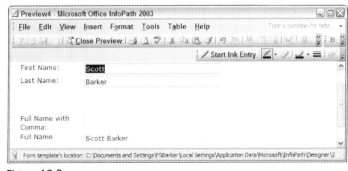

Figure 12-8

For the next task, combining last and first name with a comma, you learn how to test to make sure that both are supplied before displaying the final string. However, before seeing that code, you will add the line of code to display the error. Then using conditional branching will be discussed.

Try It Out   Displaying LastName, FirstName

To accomplish this, you will once again use the example created in this chapter.

1. While you are in the InfoPath form, choose Microsoft Script Editor from the Tools ⇨ Programming... menu.

2. Move down into the `createFullName` function you created, just above the line of code that reads:

```
fullnameField.text = firstnameField.text + ' ' + lastnameField.text
```

3. Press Enter twice to add a couple of blank lines.

4. Type in the following line of code:

```
lastfirstwithcommaField.text = lastnameField.text + ', ' +
              firstnameField.text;
```

Notice that code can wrap to another line without any special symbol. This is why the semicolon is used to designate the end of the line(s) of code.

5. Close and save the script file. You will be returned in the InfoPath designer.
6. Click the Preview Form button.
7. Type in the first name of your choice.

Notice the small detail that when the first name is entered and tab pressed, the Full Name with Comma field looks a little funky with a comma displayed with only the last name, as shown in Figure 12-9.

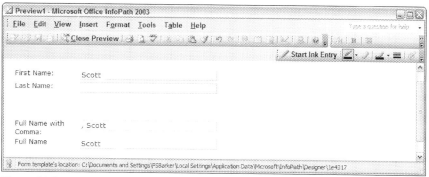

Figure 12-9

While this is a small detail, it is a great opportunity to point out how to use conditional branching in InfoPath.

Conditional Branching

The term *conditional branching* is a fancy why of saying "if this is true, perform these tasks." Conditional statements in the case of the sample in this chapter consist of the if statement. The main syntax of the `if` can be seen here:

```
if (condition)
{
    Statements here;
}
```

where the condition will be a Boolean condition of true or false. A typical condition is one that you will use in this example:

```
firstnameField.text.length>0
```

so the full initial line of the if statement is:

```
if ((firstnameField.text.length>0)
```

with the line, or lines, of code to execute following after.

> *Note that if you only have a single line of code following the if statement, the curly braces aren't required. The code used in the next Try It Out uses this syntax.*
>
> *There are a lot of operators you can use to compare values; in the script editor if you search on the if statement, you will see all of them.*

One of the issues with the line of code just displayed is that it doesn't help with the issue in the example of the comma with no last name. To truly trap for both fields would be the way to go. To accomplish this, you need to add another condition to the if statement. By doing this you will be making a complex condition, and you can do this one of two ways, by using the logical AND or OR. In JScript you will use `&&` for AND and `||` for OR. In the case of the name, you want to make sure that the first name and the last name are both included so you will use the `&&` as shown here.

```
if ((firstnameField.text.length>0) && (lastnameField.text.length>0))
```

which is added to the code just before the line that reads:

```
lastfirstwithcommaField.text = lastnameField.text + ', ' +
                firstnameField.text;
```

This way the code just mentioned is not executed unless both name fields have characters in them.

Try It Out   **Adding an Conditional If Statement**

We're in the home stretch now. Using the form and code you have been using:

1.   In the editor, add the following line of code:

```
if ((firstnameField.text.length>0) && (lastnameField.text.length>0))
```

just before the line of code that reads:

```
lastfirstwithcommaField.text = lastnameField.text + ', ' +
                firstnameField.text;
```

So, the final code looks as follows, with an extra comment line thrown in:

```
function createFullName()
{
    var firstnameField =  XDocument.DOM.selectSingleNode("//my:txtFirstName");
    var lastnameField = XDocument.DOM.selectSingleNode("//my:txtLastName");
    var lastfirstwithcommaField =
            XDocument.DOM.selectSingleNode("//my:txtLastFirstWithComma");
    var fullnameField = XDocument.DOM.selectSingleNode("//my:txtFullName");

    // Combine the last name and first name and display them in different formats.

    if ((firstnameField.text.length>0) && (lastnameField.text.length>0))

            lastfirstwithcommaField.text = lastnameField.text + ', ' +
                                    firstnameField.text;

    fullnameField.text = firstnameField.text + ' ' + lastnameField.text
}
```

2.   Save and close the form.

3.   Click Preview Form.

The form will now open and will only add the comma when both first and last names are filled in.

Summary

InfoPath and scripting give you the ability to accomplish a number of tasks that just wouldn't be possible with the two combined. Microsoft supplies the Microsoft Script Editor to help you manage the script that is used with your InfoPath form. Microsoft also provides events for the various actions on the form that developers can use for their needs.

You can create your own routines to reuse and accomplish your own tasks. JScript provides a number of programming commands that enable the developers to program as needed.

Exercises

1. Name the three events of a text box that are supplied by InfoPath.

2. What is the base object in the InfoPath form used for programming?

3. What are the programmatic, if compound symbols for AND and OR?

Working with .NET Managed Code

While there are a lot of tasks you can accomplish with scripting in InfoPath, there are a number of reasons for using .NET managed languages such as Visual Basic .NET and C#. This is especially true if you already are using those languages. This chapter is primarily for those who are not using .NET at this time. .NET is a very big development platform and can be overwhelming.

Unlike a single language such Visual Basic, the .NET platform and the managed code languages that are used with it are all based on assemblies and classes that are the same regardless of what language you use. This means they are a library of classes that include the properties, methods, and events, as discussed in the last chapter.

This chapter looks at what makes up the .NET environment. In this chapter you will:

❑   Take a look at Visual Studio .NET.

❑   Examine what it means to create InfoPath projects in .NET.

❑   Discuss the InfoPath object model in .NET.

❑   Distribute your .NET InfoPath application.

Introduction to the .NET Framework

The Microsoft .NET Framework version 1.1 consists of two main elements: the common language runtime (CLR) and .NET Framework class library. These two elements actually handle a lot of work for developers, managing threads and memory (CLR), and allowing just about unlimited expandability (class library). The CLR is used "under the covers" in that it handles translating managed code into something that can run on any platform supporting .NET. You can see how these elements fit together in Figure 13-1.

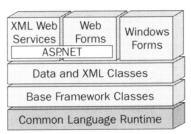

Figure 13-1

There are a number of reasons for using the .NET Framework for a development platform. Here are some of those reasons:

❏ **Guarantees Safe Execution of Code, Including Code Created by Unknown or Semi-Trusted Third Parties**: This is where the term *managed code* comes from, since the applications have to meet security standards and are managed just for that very purpose.

❏ **Allows Developers to Work in a Consistent Programming Environment Whether Creating Applications for Desktops or the Internet**: This means that although there are techniques that vary between Web and desktop applications, you can use the same languages, such as C#.

❏ **Builds All Communication on Industry Standards to Ensure That Code Based on the .NET Framework Can Be Integrated with Any Other Code**: .NET uses XML extensively, as well as other communication protocols such as SOAP (Simplified Object Application Programming), which are both industry standards.

❏ **Minimizes Software Deployment and Versioning Conflicts**: Also called DLL hell, when developing in prior platforms such as Visual Basic and using ActiveX controls. Many times when you installed new versions of your applications, controls would conflict and not work.

❏ **Eliminates Performance Problems of Scripted or Interpreted Environments**: Everything is compiled into a common language that the various parts of the platform are designed to work with.

Common Language Runtime

The common language runtime is a runtime engine that takes various languages, such as Visual Basic .NET and C#, and compiles them into a common language that is used when the applications are executed. This means that all the languages can use the same classes provided by the .NET Framework class library.

The CLR is extremely convenient and powerful in that it really doesn't matter which language you write in, because you can use the same objects and it all compiles down to the same efficient code.

.NET Framework Class Library

The .NET Framework class library is made up of various namespaces. Namespaces are actually collections of classes and interfaces, logically organized. This enables you to have multiple versions of classes with the same name, but in different namespaces, and not have conflicts.

One very interesting fact is that not only does the .NET Framework provide namespaces and classes for developer use, but it also uses those very namespaces and classes for its own purposes, including editing, compiling, and executing code.

Another big benefit of using the .NET Framework class library is the ability to use the classes in your applications consistently no matter whether you are using C# or Visual Basic .NET, Windows or Web forms. Namespaces can also be made up of other namespaces.

The best way to get into the .NET Framework class library is to take a look at some of its namespaces. You can see some of those namespaces in the following table:

Namespace	Description
System	Main system namespace that is broken into many categories.
System.Data	Makes up the classes used for ADO.NET, and overall data manipulation of just about any kind. Subnamespaces of System.Data include System.Data.SqlClient and System.Data.OleDB.
System.XML	Includes the DOM and classes for using XML in your applications.
System.Web	Namespaces and classes used for creating ASP.NET applications.
System.Windows	Namespaces and classes for creating Windows forms applications.

When you create a .NET application, Visual Studio creates references to different namespaces, based on what kind of project you are creating. You can see an example of references created in an InfoPath type .NET project in Figure 13-2.

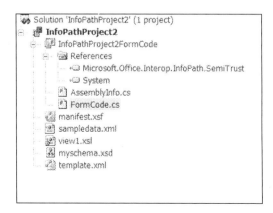

Figure 13-2

The Microsoft.Office.Interop.InfoPath.SemiTrust namespace is installed in the .NET Framework when the InfoPath 2003 Toolkit for Visual Studio .NET is installed, which is covered quickly once again in the section titled "Review: Installing the InfoPath 2003 Toolkit for Visual Studio .NET."

Using Visual Studio .NET

While you can create .NET applications using other editors, Microsoft provides Visual Studio .NET, and it rocks. With VS.NET you can create just about any type of .NET application you need to, including:

❑ **Various .NET Languages**: Visual Basic .NET and C# are both supported by InfoPath forms, as well as other available .NET language such as COBOL .NET, J# .NET, and Microsoft JScript .NET.

❑ **Create the Different Types of Projects**: Depending on the tasks, you can create Windows Applications, ASP.NET Web applications, Windows services, console applications, and ASP.NET Web services among many other choices. You can see an example of the various choices when you create a new C# application, as shown in Figure 13-3.

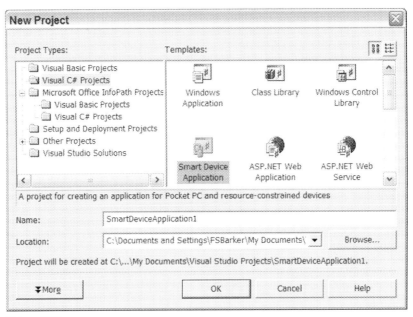

Figure 13-3

❑ **Other Application Templates Can Be Added**: For example, when the toolkit is installed, Microsoft Office InfoPath Projects also are added for Visual Basic and C#.

You can have multiple projects within a Visual Studio solution. These projects can be of different types of languages and purposes. When you "build" a solution, you are creating the runtime files necessary to make up the final application.

Try It Out: Creating a C# Windows Application Project

To get into the Visual Studio .NET editor, you will create a simple C# application. To accomplish this you will:

1. Open Visual Studio .NET 2003. If it is installed, you will find it on the Windows Start menu in the All Programs menu choices. The application shortcut is Microsoft Visual Studio .NET 2003 and can be found in a folder of the same name. When you open VS, the Microsoft Development Environment (MDE) opens with the Start Page displayed.

Which panes are displayed on your screen will vary depending on how you have used Visual Studio. For instance, the Server Explorer and Toolbox are not expanded in the screen shown in Figure 13-4.

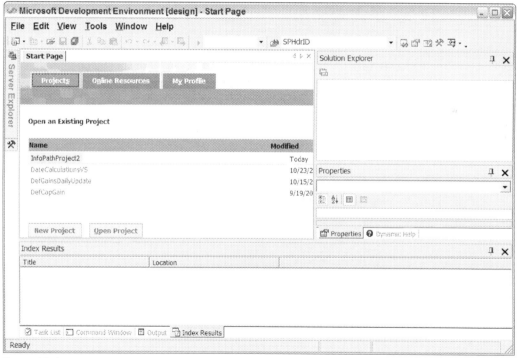

Figure 13-4

You can see some of the past projects worked on displayed in the page under Open an Existing Project. This makes it easy to go back and work on past projects.

2. Click New Project. The New Project dialog box will open.

3. Click Visual C# Projects, displayed in Project Types.

4. Select Windows Applications.

5. Locate the folder you want to place the project in, and give it the desired name. For this Try It Out, the project is named MyFirstCSharpApp and is located in the Visual Studio Project folder, which is in the My Documents folder. You can see the New Project dialog box with the specified project in Figure 13-5.

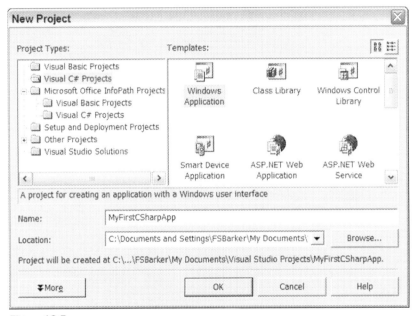

Figure 13-5

6. Click OK. The project is now created and is displayed in Visual Studio .NET 2003, with the starting windows form displayed, as shown in Figure 13-6.

Congratulations. You have created your first C# windows application. Before taking it and adding any code or controls, take a look at some of the different elements of the Microsoft Visual Studio .NET integrated development environment (IDE).

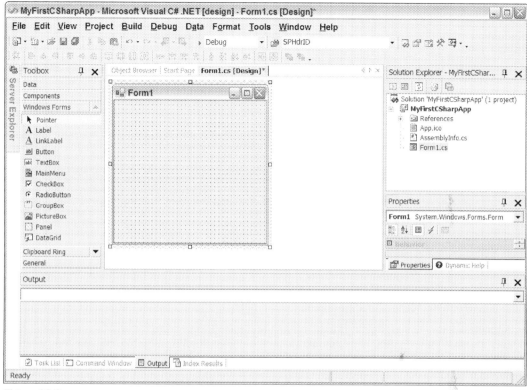

Figure 13-6

Elements of the IDE

There are actually far more elements than can be covered in a single chapter, but these following are the ones you use most.

❏ **Editing Window**: The main editing window is where your forms are displayed, or in the case of code files, where the code is displayed. You can drag and drop objects onto this window, as well as move and resize objects.

❏ **Toolbox**: This contains the controls that can be used on your windows forms and applications. Different categories of controls include data, components, and windows form. The controls available vary based on the type of project you are creating.

❏ **Solution Explorer**: This controls the various files necessary for the solution and project.

❏ **Property Sheet**: This presents various properties, depending on the object you are working with.

❏ **Output Window**: This window displays various statuses as the application is being developed, compiled, and executed.

Modifying the Project by Adding a Control and Event Code

Modifying a project consists of adding controls and writing code. When writing code in VS, you will use event programming just as you do in scripting. To accomplish this you double-click a control to add the default event.

For this section, you will use the MessageBox class in the System namespace. This class is used to display information in windows forms. The `Show` method displays requested information.

Try It Out   Adding Controls and Code

Currently the project does not do much good. Right now you have a form that only opens and does nothing. The next step is to add a button and have it display a message box when pressed.

1. Click the Windows category in the Toolbox.

2. Drag and drop a Button control from the Toolbox on the form. The editor will now be displayed as shown in Figure 13-7.

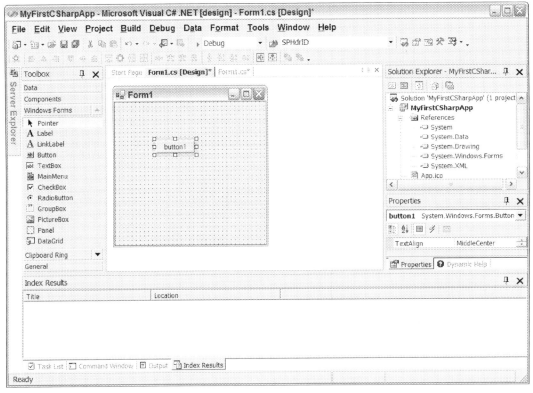

Figure 13-7

3. Double-click the button. The code file for the form opens with the new event routine created.

4. Type the following line of code in between the opening and closing brackets.

```
MessageBox.Show("Hello World");
```

The code now looks as it does in Figure 13-8.

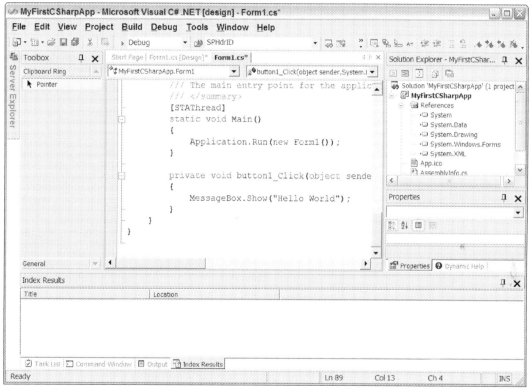

Figure 13-8

The code is now ready to test.

Executing the Application

Once you have created a project and made the desired changes, you will want to build and test the application. There are two modes for executing, or running, your application. Those modes are debug and release. You can specifically build and run applications in one or the other based on what your current purpose is.

Executing with Debugging (Debug Mode)

When you execute an application with debugging, you can use a number of options to watch how your application is running. Some of the benefits to debugging are that you can walk line by line through the code if desired or tell the code to stop at different locations in the code, much as was shown in the last chapter for scripting. Specific debugging options and techniques are discussed later in this chapter in a later section. To execute the application using this method from the project in Visual Studio, click the F5 key.

Executing without Debugging (Release Mode)

When an application is built and run without debugging, it is said to be in release mode. In this mode, you can't debug the application. You will use this mode when you are ready to distribute the application. To execute the application using this method from the project in Visual Studio, click the Ctrl+F5 keys.

Try It Out   **Running Your Application**

To accomplish this Try It Out, you will use the application you have been working in.

1.   Click F5. The application will run, displaying the traditional Hello World message, as shown in Figure 13-9.

Figure 13-9

There you go; you have now created and executed your first C# windows application.

Developing InfoPath Projects in .NET

If you are a developer using .NET for other projects, you won't find much of a difference when working with the InfoPath form and your code. Before going into details on developing InfoPath forms in Visual Studio .NET, you need to make sure that you have two development tools: Visual Studio .NET 2003 and InfoPath 2003 Toolkit for Visual Studio .NET.

Review: Installing the InfoPath 2003 Toolkit for Visual Studio .NET

You should already have VS.NET 2003 installed by this point. The downloading and installing of InfoPath 2003 Toolkit for Visual Studio .NET has already been covered in Chapter 11, "Working with Code in Your InfoPath Form" in the section titled "Managed Code with .NET."

After downloading and installing the toolkit, you can open Visual Studio .NET. When you select a new project, additional choices will be displayed, offering C# or Visual Basic InfoPath .NET projects.

Working with the InfoPath Namespaces

When creating InfoPath forms using .NET, you will be using the InfoPath object model just as you do when using scripting. However, instead of accessing the object model directly, Microsoft has created namespaces to support the object model, creating the necessary classes with methods, properties, and events. The following table contains some of the more useful classes available in the Microsoft.Office.Interop.InfoPath.SemiTrust namespace:

Class	Purpose
DataObject	Enables developers to manipulate the data sources used in a form. There are DataObjects representing the different types of data adapters used, including: ADOAdapterObject, SharepointListAdapter-Object, WebServiceAdapterObject, and the XMLFileAdapterObject object.
EmailAdapterObject	Used to represent a data adapter that is used to generate an e-mail. This object is used in the next chapter using script.
ErrorObject	Returns errors from data validation.
XDocument	Provides information about a form and its underlying XML document. This object also contains the DOM object, allowing you to get the data.

You will probably spend most of the time using the XDocument object when developing using InfoPath and .NET. Using the XDocument class you just read about, you will now create an InfoPath project that uses code to update a form.

Try It Out   Creating an InfoPath .NET Project

You will create an InfoPath .Net project and utilize the XDocument object.

1. Open Visual Studio .NET 2003.

2. Click New Project.

3. Click the Node in the Project Types tree view with the label Microsoft Office InfoPath Projects.

4. Click Visual C# Projects.

5. Locate and name the project as you wish, as displayed in Figure 13-10.

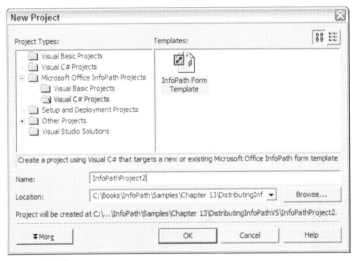

Figure 13-10

6. Click OK. The Microsoft Office Project Wizard opens, as shown Figure 13-11.

7. Click the Finish button, keeping the default choice of creating a new form template. The new project is created, along with the various C# project files as well as a new form template.

8. Click on the Controls task. The Controls task pane is displayed.

9. Drag and drop a text box onto the form. By default the name of the new control on the form will be called field1, as shown in Figure 13-12.

10. Choose Tools ⇨ On Load Event to create the event routine for the Load event.

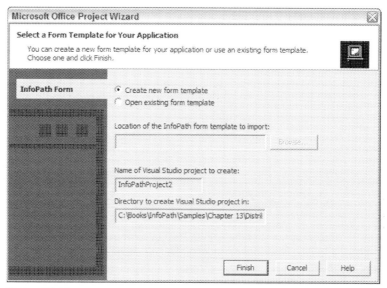

Figure 13-11

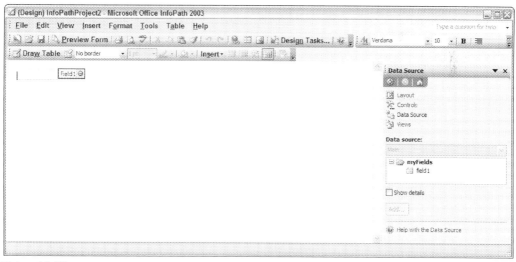

Figure 13-12

11. Type the following lines of code in between the beginning and ending brackets.

```
IXMLDOMNode Field1 = thisXDocument.DOM.selectSingleNode("//my:field1");
    if (thisXDocument.UI.Confirm("Store the word 'Test' in the field?",
                          XdConfirmButtons.xdYesNo)==XdConfirmChoice .xdYes)
        Field1.text = "Test";
```

The screen should then look as it does in Figure 13-13.

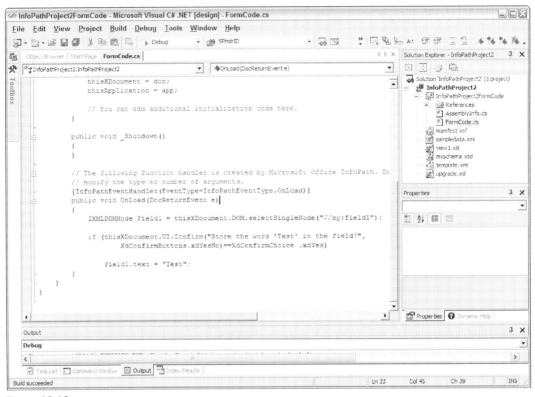

Figure 13-13

12. Click Debug ⇨ Run to test the application. The code will then run, displaying the confirm box shown in Figure 13-14.

Figure 13-14

13. Click Yes to store the word test into the field on the screen. The confirm box closes, and test is placed in the field on the form, shown in Figure 13-15.

There you have it, a simple InfoPath .NET application that updates a field on an InfoPath form. By running with this and expanding on the use of the object model using the InfoPath namespaces provided, you can create some pretty powerful applications. The next chapter shows you how to manipulate dates using C# and InfoPath. Now look at what you can do to distribute applications that you create.

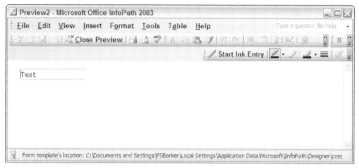

Figure 13-15

Distributing InfoPath .NET applications

While distributing .NET applications with InfoPath forms is not any different from distributing other .NET applications, as with those types of projects you will want to make sure that you build your project in release mode. There are a couple of options you can use to distribute your application.

The first option is simply to copy the objects in the Bin folder to a folder you want to use. If you are just storing the application on a LAN this is a good option. The other option is to create a distributable run-time setup program for your application. To do this use the Setup type Visual Studio .NET project.

You can create setup applications for installing from the Web or Windows desktops, creating download-able .cab files, or merge modules, which work with the Windows installer.

The setup project you will use is a wizard that walks you through specifying the files you need to include, located in the Bin folder of your InfoPath .NET project.

Try It Out   Creating the Setup Distribution Project

For the purpose of this Try It Out, you will be using the InfoPath .NET application that you created in the last exercise. In the project you just created:

1. Choose Release for the Solution Configure drop-down list, displayed on the toolbar. The drop-down list most likely displays Debug currently.

2. Click Build ➪ Rebuild Solution to create a Release version of the project. VS will then create the necessary files in a folder called Bin under your project folder.

3. Choose File ➪ Close Solution to close the current solution.

4. Click New Project. The New Project dialog box will open.

5. Click on the Setup and Deployment Project node in the Project Types tree view. The various types of setup templates will be displayed.

6. Click on Setup Wizard, and then type in the name of the new project as you want it, as shown in Figure 13-16.

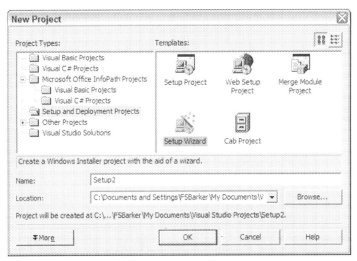

Figure 13-16

7. Click OK to start the Setup Wizard. The first page of the wizard will appear, as shown in 13-17.

Figure 13-17

8. Click Next to move on to the next page. The next page displays a dialog box asking which kind of setup application you want to create, as described in the introduction before this Try It Out. You can see the defaults in Figure 13-18.

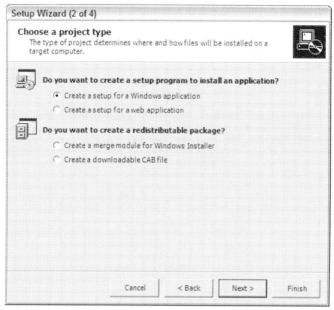

Figure 13-18

9. Click Next to accept the defaults. The next page of the wizard lets you specify which files you want to include.

10. Click Add. The Add Files dialog box will appear. Using this standard open file dialog box you can locate and select all the files you want to include in the setup.

11. Locate and highlight all the files in the Bin folder of the project. You can see from Figure 13-19 that there are only two files necessary.

12. Click Open after highlighting both files. You will then see the files listed on the third page of the Setup Wizard, as shown in Figure 13-20.

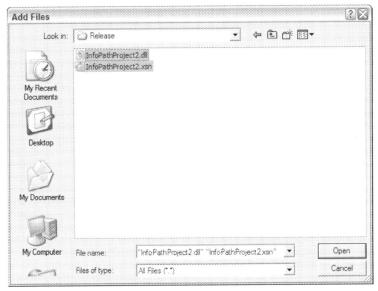

Figure 13-19

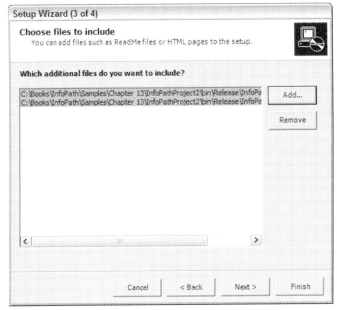

Figure 13-20

13. Click Next to display the last page of the Setup Wizard. This page, shown in Figure 13-21, displays summary information about the setup project.

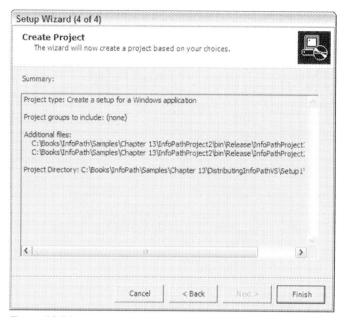

Figure 13-21

14. Click Finish to create the setup project. The project will be created, and you will be placed in Visual Studio with the project displayed. There are a lot of features you can set up using the project, but for your purposes you simply need to build the release version of the setup program.

15. Choose Release from the Solution Configure drop-down list, as displayed on the tool bar.

16. Select Build ⇨ Rebuild Solution. The release version of the setup application is created. If you look in the Release folder, located in the main setup project folder, you will see the files shown in Figure 13-22.

You can now either burn the files to a CD, or put the project out on your local area network.

17. Click on Setup.exe to start the installation program. The first page of the installation program will be displayed as shown in Figure 13-23.

You can then walk through the rest of the steps for installing the application.

Note that users still have to have a full copy of InfoPath installed on their system.

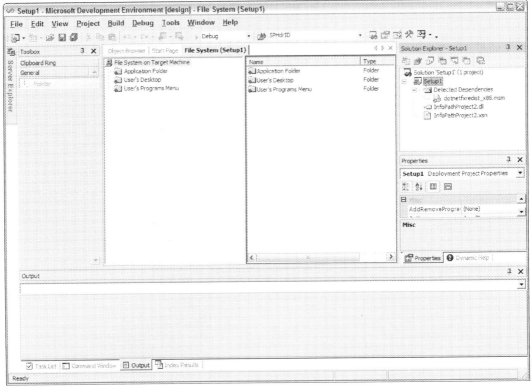

Figure 13-22

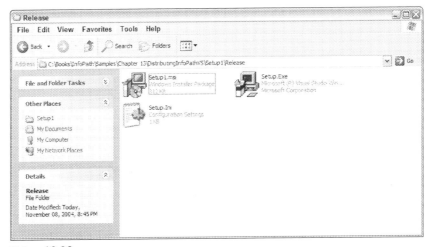

Figure 13-23

Summary

Creating InfoPath forms that take advantage of the InfoPath object model does not have to be an onerous task. The InfoPath and Visual Studio .NET teams have gone to a lot of work to make your development experience as painless and seamless as possible. By using VS with your InfoPath form you get a full-blown development environment instead of just a scripting language.

Once you've created an InfoPath application and want to distribute the files, you can use one of two methods: Copy the files into the folder you run the application to, or use a setup type .NET project to create an installation program.

Exercises

1. What are the three elements you need to create InfoPath .NET applications?

2. What are the two programming languages supported by InfoPath .NET applications?

3. What are the types of setup programs can you create using Visual Studio .NET 2003?

Real-World Tasks and Coding Examples

The last few chapters have provided enough examples for you to get an idea of how to work with the development environments that are available. Simple routines were used to show how to use events and the object model of InfoPath using scripting and managed code in .NET. Now it is time to show some more routines that you will probably find a use for in your applications. To show how to create these routines, examples will be given using both scripting and C#, so that you can have options in both development environments.

There are some techniques that come in handy when creating InfoPath forms. For instance, InfoPath doesn't provide functions or controls for handling dates, such as adding days or months, or displaying the difference between two dates. Also, how do you send an e-mail within an InfoPath form? These are a couple of the real-world examples that you will find in this chapter. In this chapter you will:

❑   See a simple way of displaying dates using scripts.

❑   See a more complete, and cleaner, way of displaying dates on a form using C#.

❑   Send a form via e-mail using code.

❑   Learn about how to provide context-sensitive help for your forms.

Date Calculations

One of the tasks that come in handy with some InfoPath forms is working with dates. The user interface doesn't really provide you with the ability to work with dates, but with scripting or managed code (C#) you can do so.

An example of date manipulation is taking today's date and displaying what tomorrow's date will be, or next week's, next month's, and even a year from today. You can see the values displayed in a form in Figure 14-1.

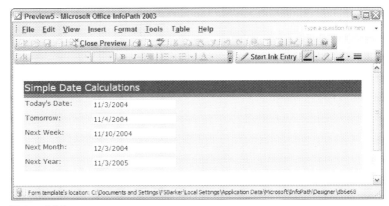

Figure 14-1

Simple Date Calculations Using Script

In both cases of creating the InfoPath form for displaying dates, you will be creating the form itself and then manipulating the InfoPath object model using code either in a script or as managed code. When discussing the code that is created using scripting, the first task to perform is to store today's date in a variable, using the following line of code:

```
var date = new Date();
```

JScript Date Object

The JScript Date object has a number of methods that can be used for extracting parts of the specified date. If you use the Date object as shown in the preceding line of code, the current system date is returned and, in this case, stored in the date variable.

Some of the methods that will be used for this section are shown in the following table:

Method	Description
getDate	Retrieves the current numeric day of the month of the Date object.
GetFullMonth	Retrieves the current month of the Date object.
getFullYear	Returns the four-digit year from the Date object.

Before using the various methods of the Date object, you must create a reference to an InfoPath control for each of the controls used.

Creating a Reference to an InfoPath Field

```
var todayField = XDocument.DOM.selectSingleNode("//my:TodaysDate");
```

Using the InfoPath object model, discussed in Chapter 12, "Getting Starting Using Scripts," you will use the main object, XDocument. The selectSingleNode method, part of the DOM (Document Object Model), is used to retrieve a reference to the XPath value of the name of the control passed to it, in this case "//my:TodaysDate".

Assigning a Value to a Variable

Everything that is now done with the `todayField` variable will be reflected in the field on the form. So, assigning a value to the `Text` property of the variable assigns the value to the field on the form, as in the following line of code:

```
todayField.text = (date.getMonth() + 1) + "/" + date.getDate() + "/" +
    date.getFullYear();
```

You also can see the Date object methods used in the last line of code. The last line of code changes based on what you are trying to accomplish. That line placed a formatted version of today's date into the todayField control. To add a day to the current date, you use the following line of code, which assigns it the variable called `tomorrowsField`.

```
tomorrowsField.text = (date.getMonth() + 1) + "/" + (date.getDate() + 1) + "/" +
    date.getFullYear();
```

Try It Out   **Creating a Form That Manipulates Dates Using Script**

The first task you have to do is create a form to display the information:

1.   Open InfoPath.

2.   Click on Design a Form.

3.   Click on New Blank Form.

4.   Lay out the form as displayed in Figure 14-2.

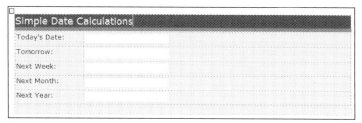

Figure 14-2

5.   Name the fields down the form as follows: **TodaysDate, Tomorrow, NextWeek, NextMonth,** and **NextYear.**

6.   Choose On Load Event from the Tools ➪ Programming... menu. The Microsoft Script Editor opens with the on load event shell displayed.

7. Type in the following code between curly brackets of the function:

```
// create a variable storing today's date
var date = new Date();

// create references to the InfoPath form controls
var todayField = XDocument.DOM.selectSingleNode("//my:TodaysDate");
var tomorrowsField = XDocument.DOM.selectSingleNode("//my:Tomorrow");
var nextWeekField = XDocument.DOM.selectSingleNode("//my:NextWeek");
var nextMonthField = XDocument.DOM.selectSingleNode("//my:NextMonth");
var nextYearField = XDocument.DOM.selectSingleNode("//my:NextYear");

// create the new date values and store them in the controls.
todayField.text = (date.getMonth() + 1) + "/" + date.getDate() + "/" +
    date.getFullYear();
tomorrowsField.text = (date.getMonth() + 1) + "/" + (date.getDate() + 1) + "/" +
    date.getFullYear();
nextWeekField.text = (date.getMonth() + 1) + "/" + (date.getDate() + 7) + "/" +
    date.getFullYear();
nextMonthField.text = (date.getMonth() + 2) + "/" + date.getDate() + "/" +
    date.getFullYear();
nextYearField.text = (date.getMonth() + 1) + "/" + date.getDate() + "/" +
    (date.getFullYear() + 1);
```

The screen will then look as shown in Figure 14-3.

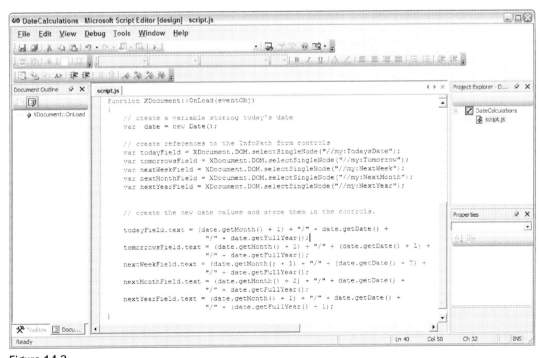

Figure 14-3

8. Save and close the editor.

9. Click Preview Form. The form is displayed with the various dates, as shown in Figure 14-1.

The reason that these are simple date calculations is that you are really just adding values to the parts of the dates, not looking at the date values. For instance, if you add a month to the current month, and the month is December, then you see an error in the displayed field. Now check out how to do it using C# and Visual Studio .NET to resolve this issue.

Date Calculations Using C# and Visual Studio .NET

One of the huge benefits of using C# instead of JScript is that with C# you have the power of the classes in .NET. Instead of using the limited Date object in JScript, you get to use the powerful DateTime .NET class, including all the properties and methods belonging to it. These methods include specific operations for adding days, months, and years to dates.

As with the script example, you will assign today's date to a variable, as shown here:

```
System.DateTime date = System.DateTime.Today;
```

System.DateTime Class

The DateTime class has a number of very nice methods for working with dates. You can see a number of them in the following table, which are used for this example:

Method	Description
Today	Returns a DateTime object representing today's date.
ToShortDateString	Returns a string value formatted in the short date format of mm/dd/yy.
AddDays	Adds the number of days passed in an argument to the DateTime object it is called from.
AddMonths	Adds the number of months passed in an argument to the DateTime object it is called from.
AddYears	Adds the number of years passed in an argument to the DateTime object it is called from.

Remember that these are methods of a DateTime object. You will see them used shortly. First check out how to create a reference in your InfoPath form fields.

Creating a Reference to an InfoPath Field

Unlike using Jscript, when you use a variable in C# you need to declare it as a specific type. In the case of assigning a reference to a field on the InfoPath form, it will be a IXMLDOMNode type. The command itself looks very similar to the same line of code in JScript. Here is one of the lines of code you will use:

```
IXMLDOMNode todayField = thisXDocument.DOM.selectSingleNode("//my:TodaysDate");
```

Using the InfoPath object model in C#, discussed in Chapter 13, "Working with .NET Managed Code," you will use the main object, XDocument. The selectSingleNode method, part of DOM, is used to retrieve a reference to the XPath value of the name of the control passed to it, in this case "//my:TodaysDate".

By declaring the variable as an IXMLDOMNode object you will be able to see the properties and methods using Intellesense, also introduced in earlier chapters.

Assigning a Value to a Variable

Everything that is now done with the todayField variable will be reflected in the field on the form, as can be shown the following line of code:

```
todayField.text = date.ToShortDateString();
```

This line of code stores the value in the date variable in the text property of the todayField, formatting it using the ToShortDateString method. The line of code after this one varies depending on which field is being assigned.

Try It Out   **Manipulating Dates Using C#**

As with the last Try It Out, the first task you have to do is create a form to display the information:

1. Open Visual Studio .NET 2003.

2. Click New Project. The New Project dialog box will open.

3. Choose Microsoft Office InfoPath Projects.

4. Click Visual C# Projects. The InfoPath project will be displayed as shown in Figure 14-4.

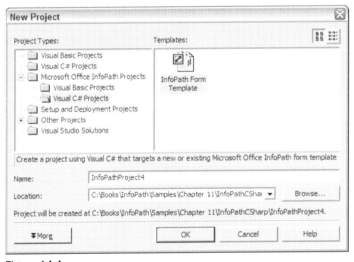

Figure 14-4

5. Click OK. The Microsoft Office Project Wizard will be displayed.

6. Click the Finish button, accepting the defaults. The project will be created with a new blank form displayed.

7. Lay out the form as displayed in Figure 14-5.

Date Calculations

Today's Date:	
Tomorrow:	
Next Week:	
Next Month:	
Next Year:	

Figure 14-5

8. Choose On Load Event from the Tools ➪ Programming... menu choice. The new event will be created, and you will be placed in the routine.

9. Type the following between the opening and closing brackets.

```
// Assign today's date to a variable.
System.DateTime date = System.DateTime.Today;

// Assign the field references.
IXMLDOMNode todayField = thisXDocument.DOM.selectSingleNode("//my:TodaysDate");
IXMLDOMNode tomorrowsField = thisXDocument.DOM.selectSingleNode("//my:Tomorrow");
IXMLDOMNode nextWeekField = thisXDocument.DOM.selectSingleNode("//my:NextWeek");
IXMLDOMNode nextMonthField = thisXDocument.DOM.selectSingleNode("//my:NextMonth");
IXMLDOMNode nextYearField = thisXDocument.DOM.selectSingleNode("//my:NextYear");

// Assign the new values to the form fields.
todayField.text = date.ToShortDateString();
tomorrowsField.text = date.AddDays(1).ToShortDateString();
nextWeekField.text = date.AddDays(7).ToShortDateString();
nextMonthField.text = date.AddMonths(1).ToShortDateString();
nextYearField.text = date.AddYears(1).ToShortDateString();
```

10. Choose Debug ➪ Start. The form will then open in Preview Mode, shown in Figure 14-6.

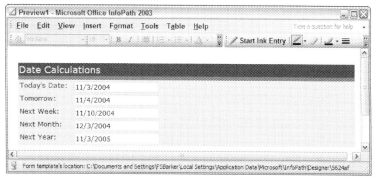

Figure 14-6

235

If you change the system date to a later month, you will notice that unlike the form created in the script version, all the dates are displayed correctly. Again, this is one of the benefits of using C# over scripting. While you could jump through more hoops (meaning create more code) to accomplish the same goal, it is easier to use .NET to accomplish the task.

Sending a Form in an E-Mail

Another useful feature is to be able to send forms to other users via e-mail. While you can accomplish this using the menu choices, it is also more professional and convenient to be able to create code to accomplish the same thing.

To send a form using e-mail, you will need to perform a couple of steps: First, you need to create a data connection for your form, but in this case it will be used for sending e-mail instead of submitting and retrieving data to and from a database. You can see the Data Connection Wizard used for setting up the data connection in Figure 14-7.

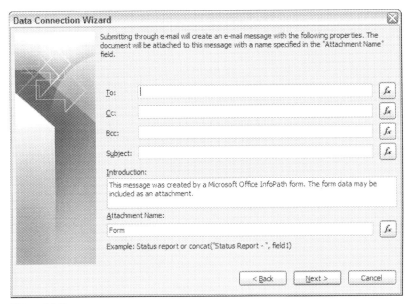

Figure 14-7

Although you have to specify someone for the To field when creating the data connection, you can change all the properties using code at runtime.

The next step is to create the form you want to send. Finally, you have to write the necessary code, added to a command button on the form. The code created will use a DataAdapter from the DataAdapters collection off the XDocument object. You can see the line of code here:

```
var objEmail = XDocument.DataAdapters("Submit");
```

Because you set the data adapter up to work with e-mail, InfoPath knows how to use it. The following table contains some of the properties for the Email Adapter:

Property	Description
AttachmentFileName	Sets or returns the name of the attachment that will be made of the for.
BCC	BCC recipient
CC	CC recipient
Intro	Introduction of the form
Name	Name of the data adapter
Subject	Subject of the e-mail message
To	To recipient

The method you use will use here is the Submit method. You can see some of its properties displayed in the table, along with the Submit used in the following lines of code:

```
objEmail.To = XDocument.DOM.selectSingleNode("//my:ToField").text;

objEmail.Subject = XDocument.DOM.selectSingleNode("//my:SubjectField").text;

objEmail.Submit();
```

Try It Out   Creating a Form That Can E-Mail Itself

You will create a new blank InfoPath form for this Try It Out.

1. Open InfoPath.
2. Choose Design a Form.
3. Click New Blank Form. A new form is displayed.
4. Lay out the form as shown in Figure 14-8. The field names for the text boxes will be ToField and SubjectField.

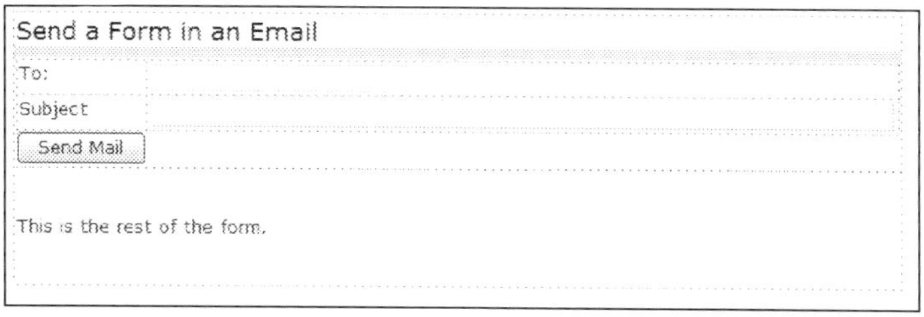

Figure 14-8

5. Choose Tools ➪ Data Connections. The Data Connections dialog box appears.

237

6. Click the Add button. The Data Connection Wizard starts, with the first page asking if you would to Submit or Receive data. The default is Submit.

7. Click Next. The next page asks how you would like to submit the data: To a Web Service, to a SharePoint Library, or As an Email message.

8. Select the As an Email Message choice, then click Next.

9. Fill in the To text box with an e-mail address. The dialog box will then look like Figure 14-9.

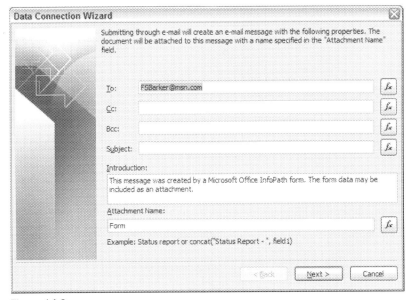

Figure 14-9

10. Click Next. The last page of the Data Connection Wizard is displayed.

11. Click Finish, remembering the name of the data connector, Submit.

12. Click Close. The Data Connection dialog box closes.

13. Double-click the command button. The property sheet will open.

14. Change the Label of the button to Send Mail, and the ID to btnSendMail. The property sheet will then look like Figure 14-10.

15. Click the Edit Form Code button. The Microsoft Script Editor will open, and a new Click event subroutine will be created.

16. Type the following line of code in between the opening and closing brackets:

```
var objEmail = XDocument.DataAdapters("Submit");

objEmail.To = XDocument.DOM.selectSingleNode("//my:ToField").text;

objEmail.Subject = XDocument.DOM.selectSingleNode("//my:SubjectField").text;

objEmail.Submit();
```

In the editor, the routine will now look as it does in Figure 14-11.

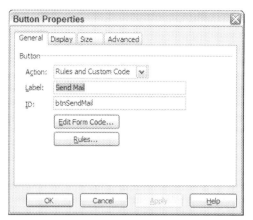

Figure 14-10

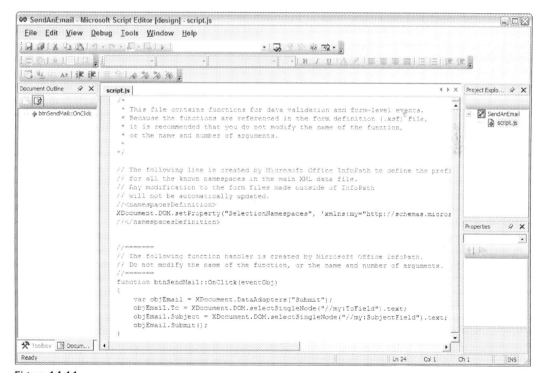

Figure 14-11

17. Close the Microsoft Script Editor, saving the script file.

18. Click Preview Form. The form opens.

19. Fill in the To and Subject fields, then click Send. The message box is displayed, as seen in Figure 14-12.

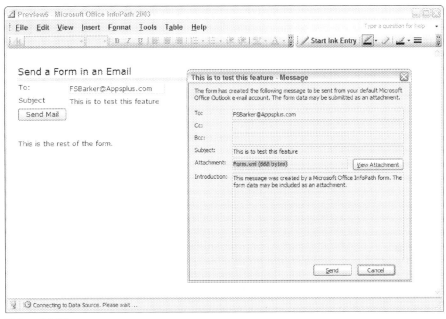

Figure 14-12

After clicking Send, the e-mail will be sent to the recipient. There you have it! You can send forms to your users and have them send the form back to you after they have filled in the information needed.

Providing Context-Sensitive Help

Besides displaying view choices in a custom task pane as shown back in Chapter 11, "Working with Code in Your InfoPath Form," you can also use the custom task pane to display context-sensitive help. Context-sensitive help is information displayed based on where the user is on a form. For example, when a customer is in a field such as Customer ID, you can display a description for the field or give instructions on how to enter certain types of data. In Figure 14-13, you can see an example of the form taken from Chapter 6, "Working with Controls in General," modified to use context-sensitive help.

Just as when you're using the custom task pane for displaying views, you specify the custom task pane properties using the Advanced tab of the Form Options dialog box. In addition to this, you will supply an HTML page providing the information in the task pane. Finally, you will add code to the ContextChange event so that as you are moving to each part of the form, the task pane will change the description text to match.

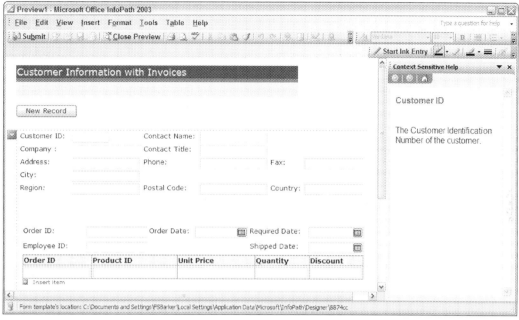

Figure 14-13

The actual steps are:

1. **Create the Form**: In the case of this example, the form from Chapter 6 is used.

2. **Create the HTML Web page**: In creating the HTML Web page, you will use standard HTML statements (tags) in a format that can be used by the code written for the `ContextChange` event. You can see an example of the code in Figure 14-14.

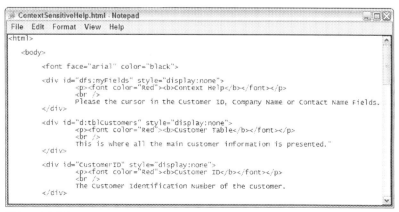

Figure 14-14

The main object to notice is the <div> object. This object is used to display HTML in a specific section. In this case the code will look up the ID of the object and display the HTML in task pane. The other tags specify different formatting commands.

Notice also the first two DIVs, dfs:myfields and d:tblCustomers. The first node, dfs:myfields, displays its message when you are on the blank part of the form and the heading. d:tblCustomers is displayed when you are on the tblCustomers table part of the form, when the individual fields aren't being displayed.

Tag	Description
<p>	Specifies the start of a new paragraph.
<b>	Sets text between the beginning and end tags to bold.
<font>	Set different properties of the font of text between the beginning and end tags.

3. **Create the Code in the ContextChange Event**: Using the Microsoft Script Editor, you will create the following code on the ContextChange event:

```
var strHelp = null;
function XDocument::OnContextChange(eventObj)
{
if (eventObj.Type == "ContextNode")
{
        var objTP = XDocument.View.Window.TaskPanes.Item(0);
        var objDoc = objTP.HTMLDocument.all;

        if (strHelp)
                objDoc.item(strHelp).style.display="none";

        objDoc.item(eventObj.Context.nodeName).style.display="";

        strHelp=eventObj.Context.nodeName;

        return;

    }

}
```

After testing for the context node, a reference is created for the task pane in the line of code that reads:

```
var objTP = XDocument.View.Window.TaskPanes.Item(0);
```

Next, a string variable called strHelp is queried to see if it was set to a value; if not, then it is cleared.

```
if (strHelp)
        objDoc.item(strHelp).style.display="none";
```

Finally, set the task pane to the current node of data, and store the node name for later use.

```
objDoc.item(eventObj.Context.nodeName).style.display="";

strHelp=eventObj.Context.nodeName;
```

That's it. Now try it out yourself.

Try It Out   Creating a Context-Sensitive Help Task Pane

For the purposes of this Try It Out the Chapter 6 form has been copied into the Chapter 14 folder for this book on the WROX Web site (`ContextSensitiveHelp.xsn`) and `ContextSensitiveHelp.htm` with the commands in it.

1.   Open InfoPath.

2.   Create the InfoPath form as desired. You can see the form used for this example in Figure 14-15; you will want to make note of the field names.

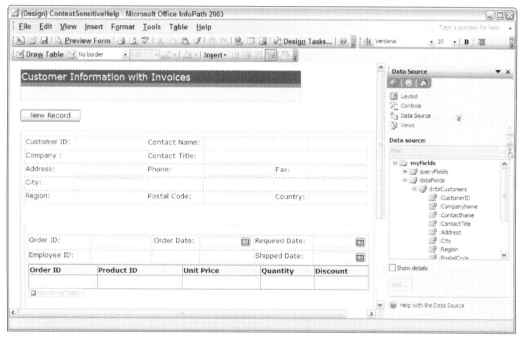

Figure 14-15

3.   Using NotePad or your favorite editor, create the HTML Web page containing the help text. If using the form with the layout displayed in Figure 14-15, the text would look as follows:

```html
<html>
  <body>
    <font face="arial" color="black">
  <div id="dfs:myFields" style="display:none">
    <p><font color="Red"><b>Context Help</b></font></p>
      <br />
```

```
         Place the cursor in the Customer ID, Company Name or Contact Name Fields.
       </div>
       <div id="d:tblCustomers" style="display:none">
          <p><font color="Red"><b>Customer Table</b></font></p>
          <br />
          This is where all the main customer information is presented."
       </div>
       <div id="CustomerID" style="display:none">
          <p><font color="Red"><b>Customer ID</b></font></p>
          <br />
          The Customer Identification Number of the customer.
       </div>
       <div id="CompanyName" style="display:none">
          <font color="Red"><b><p>Company Name</p></b></font>
          <br />
          Company Name of the Customer.
       </div>
       <div id="ContactName" style="display:none">
          <font color="Red"><b><p>Contact Name</p></b></font>
          <br />
          Name of the Contact.
       </div>
       <div id="ContactTitle" style="display:none">
          <font color="Red"><b><p>Contact Title</p></b></font>
          <br />
          Contact's Title.
       </div>
       <div id="Phone" style="display:none">
          <font color="Red"><b><p>Phone</p></b></font>
          <br />
          Contact's Phone.
       </div>
       ...
  </body>
<html>
```

Note that you can fill out the HTML Web page with as many of the fields as you want to cover.

4. Save and close the HTML Web page, noting where it is saved.

5. Choose Tools ➪ Form Options.

6. Click the Advanced tab.

7. Put a checkmark in the check box labeled Enable custom task pane.

8. Click on the Resource Files ... button. Using this form, you will locate and specify the HTML Web page you created in Steps 3 and 4.

9. Click Add....

10. Locate the HTML Web page you created.

11. Click OK. You can see the HTML Web page specified in the Resource Files dialog box in Figure 14-16.

Figure 14-16

12. Click OK. You will be taken back to the Form Options dialog box on the Advanced page.

13. Type the name you want to use in the Task pane name field.

14. Pick the name of the HTML Web page you specified in Task pane location. You are now done filling out the Form Option for the task pane information, as shown in Figure 14-17.

Figure 14-17

15. Click OK.

16. Click Preview Form. The form opens. If you click various parts of the form, help will be displayed, as shown in Figure 14-18. The cursor is placed on the table called tblCustomers.

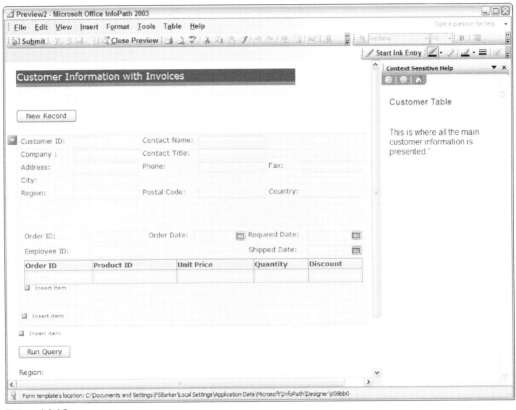

Figure 14-18

Make sure you test all areas of the form. If you don't have a node entered into the HTML Web page, an error will occur.

Summary

One of the areas that InfoPath forms don't cover using the user interface is the manipulation of dates. Even in JScript there are hoops you have to jump through, meaning additional code you need to write, to handle cases where months and years overlap. You learned how you can take care of this using C#'s DateTime methods to handle any date manipulation needed. You also learned how to handle additional tasks such as sending a form using scripting and creating context-sensitive help using a custom pane.

There is virtually nothing you can't accomplish using InfoPath forms with scripting or managed code. Of the two language platforms scripting is provided by InfoPath, but C# gives you more flexibility.

Exercises

1.   Name three methods of the JScript Date object used in this chapter.

2.   What object is used to send e-mail using code?

3.   What is the HTML element used to specify an area on Web page?

4.   Where on an InfoPath form do you specify information about the HTML Web page you want to use for context-sensitive help?

Creating and Working with Web Services

Web services, sometimes called XML Web services, have been mentioned several times in this book. Web services are fast becoming a very popular technology and are surprisingly easy to use and create. Once created, you can expose the Web service to either your intranet or the Internet. If the Web service is exposed to the Internet, other applications can access it regardless of if they are desktop — or Web browser — based. They can be used (known as being *consumed*) using standard Internet protocols.

Along with databases, such as Access and SQL Server, and XML documents and schemas, you can use a Web service for InfoPath data sources. You may ask why you would bother if you can just hook into the database just mentioned, but there are a number of other databases that you may want to connect to over the Internet, and Web services are the way to accomplish that. In this chapter you will:

- ❑ Be introduced to Web services and the technologies behind them.
- ❑ Get an overview of ASP.NET.
- ❑ See how to create a Web service.
- ❑ Create a Web service and use it as a data source for an InfoPath form.

For the purposes of installing and testing the Web service provided in this chapter, you must have Internet Information Services 5.x installed and ASP.NET 1.1 loaded for the local host. When creating the sample Web service in the chapter, you will use Visual Studio .NET 2003 with C#.

Web Services Overview

Web services are fast becoming an essential part of various applications in use, including Windows itself. Now in the later versions of Windows when you click a file using Explorer and the system doesn't recognize the file format, a dialog box such as the one in Figure 15-1 will appear.

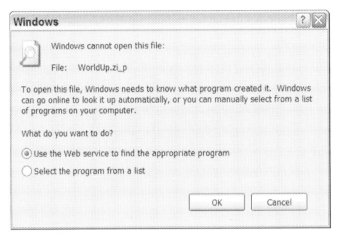

Figure 15-1

Notice that the first option in the dialog box is to use a Web service to locate the appropriate program for the file. To use the service, or communicate, the consumer (local machine or application) will use XML Messaging and HTTP. The same is true when the Web service is communicating back to the consumer.

One of the great things about using XML Web services is that as long as the consumer can create and consume messages defined for the Web service, it doesn't matter what the consumer is written in, or what even what platform. The term used for this is loosely coupled, or in other words, nonproprietary. Figure 15-2 displays this concept.

Notice that no specific languages or platforms are named in this graphic, except to point out ASP.NET of course. The Web service can be created using ASP.NET or any other language that works with Simple Object Access Protocol (SOAP).

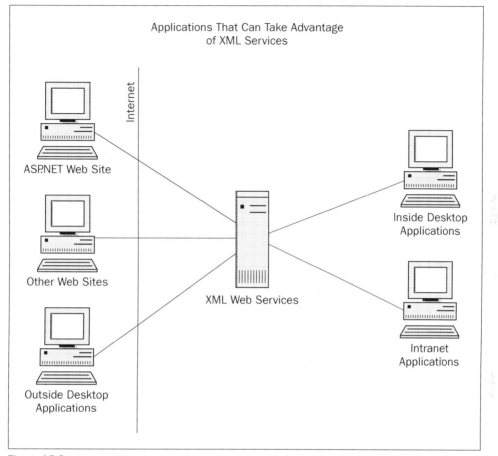

Figure 15-2

Web Services Infrastructure

When talking about the infrastructure of Web services, there are four main areas. They are:

❑ **XML Web Services Directories**: The central location to locate XML Web services created by outside organizations. The UDDI registry is an example of one of these directories. Your Web service client may not even need to use these if you know the address of the Web service you are accessing.

❑ **XML Web Service Discovery**: Discovering documents that describe a particular XML Web service using the Web Services Description Language (WSDL). The DISCO specification defines an algorithm for locating service descriptions. Again, if you know the location of the service description you can avoid this process.

❑   **XML Web Service Description**: Defines what types of methods the XML Web service uses. Tells clients how to interact with an XML Web service so that they know how to use it.

❑   **XML Web Service Wire Formats**: To be able communicate with all platforms and languages, XML Web services use open wire formats. These protocols are understood by any system capable of supporting the most common Web standards. SOAP is the main protocol used.

You can see each of these parts of the infrastructure displayed in Figure 15-3.

Don't panic. These steps are performed for you in most cases after you set up the Web reference, or in the case of InfoPath, after you specify which Web service to use as a data source. You get a chance to practice this in upcoming sections.

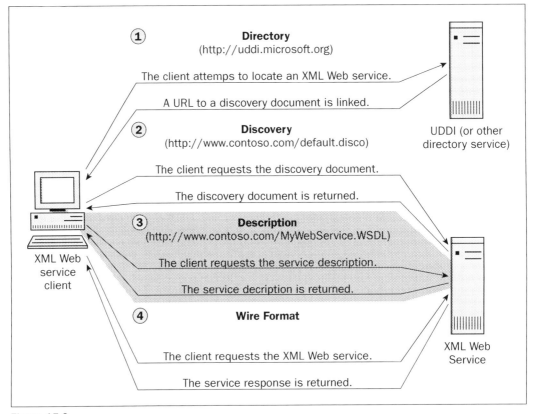

Figure 15-3

Using Web Services Locally

This section walks you through setting up a Web service locally to practice connecting to and creating Web services. To accomplish this, you should download the final version of the Web service for this chapter, called `Chapter15WebService`, into the root directory of your local host, using:

> *drive*: \inetpub\wwwroot

Once the whole folder is copied to the specified folder, you will open up IIS and then make the folder into a virtual directory by creating a default application for the folder using a property sheet.

Try It Out   **Setting Up a Web Service Locally**

You will need to have downloaded the Web service from the Chapter 15 folder on the WROX Web site. When you have done so:

1. Copy the folder of the Web service into the default folder of your local host. In the case of the authors machine: c:\inetpub\wwwroot.

2. Choose Adminstrative Tools ⇨ Internet Information Services from the Start menu. In IIS you will see the default machine displayed.

3. Click the machine node to expand the tree view. You will then see the Web Sites nodes displayed. You may see other services listed such as SMTP and FTP if you installed them.

4. Click the Web Sites node. The Default Web Site node is displayed.

5. Click the Default Web Site node. You will then see a list of current Web sites and services on your machine, as displayed in Figure 15-4.

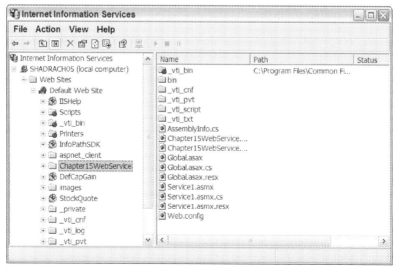

Figure 15-4

6. Right-click the Web service folder Chapter15WebService and choose Properties from the pop-up menu. There are a number of properties listed here for the various types of Web sites.

7. Click the Create button, located under the application settings. The caption of the button changes to Remove, and the name of the Web service is displayed in the Application Name property, shown in Figure 15-5.

8. Click OK to close the property sheet. The Web service is now displayed in IIS with the virtual directory icon displayed as displayed in Figure 15-6.

You can now close IIS, and the Web service will now be available as needed for use locally.

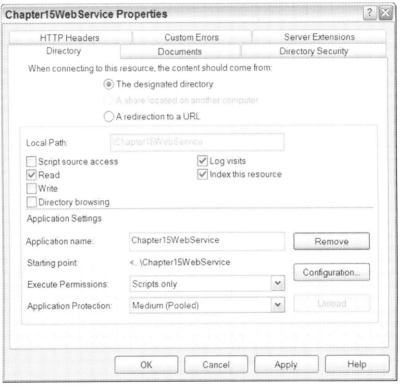

Figure 15-5

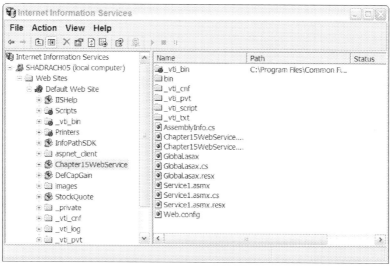

Figure 15-6

Using Web Services for Data Source

The steps for specifying a Web service as a data source for an InfoPath form are almost as easy as, if not easier, than those used for specifying a table in a database for a data source. InfoPath performs a number of the steps for you.

The first thing you have to specify is whether you are receiving (querying) or submitting data. For now you will see quickly how to specify a Web service for viewing data.

After specifying what you want to do with the data (receive and/or submit), you will need to specify where the Web service you want to use is located. For the purpose of locating the Web service, you can utilize the UDDI directories, displayed in Figure 15-3, on the prior page. To help you locate the Web service, Microsoft supplies a dialog box, displayed in Figure 15-7.

Figure 15-7

For the purposes of this chapter, the Web services used will be located on the local machine at `http://127.0.0.1`, so the dialog box displayed in Figure 15-7 will not be used. You can also test using `http://localhost`.

Once you have specified the Web service, the wizard will walk you through the steps to specify which methods to use. After the wizard is completed, you will then need to bind the fields displayed to the various controls just as you do when using other types of data for data sources.

Try It Out   Basing an InfoPath Form on a Web Service

To start off, you will be using an InfoPath form to display information from a Web service. While here you will be seeing how to specify a Web method as an InfoPath data source, in the following sections you will see the code on the Web service side that makes up the data connection. To start:

1.   Open InfoPath.

2.   Click Design a Form. The Design a Form task pane will be displayed on the right-hand side of the application.

3.   Click the task New from a Data Connection in the Design a Form task pane. The first page of the Data Connection Wizard will be displayed.

4.   Select Web Service from the first page, as shown in Figure 15-8.

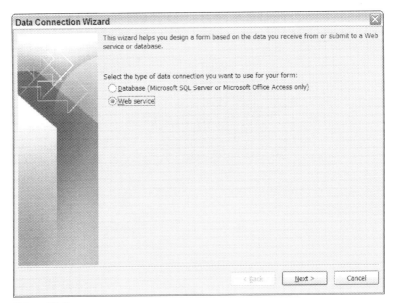

Figure 15-8

5.   Click Next to continue with the Data Connection Wizard. The next page asks you if you want to receive and submit data, submit data, or just receive data. For the purposes of this task, you will just receive data.

6.   Choose Receive data, as shown in Figure 15-9.

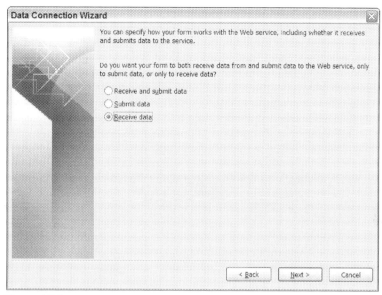

Figure 15-9

7. Click Next. The page displayed is where you will supply information about the Web service you want to use. In this case, you will be using your localhost service, or IP address, 127.0.0.1.

You will next be supplying the Web service name, in this case `Chapter15Webservice`, and the main page of the Web service `Service1.asmx`. Finally, you add the `?`, which tells Web pages you are sending a query, and the letters WSDL, which informs the Web service that you want the descriptions of the available methods and properties of the Web service. You can see the full string supplied for this example in Figure 15-10.

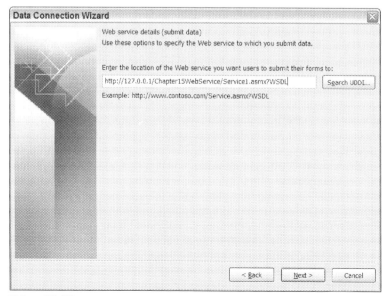

Figure 15-10

8. Click Next. The wizard queries the URL you specified to see if it can read the WSDL. If so, you see the list of methods provided by the sample application, as shown here in Figure 15-11.

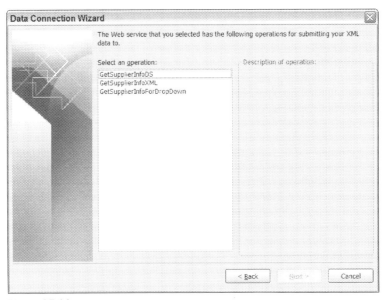

Figure 15-11

If you have specified the URL incorrectly, then a message box will appear, and you will need to click Back in the wizard.

9. Select GetSupplierInfoDS, and click Next. The next page displays all the parameters that will be used for querying the data. In this case, SupplierID will be used. To have InfoPath understand how to query the data correctly, you have to supply a sample for the query. In this case supply the value of 1, then InfoPath can do the rest of the work.

10. Click Set Sample Value.... The Parameter Details dialog box opens.

11. Type in **1**, as shown in Figure 15-12.

12. Click OK to accept the value, and then click Next in the Data Connection Wizard. The summary page, which is also the last page of the wizard, is displayed, as shown in Figure 15-13. You can also change the name used for the data connection you want on this page.

13. Click Finish. The wizard is now complete and a query form template is displayed.

14. Click the Data Source task pane, and then expand the two branches queryFields and dataFields, as shown in Figure 15-14.

    These should look familiar because they also are using a database for the data connection.

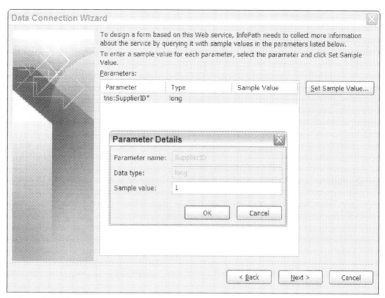

Figure 15-12

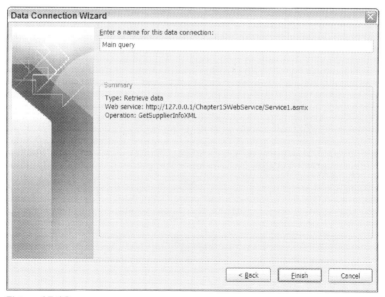

Figure 15-13

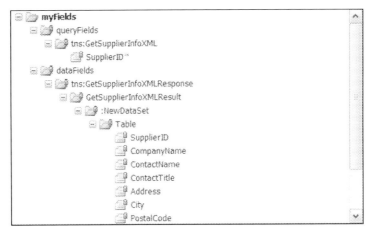

Figure 15-14

15. Drag the SupplierID field from the queryFields into the table under the button labeled Run Query.

16. Drag and drop the Table node from dataFields data source branch under the table that has the label Click to add form content. You will then see the sections menu appear, letting you choose how you want to set the section up.

17. Pick Controls in Layout Section from the displayed menu. The fields will now all be displayed as shown in Figure 15-15.

That's all there is to it. Now, the last step is to preview the form just as would any other form.

18. Click Preview form. The empty form is now displayed, ready for you to enter a supplier ID to query.

19. Type **1** in the text box under the label Supplier ID.

20. Click Run Query. The parameter is supplied to the Web service, and the result is returned to the form to be displayed, as shown in Figure 15-16.

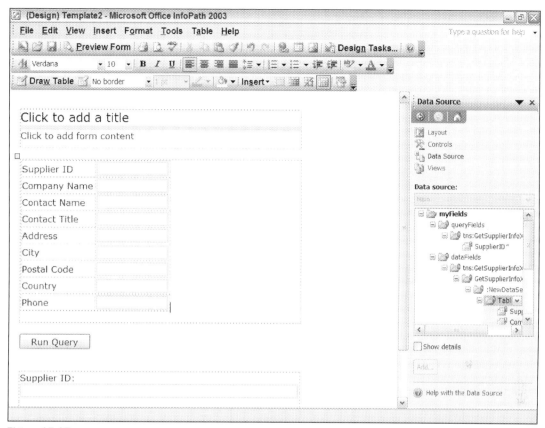

Figure 15-15

Now comes the fun part. If you've read Chapter 13, "Working with .NET Managed Code," along with the Chapter 14, "Real-World Tasks and Coding Examples," you should be somewhat comfortable with Visual Studio .NET 2003. One of things not covered was using ASP.NET and developing for the Web. This next section provides an introduction to just that.

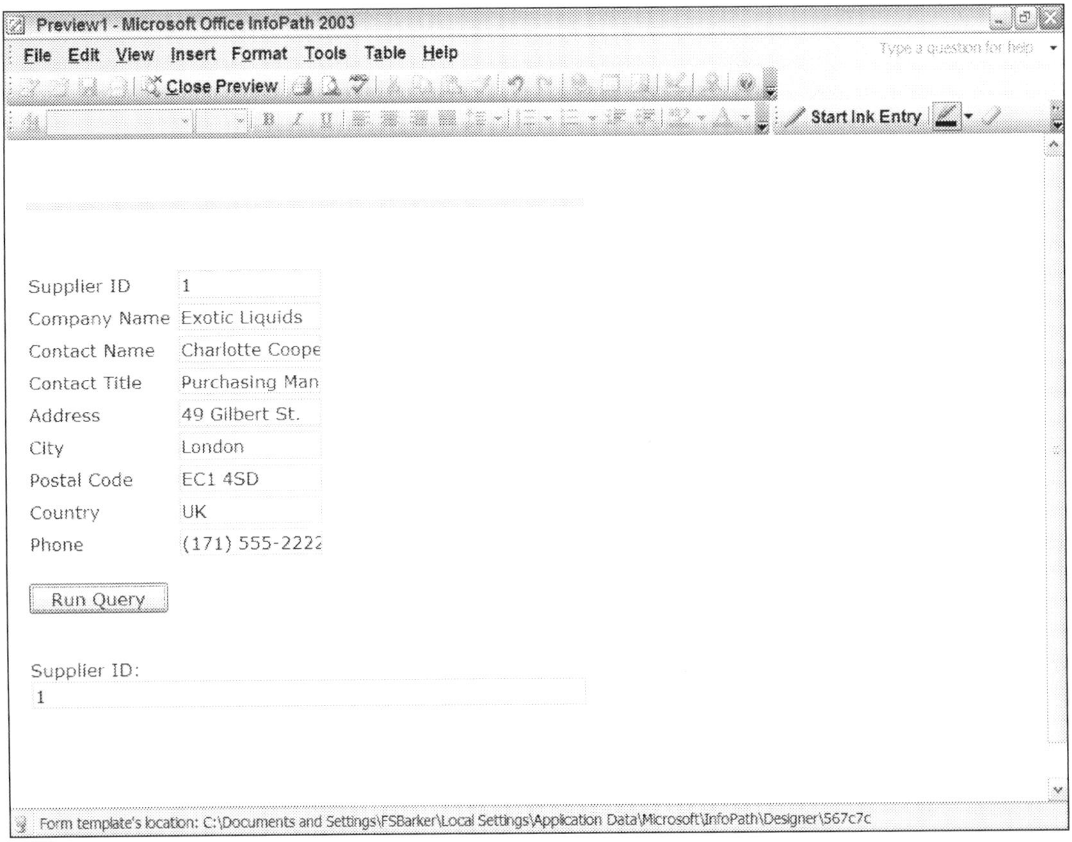

Figure 15-16

Creating a Web Service Using ASP.NET

In the prior chapters you have see how to use C# to manipulate the InfoPath object model and create functions to accomplish tasks using Visual Studio .NET. Although some of your InfoPath development thus far has used HTML and scripting to perform some of those tasks, none has used the Web. It is now time to remedy that.

While there are many languages and platforms you can use to create Web services, to develop Web services for this book you will be using ASP.NET.

Introducing ASP.NET

With .NET developing for the Web becomes easier than ever. ASP.NET is actually even fun to work with. In the past, it has been quite a task to develop applications in ASP. Now you can develop your Web applications in much the same way you do Windows desktop applications, with a few major differences.

Those differences really won't even be felt when you create the Web service for this chapter, because you will really just be taking parameters and passing back data.

ASP.NET combines HTML and server-side code such as C# that helps to create dynamic Web pages, which not only provide static Web presentations but also allow user interaction with data. In this chapter, you use Web services for sending and receiving data, not only for the data presentation itself.

Note that when you use Web services Visual Studio (VS) does a lot of the work with setting up how the Web service communicates using SOAP, which is used to transfer the data via XML. SOAP was created originally by the W3C group, mentioned in Chapter 5, "Utilizing XML and Web Service Data Sources."

Try It Out   Creating an ASP.NET Web Service Project

When you create a new project in Visual Studio .NET, there are a number of choices of project types to create; one of those is the ASP.NET Web Service project:

1. Start Visual Studio .NET.

2. Click New Project. The New Project dialog box will appear.

3. Select ASP.NET Web Service, as shown in Figure 15-17.

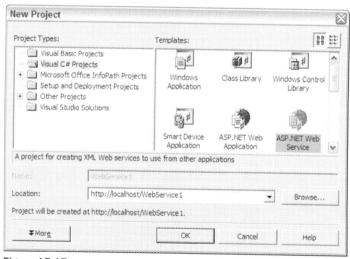

Figure 15-17

When you specify the name of the Web service you want to create, Visual Studio will create a folder under the Web server you specify. In the case of Figure 15-17, the majority of the project files will be stored in the folder called WebService1 under the localhost Web server. Remember the default location for localhost is drive:\inetpub\wwwroot. WebService1 will also be set as a virtual directory.

4. Click OK. Visual Studio .NET creates the project. By default you see the Solution Explorer on the right and a blank *.cs file in Design view, shown here in Figure 15-18. The reason that you don't have a design surface to work with is that Web services don't have a user interface.

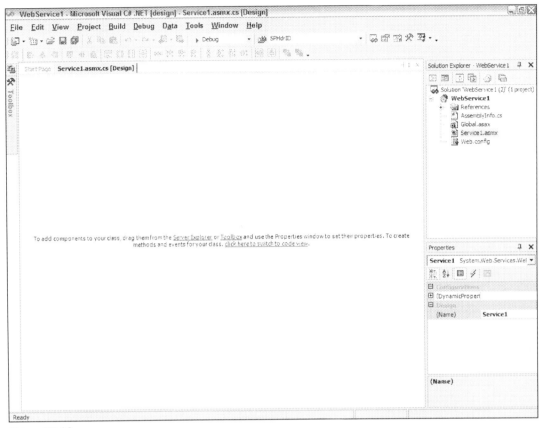

Figure 15-18

5. Click the link that says *click here to switch to code view*. You will then see the code created for you, as shown in Figure 15-19.

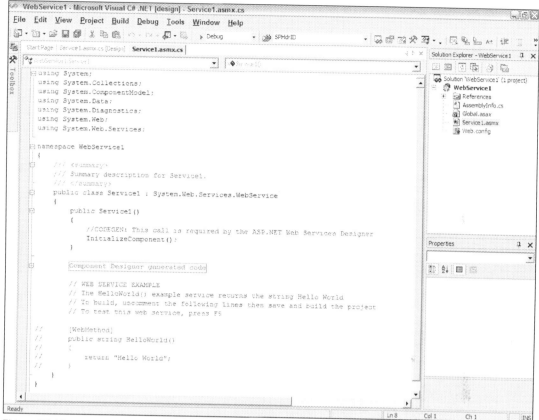

Figure 15-19

Looking at the Initial Template

When looking at the file displayed in 15-19, the actual code that you will be modifying is at the bottom of the code, and can be seen here:

```
//          [WebMethod]
//          public string HelloWorld()
/           {
//              return "Hello World";
//          }
```

You will be removing the comment markers (//) and modifying the code to create a method that will be used by InfoPath. Microsoft provides a template to return a class message of "Hello World." Before checking this code out, take a look at the various parts of the file that are common in Web services, as well as other C# applications.

The Using Directive

In the first section, you will specify which classes and namespaces you need to import into your Web service with the `using` directive as follows:

```
using System;
using System.Collections;
using System.ComponentModel;
using System.Data;
using System.Diagnostics;
using System.Web;
using System.Web.Services;
```

VS puts in the namespaces displayed here by default, and you can add your own as needed. For instance, if you need to use commands that manipulate XML, then you will want to add a `using` directive as follows:

```
using System.Xml;
```

By specifying these namespaces, you can then utilize the classes within the namespaces without giving the complete name path in your code.

Namespace and Class Directives

Already discussed in Chapter 13, the following code specified the namespace for the Web service, as well as the name of the Web service itself, designated with the class.

```
namespace WebService1
{
    /// <summary>
    /// Summary description for Service1.
    /// </summary>
    public class Service1 : System.Web.Services.WebService
    {
```

Notice that the type of class of `Service1` is `System.Web.Sevices.WebService`. VS designats this class to perform a ton of work for you, and it allows you to use all the methods and properties available to the WebService class.

Initialization Code

The following method is run when the Web service is first run. When you have code that you want to run whenever the Web service object is instantiated, you will put the code here. For the purposes of the code used in this chapter, you won't be using this method.

```
public Service1()
{
    //CODEGEN: This call is required by the ASP.NET Web Services Designer
        InitializeComponent();
}
```

The Sample Web Service

The following code is what you will be modifying and using for your own methods that will be created for the Web service:

```
//          [WebMethod]
//          public string HelloWorld()
//          {
//                return "Hello World";
//          }
```

As you can see, the code looks a lot like other C# methods introduced earlier in the book. The big difference is the [WebMethod] attribute added just before the method declaration. Everything else will be the same.

Try It Out   Creating and Testing Your First Web Method

To get started as quickly as possible, you will start small by removing the comment symbols in the current code listed in the *.cs file created in the last Try It Out.

1.   Highlight each of the comment symbols (//) in the code just presented, and press the Delete key.

```
[WebMethod]
public string HelloWorld()
{
    return "Hello World";
}
```

That's it. Now it's time to test the code.

2.   Choose Debug ⇨ Start. The Web Service project is built, or rebuilt, and then the test harness that VS creates is started in Internet Explorer. You can see the test page in Figure 15-20.

Besides the name of the method to test, HelloWorld, there are some explanations on how to implement the Web service and its methods. To see what the SOAP that VS creates looks like, click the Service Description link. You will then see the page displayed in Figure 15-21.

Again, be thankful that Visual Studio does all that work for you. Click the Back button to return to the test harness page.

3.   Click the HelloWorld link. A test Web page with an Invoke button is displayed along with the sample SOAP request and response, shown in Figure 15-22.

You won't be using the SOAP at all. If you had any parameters required by the method, they would also be displayed on this page.

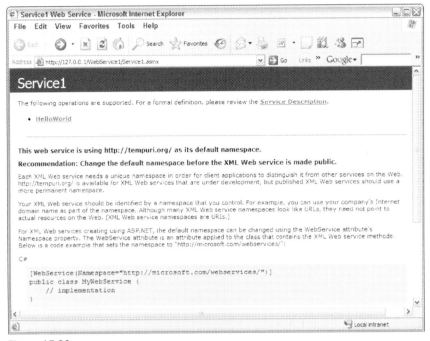

Figure 15-20

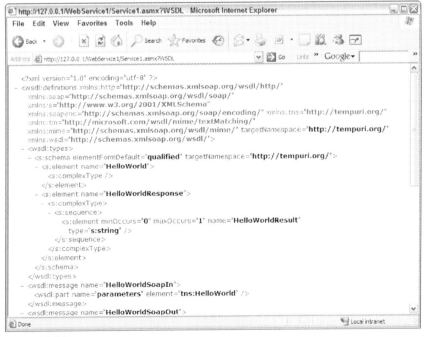

Figure 15-21

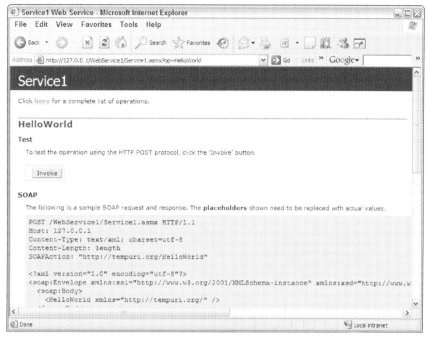

Figure 15-22

4. Click the Invoke button. The final page is displayed with the XML returned from the Web service and can be seen in Figure 15-23.

Figure 15-23

If it seems like a lot of work for the little return of "Hello World," the good news is that to return more data doesn't take much more effort. However, there are some more things you will need to cover that apply not just to Web services, but to working with data overall.

Working with Web Service Methods That Return Data

Everything you have read in the preceding chapters on coding in Visual Studio .NET applies to creating Web services. In addition to the commands covered already, .NET provides classes to help you work with data. In comes ADO.NET.

Introducing ADO.NET

In Chapter 13, you were introduced to the concept of assemblies, namespaces, and classes. One of the namespaces that can be found in .NET is the System.Data namespace. This namespace makes up ADO.NET, which is a set of classes created to assist developers who work with data using the .NET Framework.

If you have done any development for the desktop using Visual Basic or VBA in the last couple of years, especially when dealing with data, then you have probably used ActiveX Data Objects (ADO). ADO has an object model created for the purpose of manipulating data using code. On the .NET platform ADO.NET is used.

Differences between ADO and ADO.NET

The main difference between ADO and ADO.NET, besides specific objects, is the concept of connected data (ADO) versus disconnected data (ADO.NET). In both versions of ADO, you will use a Connection object, but in .NET the data is loaded either on the local computer or on the server using XML. The connection is then broken until the data is resubmitted to the source data. The ADO.NET objects, using properties, handle synchronization of data.

In ADO the main object was the Recordset, whereas in ADO.NET it is the DataSet. Unlike the Recordset from ADO and DAO, the DataSet actually brings back a hierarchical view of the data. Using properties and collections in the DataSet object, you can get from overall relations all the way down to individual tables, rows, and columns. You will read more about the DataSet object in the section in this chapter called "ADO.NET Objects."

Rather than going class by class through both ADO and ADO.NET, you will read about the classes used to work with the data in ADO.NET.

ADO.NET Data Provider Classes

.NET provides classes called data providers that will work with ADO.NET objects to provide access to data. You can see some of those objects in Figure 15-24.

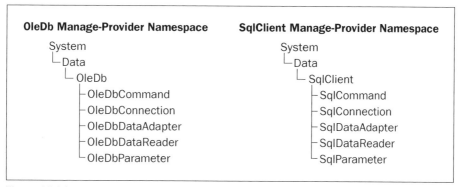

Figure 15-24

As mentioned, Visual Studio .NET applications are made up of one or more assemblies. Each assembly contains one or more namespaces. Namespaces are then made up of one or more classes (objects). Hence the namespace for OleDb objects is System.Data.OleDb. You can find these objects using the Object Browser. In the following table you can see a brief description of two of the OleDb objects that you will use in creating the Web service method for supplying data.

Object	Purpose
Connection	This object opens a connection to the server and database you want to work with. Unlike the ADO Connection object, how the connection remains open depends on the object you are working with, such as a DataReader or DataSet.
DataAdapter	A real workhorse, the DataAdapter lets you create SQL statements and fill DataSets with the data. It also will create other action queries necessary such as Insert, Update, and Delete ADO.NET command objects.

ADO.NET Objects

As mentioned in the previous section, the main object used with ADO.NET is the DataSet object. You can see the DataSet object, and its properties, methods, and additional objects, in Figure 15-25.

The DataSet object is used in conjunction with the other data controls, storing the results that are returned by commands and DataAdapters.

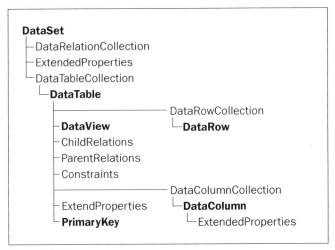

DataSet
├─DataRelationCollection
├─ExtendedProperties
└─DataTableCollection
    └─**DataTable**
        ├──────────────────────────── DataRowCollection
        ├─**DataView**   └─**DataRow**
        ├─ChildRelations
        ├─ParentRelations
        ├─Constraints
        ├──────────────────────────── DataColumnCollection
        ├─ExtendProperties   └─**DataColumn**
        └─**PrimaryKey**   └─ExtendedProperties

Figure 15-25

Try It Out   Creating the Method to Return Supplier Information

For this Try It Out, you can replace the HelloWorld method created in the last Try It Out.

1. Open the project just created.

2. Add the following statement in the top of the *.cs file with the other using statements:

```
using System.Data.OleDb;
```

3. Add the code displayed here just after the last curly brace for the HelloWorld method:

```
[WebMethod]
public DataSet  GetSupplierInfoDS( long SupplierID )
{

        //Create a connection to the local Access Database.
        string strCnn = "Provider=Microsoft.Jet.OLEDB.4.0; ";
        strCnn += "Data Source=" + Server.MapPath("/Chapter15WebService");
        strCnn += "\\Chapter 15.mdb";

        OleDbConnection cnn = new OleDbConnection();

        cnn.ConnectionString = strCnn;

        //Create an SQL DataAdapter to read the data.
        string strSQL = "SELECT SupplierID, CompanyName, ContactName, ";
        strSQL += "ContactTitle, Address, City, Region, PostalCode, ";
        strSQL += "Country, Phone, Fax FROM tblSuppliers ";
        strSQL += "WHERE SupplierID=" + SupplierID;

        OleDbDataAdapter daSuppliers = new
                    OleDbDataAdapter(strSQL, cnn);
```

```
                      // Create a DataSet and Fill it.
                      DataSet dsSuppliers = new DataSet();
                      daSuppliers.Fill( dsSuppliers);

                      return dsSuppliers;

        }
```

4. Press F5 to rebuild and run the application. The introduction page to the test harness will display both HelloWorld and your new Web method.

5. Click on the GetSupplierInfoDS link. You will then see the launch page for the Web method displayed with a text box to accept the Supplier ID parameter.

6. Enter the parameter, as shown in Figure 15-26.

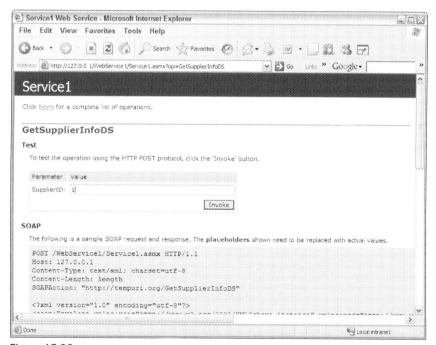

Figure 15-26

7. Click Invoke. The Web method is now executed, and the XML for the resulting data is displayed as shown in Figure 15-27.

Notice that the Web service returned not only the data, but also the schema for the data. This is what makes Web services so easy to use with InfoPath. Now you are ready to create other Web methods for various purposes.

For more information and practice with creating Web services for InfoPath check out the POWebService project, which is installed when you installed the Microsoft InfoPath 2003 SDK. This project displays more complicated methods for receiving and submitting data between InfoPath and Web services.

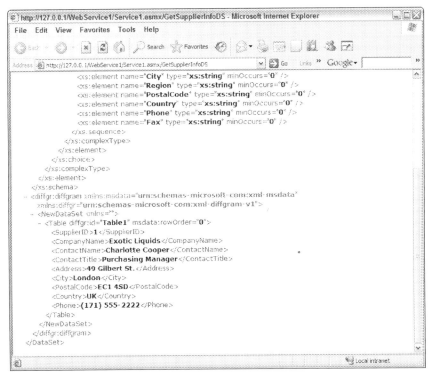

Figure 15-27

Summary

Web services enable developers to work with data from databases other than Access and SQL Server. They also make data that would be normally be off limits to outside systems available. Web services pass the data via XML to both Web- and desktop-based applications.

Visual Studio .NET can be used to create Web services, and it performs quite a bit of the work in creating the project. You can use the language of your choice, for example C# or Visual Basic .NET, with ASP.NET. In addition, .NET provides ADO.NET classes for manipulation of data within your Web services.

InfoPath interfaces with Web services the same as it would Access and SQL Server, using the Data Connection Wizard.

Exercises

1. What is the other name for Web services?

2. What does the acronymn SOAP stand for?

Implementing Security

Security is always the last thing developers seem to look at, when in fact security should be thought about even before the first InfoPath solution is designed. Developers often get excited about the possibilities of forms, or applications, and fail to pay attention to the integrity of the system as a whole.

While security is not as exciting as developing the actual form, it is more important than just about every aspect of the forms you create, because poor security could allow hackers to get into your system and network. In this chapter you will:

❑ See an overview of security and how it is handled in InfoPath.

❑ Create fully trusted forms automatically and using a special utility called RegForm.

❑ Learn how .NET defines security.

❑ Find out what digital signatures are and how to best use them in InfoPath forms.

What Does Security Mean?

As a developer, you may not have had to worry too much about security. This is especially true if you have been working just on applications that are used primarily on your machine or in your department in the office. If this is the case, then you may not have to read the rest of this chapter. However, if you are creating InfoPath forms and distributing those forms around your company, you need to have more information about what you have to do to secure those forms and what it takes to work with Windows and Internet security. There are four major pieces to developing a good secure application that define security itself. They are:

❑ **Authentication**: This is kind of like a secret handshake. The typical network handshake uses authentication such as the challenge response approach, where the challenge is sent by the server and the user's machine creates the response with no intervention from you. Custom-built security solutions challenge a person with the user credentials, and he/she has to log in.

❑ **Authorization**: A way of giving authenticated users no, partial, or full trust over the resource being requested. For example, on a network, certain people have certain permissions to change, edit, and delete files on shared areas; others have no authorization to do anything but read files.

❑ **Data Integrity**: This is very important in this day and age as hackers are finding more and more ways to break down the security barriers we strive to implement, which results in personal privacy being violated, monetary losses, and so on.

It is truly important that we set up secure barriers to protect the integrity of our data. This is very important especially with the invention of HIPAA, which is a government regulation on the handling of private information.

❑ **System Availability**: Will it be possible to log on to the server or to use the domain logon? These questions need to be considered up front. If you build the most secure InfoPath form in the world, but the network it is used on doesn't support security, you will have wasted your time.

InfoPath Security

InfoPath has its own built-in security model that is exposed to developers to allow them to start with some in-place baseline security and then customize it according to their needs. InfoPath's security model is different from most; it uses some settings from Internet Explorer as well as some of the .NET security model. InfoPath works closely with Internet Explorer's security model to closely guard your local resources against malicious attacks from hackers

InfoPath is a client-side application, meaning it runs on your local machine. Because of being a client-side application, it is not allowed to do certain things to your machine, for example, reformat your hard drive. It must obey all security laws that regulate your machine. This allows the user of the forms to feel assured that InfoPath or your custom-built form will not violate any security issues. Realize that InfoPath, as a data-driven type of application, provides additional levels of security to protect the data that is coming in and out of the custom-built InfoPath form.

The default behavior of InfoPath is to use Uniform Resource Locator (URL) based forms; the second behavior is to use Uniform Resource Names (URN) based forms. These types of forms may look, act, and feel the same, but there are some significant differences in the two models.

URL-based forms are the default form type used with InfoPath. These forms are created by publishing a form to a Web server, a Microsoft SharePoint site, or file share. They are called URL-based because typically a user will open these InfoPath forms by using a URL pointing to the location of the published form. URL-based forms are considered "sandboxed" forms. A *sandbox* is a location on your computer that is controlled highly by IE's security settings, in particular, the zones discussed in the next paragraph.

Internet Explorers security is based on the Zones theory. There are five zones in the IE model, with 1 being the most restrictive and 5 being the least: Restricted, Internet, Intranet, Trusted Sites, and the Local Machine zone. You can see the icons in Figure 16-1.

Figure 16-1

For example, if a Web page you visit has a script that tries to create an unsafe ActiveX control, it will cause an error on every zone except Local Machine and Trusted Sites, which will prompt you first.

Local Machine is not listed in the choices in Figure 16-1 because everything on your local machine is trusted.

Consider another example. Just as InfoPath forms can use scripts you create, other applications, such as those created in HTML, use script as well. If an application that uses script tries to call a resource on another domain, you will get the following Access Is Denied message: "This page is accessing information that is not under its control. This poses a security risk. Do you want to continue?" This dialog box will appear if you are in the Intranet Zone, but in the Local Computer or a Trusted Site zone your script will run just fine. Script in InfoPath's HTML task pane is subject to these rules as well.

Form-Based Security

As shown in Chapter 9, "Managing Views," you can run script in the HTML custom task pane of InfoPath. In Chapters 11, 12, and 13 you saw how to create scripts in InfoPath forms as custom business logic, for example, scripting the On Load event of the form or the On Click event of a control. Each property or method used from the InfoPath object model has its own security measures. These models are numbered 1 to 3:

❑ **Level 1**: Properties and methods can be called by anyone. These are methods that are considered safe no matter who or what calls them.

❑ **Level 2**: InfoPath forms can communicate with each other. For example, you can write the following and get access to another form running on the machine:

```
Application.XDocuments.Item(1)
```

Whether this works or not is based solely on where the .xsn file is located. Most of InfoPath's Object Model resides in this zone.

❑ **Level 3**: These calls are considered unsafe no matter who is calling them. The only way to call these methods is to use Full Trust on the form. This means that you must register the form or digitally sign the form. You also can use the regform.exe utility to register the form with full trust for you.

InfoPath's default security model restricts all access to local system resources and is not allowed to use components that are not built to be safe for scripting.

Form templates (*.xsn) files based on a URL are thrown into what is commonly known as a *sandbox*. As mentioned in the last section, the sandbox model means that the form is thrown into a local system cache that inherits its security from Internet Explorers security settings, as shown in the following Try It Out.

Try It Out   **Looking at IE's Security Settings**

1.   Open Internet Explorer.

2.   Select Tools ➪ Internet Options, and then select the Security tab. You will be presented with the dialog box for editing IE's Security levels.

Usually InfoPath forms run in the Local intranet zone of IE, using permissions that you set for that particular zone. You can see those permissions in Figure 16-2.

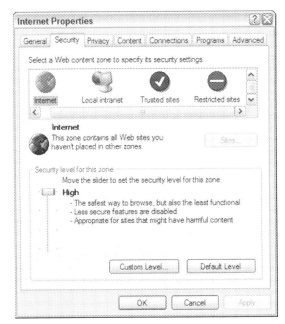

Figure 16-2

Remember that InfoPath security is based on the location of the .xsn form template, not the client location. You will need to keep that in mind as you are developing the InfoPath forms. This means that any local resources to which you allow permission on your machine will and can be accessed by InfoPath over the network from other machines. So, if you give access to a resource just as specific folders on your machine, other users will be able to access that folder on your machine. This is not good in most cases.

Fully Trusted Forms

It's possible to allow InfoPath forms to run in a fully trusted context. The InfoPath form needs to be installed locally and then given access to local system resources. Fully trusted forms have more privileges on a local machine than cached or sandboxed forms. Being trusted on your system allows the InfoPath to access:

❑ Objects external to the InfoPath form but on the same system

❑ Microsoft ActiveX controls that are marked safe for scripting

❑ Custom logic within the Component Object Model (COM) and additional object models

The higher the trust level the more resources the InfoPath form has access to. For this reason, the next Try It Out shows you how to create fully trusted form on your machine.

Try It Out   How to Create a Fully Trusted Form

The first step in creating a fully trusted form is to make sure the InfoPath IDE has an option checked.

1. Open InfoPath.

2. Go to Tools ⇨ Options. In this dialog box you will see a check box on the bottom of the dialog box.

3. Check Allow fully trusted form to be have access to files and settings on my computer, shown in Figure 16-3.

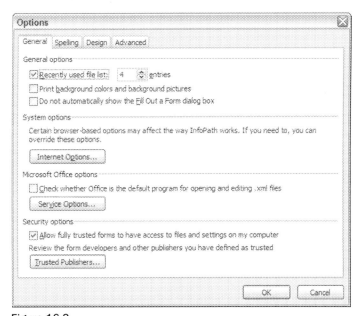

Figure 16-3

Once there you can also view all of your trusted publishers by clicking the Trusted Publishers button. This dialog box shows you what particular publishers you give full access to, as shown in Figure 16-4.

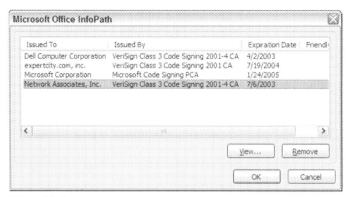

Figure 16-4

Using the SDK Regform Utility

Although you can manually create a fully trusted form, it is not good practice because there are too many little details that all need to be in place for it to work correctly. Microsoft realized quickly that this would be the case so they packaged a nice little utility for us called RegForm. This utility is included in the InfoPath 2003 Software Development Kit (SDK).

```
http://www.microsoft.com/downloads/details.aspx?FamilyId=351F0616-93AA-4FE8-9238-
D702F1BFBAB4&displaylang=en
```

Once you install the SDK, you can find the RegForm utility at `C:\Program Files\Microsoft Office 2003 Developer Resources\Microsoft Office InfoPath 2003 SDK\Tools`, wherever you installed the SDK.

`regform.exe` is a command-line tool that simplifies the creation of fully trusted forms by automatically:

❑ Making a backup copy of your form template

❑ Making the necessary changes to the .xsf file and XML template files to make them fully trusted

❑ Updating the version of the form template

❑ Repackaging the files into an .xsn file template

❑ Creating a custom installation program

Imagine what a pain this would be to have to do all of that yourself. The RegForm parameters are very straightforward, as shown in the help display of the tool:

Usage:

```
RegForm [/U urn] [/FT formtemplatename] [/C companyname]
        [/V [0-9999.0-9999.0-9999.0-9999]] [/T Yes|No] [/O outputfile]

        [/MSI] [/?|/h|/help] formtemplatefile
```

The following options can be seen in the command window by typing:

```
RegForm /?
```

Option	Description
/U	The URN to use for the form template. Must be in the form of "urn:<string>:<string>". If the URN is not specified, it is built using the specified form template and company name parameters. If the form template or company name parameters are not specified, a GUID value is used.
/FT	The form template name.
/C	The company name.
/V	The version number [0-9999.0-9999.0-9999.0-9999] of the form template. If the version number is not specified, the version number of the specified form template file is used. If no version number is present in the form template file, the default version number "1.0.0.1" is used.
/T	Specifies that the form template is fully trusted. This sets the requireFullTrust attribute in the form definition (.xsf) file to Yes. The default value is No.
/O	The path and name of the output installation file that is to be created. If the path and name are not specified, the name of the form template file is used.
/MSI	Specifies that the output installation file is a Microsoft System Installer (.msi) file. The default is a Microsoft JScript (.js) file.
/?|/h|/help	Displays information about using the RegForm tool.
formtemplatefile	The full path to the InfoPath form template to process.

Examples:

```
RegForm /U urn:MyForm:MyCompany /T Yes /MSI MyForm.xsn

RegForm /FT myForm /C myCompany /MSI myForm.xsn
```

Creating a fully trusted form this way is very simple:

```
Regform /U urn:FormName:CompanyName /T Yes C:\Directory\FormName.xsn
```

Using the tool this way, the /T indicates that the form should be fully trusted, and the last parameter is the path of the form to be converted to fully trusted. If you have Visual Studio .NET installed on the local machine, then you can also create an .MSI installation program using the /MSI switch:

```
Regform /U urn:FormName:CompanyName /T Yes /MSI  C:\Directory\FormName.xsn
```

This will place an `.msi` file in the forms directory containing the setup files needed, as well as create a Visual Studio solution file for you to modify. Using Visual Studio to create a custom installation program was discussed in the "Distributing InfoPath .NET applications" section of Chapter 13, "Working with .NET Managed Code."

To get some experience with the RegForm utility, work through the following Try It Out.

Try It Out   **Creating a Fully Trusted Form Using the RegForm Utility**

Start by creating a fully trusted form using an existing InfoPath template, and then save the form. For the purpose of these instructions, `Chapter 16.xsn` will be used.

1. Choose Start ➪ Run from the Windows Start menu.

2. Type in **CMD.EXE**, and click OK. The Command Window opens.

3. Navigate to the `regform.exe` folder using the CD command, as shown in Figure 16-4. For this example:

```
cd "C:\Program Files\Microsoft Office 2003 Developer Resources\Microsoft Office
InfoPath 2003 SDK\Tools"
```

4. Type **regform /U urn:Chapter16:Appsplus /T Yes "C:\Books\InfoPath\Samples\Chapter 16\Chapter 16.xsn"**. The command line will report back any errors that may arise from running the regform utility against the InfoPath template. If this is successful, you will see the text shown in Figure 16-5.

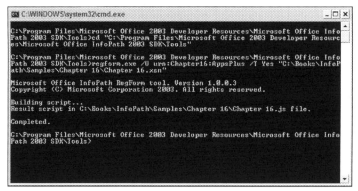

Figure 16-5

How It Works

The `Chapter 16.xsn` form is now fully trusted by InfoPath and Internet Explorer. This will also result in the RegForm utility creating a `Chapter 16.bak` file, and a `Chapter 16.js` file in the directory that the original template is located in, as shown in Figure 16-6.

Figure 16-6

The .bak file is a backup copy of the original template but without full trust, and the .js file is a script run on machines where the form will be installed. To have this be fully trusted on another person's machine, you must send the *.js file, and that person must run it by double-clicking it. This script sets the permissions on that person's machine. When the file is double-clicked, the user receives the dialog box shown in Figure 16-7.

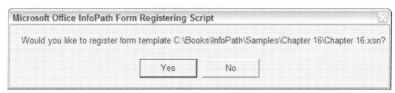

Figure 16-7

Creating an MSI to Automatically Set Up Full Trust

If you have Visual Studio .NET 2003 installed on your local system, you are allowed to specify the /MSI attribute when using the RegForm utility. This causes Visual Studio to create an MSI setup project, discussed in Chapter 13, based on your form template. This will result in creating a Windows installer package. The following Try It Out walks you through using the /MSI attribute.

Try It Out   Use the RegForm Utility to Create an MSI

Using the command window navigate to the regform.exe folder as in the last Try It Out:

1. Type regform /U urn:Chapter16:Appsplus /T Yes **/MSI** "C:\Books\InfoPath\
    Samples\Chapter 16\Chapter 16.xsn". The RegForm utility will then complete as before,
    and you will receive the completion messages.

2. Navigate to the form templates directory. You will now see an additional file with the extension
    of .msi.

Distributing the .msi file to clients will allow them to set up the InfoPath form on another machine and create the fully trusted form for you.

One of the exciting parts about using the /MSI switch is that in your users' temporary directory under the RegForm directory you will find a Visual Studio setup solution ready for you to open up in Visual

Studio and modify as you wish. This allows for more control over the setup process on the users' local machines.

Navigating to your user `temp` *directory can sometimes be difficult as it is hidden away for obvious reasons. The best way to figure out how to get to your user's* `temp` *directory is to open up the command line and type* `cd %temp%`.

This will navigate to the directory where the `temp RegForm` directory lives. Usually it is `C:\Document and settings\user\Local Settings\RegForm`. You are encouraged to navigate to that directory and discover what and why files are placed in that location.

This solution can be modified as you wish then recompiled to create your custom `.msi` file for distributing your fully trusted form.

Defining Security with the .NET Framework

The .NET Framework has several procedures and namespaces to help you build secure applications. The term *managed applications* is used to refer to applications written to run within the common language runtime (CLR), the engine used to process and run all .NET assemblies. Assemblies are the core of all .NET Framework applications, be they a Web application or a Windows-based application. An assembly is actually a collection of types and resources that are compiled and built to work together to form a complete application. Assemblies provide the CLR with the information needed during the runtime of your application.

Defining Assemblies

Defining .NET assemblies is basically just coding. When you create types, enums, properties, and so on, you are defining the .NET assembly. A .NET assembly can be a single code class or can be spread out over multiple code classes and then compiled into a new language called Microsoft Intermediate Language (MSIL). The CLR uses this as its base for figuring handle versioning, deployment, reuse, security, and scoping.

The advantage of using MSIL is that when an assembly is loaded the MSIL is interpreted and run by the CLR for the platform on which it is residing. The advantage of this is that CLR can handle file validation, code verification, integrity checking, and code security.

Assemblies in Web Services

A Web service is basically an assembly with an `.asmx` file (ASP.NET Web page) that is loaded into an IIS instance. When you call a Web service, you're basically asking the ASP.NET runtime to grab the assembly and process the instructions there using the CLR. A Web service file, an `.asmx`, contains a directive that tells the CLR where the Web service can be found. This directive is used by ASP.NET to bind the Web service to the `.dll` that contains the actual code to be run. Think of using a pointer; you call the `.asmx` file (the Web service), which tells your application to use a particular `.dll` (library file) and where to find it.

Creating Web services and how to use them with InfoPath is discussed in Chapter 15, "Creating and Working with Web Services."

User versus Code Security

The .NET Framework holds two types of security models. The first is Code Access Security (CAS), which is used to figure out if the code has the right permissions and to verify the origin of the assembly. The second is a group of role-based permissions. This model is based on having users make a request, and then figuring out if they have the right permissions to access the requested assembly or resources.

Code-Based Security

Coding your security levels is a very common practice. This allows the developer to grant access to certain resources without having to worry about what machine the assembly is running on. CAS isn't concerned with the user because the code has sent the request and has passed the correct credentials.

Role-Based Security

Role-based security is exactly what the name implies. You define particular groups, each of which has its own security policies; your application is then coded to join one of those groups. For example, when you use Windows authentication in your application, the CLR pushes security onto Active Directory or even SQL Server to handle. There are three types of Authentication objects available for your use:

❑ **Windows**: Windows authentication verifies credentials using the Security Accounts Manager (SAM) or Active Directory. Windows or Domain groups are used for these types of roles.

❑ **Forms**: Forms authentication requires you to add code to verify credentials and retrieve the role from some sort of security store, usually held in a database table.

❑ **Passport**: Passport authentication relies on the Microsoft Passport SDK to authenticate the user against the .NET passport role, equivalent to MSN/Windows Messenger.

System.Security Namespace

The System.Security namespace is the base assembly that handles all security for the CLR. One thing to remember is that the CLR enforces security on the location where the code is run from rather than on the location where the user logged in. There are many classes that can be used in the System.Security namespace. You can see the classes that apply to InfoPath in the following table:

Class	Description
AllowPartiallyTrusted CallersAttribute	Allows signed assemblies to be called by InfoPath.
CodeAccessPermission	Base class for all access permissions.
NamedPermissionSet	Defines permissions with name and description attributes.
PermissionSet	Collection of different types of permissions.
SecurityManager	Main class for security interaction between InfoPath and CLR.
VerificationException	The exception raised if anything goes wrong.

You can implement the following interfaces in your classes created with Visual Studio to use in your custom security model for InfoPath.

Interfaces	Interface Description
IEvidenceFactory	Gets an object's Evidence (property value).
IPermission	Defines methods implemented by permission types; can be inherited for utilizing methods and properties of a permission object.

Digital Signatures

You have probably seen digital signature dialog boxes in the various Microsoft Office applications, as well as other applications you have created.

Digital signatures enable developers to create a public/private key pair set to use for authentication purposes. This is much like a driver's license: You show it to the police officer when you are pulled over, he goes to his car and runs it, and the computer tells him that yes you are in fact so and so and that your record is clear. In the same way, a digital signature is a way for software to verify the identity of the creator or publisher of the form, application, and so on.

Using Digital Signatures with InfoPath

InfoPath enables you to sign your forms with a digital signature to assure others that the form did in fact did come from you or your company.

Try It Out   Creating a Test Digital for Testing

To create a test signature used on the local machine, you must follow a few simple steps.

1. Download and install the Authenticode for Internet Explorer from:

    http://www.microsoft.com/downloads/details.aspx?FamilyID=2B742795-D0F0-4A66-B27F-22A95FCD3425&displaylang=en

2. Open up the command-line utility and navigate to the C:\inetsdk\bin directory, or wherever the makecert.exe utility is located.

3. Type in the following to create your certificate; take note that you can replace the string "CN:TestCertificate" with "CN:" and whatever name you want to use for the signiture, that would have more meaning for you, and not imply that it was a test certificate.

    ```
    makecert -n "CN:TestCertificate" -cy end -a sha1 -sky Signature -m 1 -iv
    certRoot.pvk -ic certRoot.cer -ss MY
    ```

    This will add the TestCertificate into the users Personal store.

Now the new digital signature can be used to sign forms. You get a chance to use it in the following Try It Out.

Try It Out   Sign the Form with the Digital Signature

Using the form `Chapter 16.xsn` in Design view:

1. Select from the Tools ⇨ Digital Signatures. You will be prompted with the dialog box in Figure 16-8. This dialog box will enable you to view and Add/Remove Digital Signatures from your form.

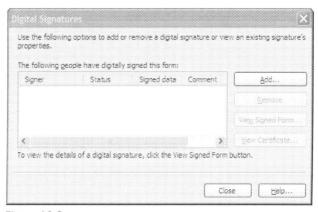

Figure 16-8

2. Click the Add... button. The Digital Signature Wizard appears and walks you through some simple steps in getting your form signed. You can see this page in Figure 16-9.

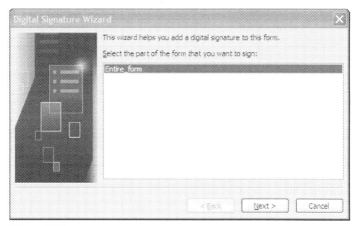

Figure 16-9

3. Click Next. On this page, you will see the Test Certificate created in the previous Try It Out, as displayed in Figure 16-10.

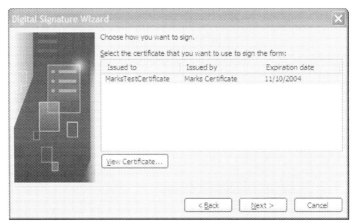

Figure 16-10

4. Click the Next button, choosing the test certificate. The next page of the Digital Signature Wizard is shown in Figure 16-11 and lets you specify some comments and summarize the digital signature.

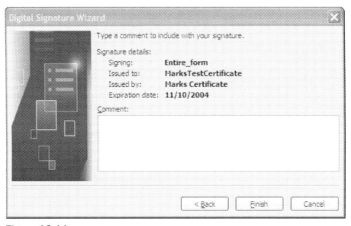

Figure 16-11

5. Click Finish. The last page of the Digital Signature Wizard prompts you to review and verify all your information as well as the information regarding your digital signature, as shown in Figure 16-12.

6. Check the box labeled I have verified this content before signing.

7. Click the Sign button.

You have now digitally signed your InfoPath form, and it is ready to be used.

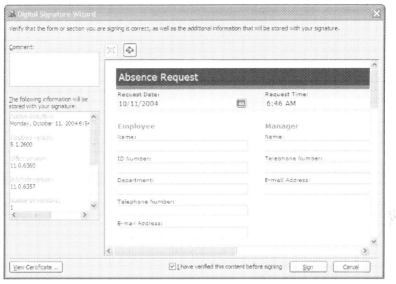

Figure 16-12

Summary

Now you know more than you ever wanted to know about security in Windows, .NET, and InfoPath. Depending on how you are going to be using your InfoPath forms, you will need to have an understanding of the different options available in the area of security.

While you can add security to your forms in a number of different ways, you will have to set up security to match the location where your forms are going to be deployed. This chapter showed you how to set up your forms, including how to use of digital signatures.

Exercises

1. Name the four major pieces in developing a good secure application that define security itself.

2. What is a sandbox in regard to security?

3. What are the two ways to create a fully trusted InfoPath form?

4. Name the two types of security models in .NET Framework.

Working with InfoPath and Windows SharePoint Services

One of the major features of InfoPath is that it is a collaborative product, dealing with data from various sources including databases, XML, and Web services. You have seen how to use this feature throughout the book. Now get ready for another major collaborative feature of InfoPath: The ability to take advantage of integrating your InfoPath form with Microsoft's collaborative technology called Windows SharePoint Services.

Windows SharePoint Services enable companies to create collaborative Web sites that can be used for a number of different purposes that will be covered in this chapter. In this chapter you will:

❑   See what Windows SharePoint Services are all about.

❑   Take a look at a SharePoint Web site.

❑   Learn about creating your own SharePoint Web site.

❑   Look at ways to use InfoPath and SharePoint.

❑   Publish an InfoPath form to a SharePoint site.

❑   Fill in an InfoPath form based on a SharePoint site.

❑   Add a SharePoint Web component to your InfoPath document library.

To perform the tasks in this chapter, you have to have access to Windows SharePoint Services, which instalsl on Windows Server 2003. If you have a Windows 2003 Server you can use, then download Windows SharePoint Services from the following link: www.microsoft.com/ windowsserver2003/techinfo/sharepoint/wss.mspx.

What Are Windows SharePoint Services?

Quickly becoming a popular solution for creating collaborative Web sites, Windows SharePoint Services (WSS) enable companies to generate such sites rapidly and with a great deal of customization. At last count, Microsoft itself had over 80,000 internal SharePoint sites used by various product teams. This is a great example of what is referred to as "eating your own dog food."

A collaborative Web site is a site that enables groups of people such as teams or departments in a company to collaborate among themselves in a number of different ways. SharePoint facilitates this by providing templates for various features that are necessary for collaboration.

Windows SharePoint Services Site Features

With WSS sites you can:

❏   Store working documents in centralized locations called document libraries, including using various Office solutions.

❏   Assign various users different roles, from a casual browser to an advanced author or administrator.

❏   Create and maintain various lists including but not limited to contacts, announcements, pictures, tasks, and meetings.

❏   Make discussion areas that can include general discussions, notifications, and surveys.

❏   Use Search capabilities within the site, subsites, and documents within the site.

❏   Use a programmable object model to create your own custom solutions.

WSS is very scalable, whether you are creating a site for a single group or multiple sites combined using a SharePoint portal. The sites also are highly modifiable using ASP.NET and Web parts, discussed in the section titled "Customizing the Windows Services SharePoint Services Team Site"

The Difference between Windows SharePoint Services and SharePoint Portal Services

A question that people frequently ask when learning about SharePoint is what is the difference between Windows SharePoint Services (WSS) and SharePoint Portal Services (SPS)? Both are key components of Microsoft's SharePoint products and technologies.

Windows SharePoint Services are used to create collaborative Web sites that let teams, site managers, and users work together on Office documents, as well as use the other features mentioned in the last section. Windows SharePoint Services are downloadable for Windows Server 2003, and can be used either on an intranet or the Internet.

SharePoint Portal Services are a portal product that allows companies to create more than one SharePoint site and then link them together. SharePoint Portal Services are a separate product that can be purchased. It provides an environment for managing multiple SharePoint sites and creating applications.

Touring a SharePoint Site

You can see an example of a default WSS site in Figure 17-1.

The WSS site can be broken down into four or five main areas, some of which are repeated in various areas of the site. An example of this is using task lists in subsites you create.

Default Lists of the Site

A good portion of WSS sites is handled as lists. These are not the lists of old that had a few columns going across the page. While they display data in a list type format, they can be made up of various types of controls, including drop-downs lists and hyperlinks. When you click a list item, you are generally brought to a view of the specific item, with a menu displayed to let you edit the item, and perform other tasks.

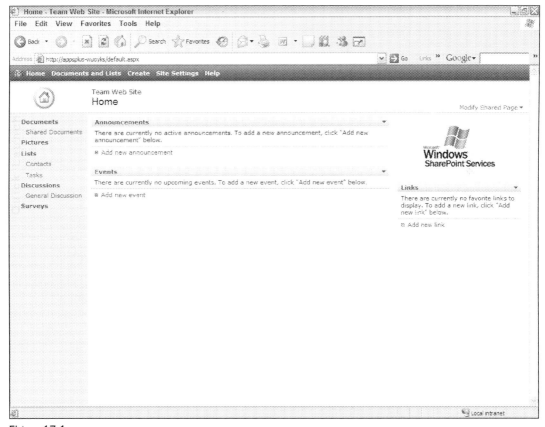

Figure 17-1

The default lists in SharePoint include:

❑ **Announcements**: Can be set up to alert you to various changes and can be set to expire. Alerts can be in the form of e-mail and can be set up as a one-time alert, or as daily or weekly updates. An example of an announcement being edited is shown in Figure 17-2.

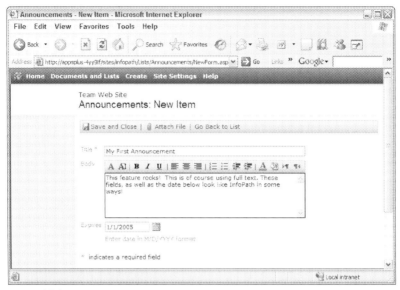

Figure 17-2

Once added, the announcements are displayed on the home page by default until the date specified passes. You can see the announcement added in Figure 17-3.

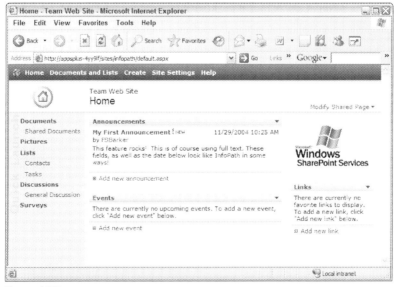

Figure 17-3

You need to specify which sections are displayed on the home page. Sections are actually Web parts. Each of the lists discussed here are Web parts that are provided by WSS. Modifying the home page for the site is discussed in the section titled "Customizing the Windows SharePoint Services Team Site," found later in the chapter.

❏ **Contacts:** Much as with the Outlook contacts, various data can be stored for contacts for a team or project such as Name, E-Mail, Phone, and the like. Information can be exported, imported, and linked to from Outlook. These options can be seen in Figure 17-4.

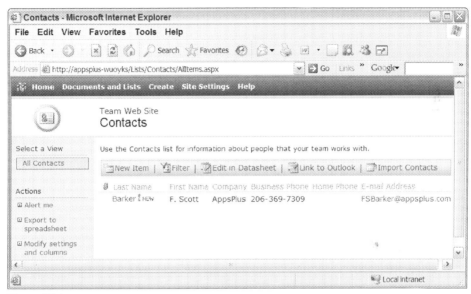

Figure 17-4

❏ **Events**: There are quite a few areas to work with under an event. Besides listing and editing the various properties of the event itself, including; title, beginning and ending date/times, location, and reoccurrences, you can create a workspace that is actually a subsite under the main team site.

The workspace site has its own lists, consisting of Objectives, Attendees, and Agendas. You also can modify the workspace, just as you can on the main site, including the theme. This gives you the ability to allow your workspaces to have their own "feel." So, for example, if you were planning a party, you could have a party theme for the workspace.

❏ **Links**: Links let you add hyperlinks to various other Web sites you want to have linked to your site. Links are displayed on your main home page, but like the rest of the lists (which are in essence Web parts), they can be added to different areas of your WSS site. As with other lists they can be exported to other applications.

❏ **Tasks**: You can assign tasks to be performed and track the current status, the percentage of the task that has been completed, and whether or not to include attachments. Alerts can be set up to let you know when the status of your tasks changes. In the list view of tasks you can view for all tasks, only your tasks, tasks due today, tasks that are active, and tasks by assignment.

Although the other areas are displayed in list format at times, they contain more information than that listed in these sections.

Try It Out   Touring the Different Areas

Once your IT administrator has downloaded and installed Windows SharePoint Services or SharePoint Portal Services, it's time to create the default Web site:

1.   Click the Announcements link. The announcements list is displayed, with only the getting started announcement shown, as illustrated in Figure 17-5.

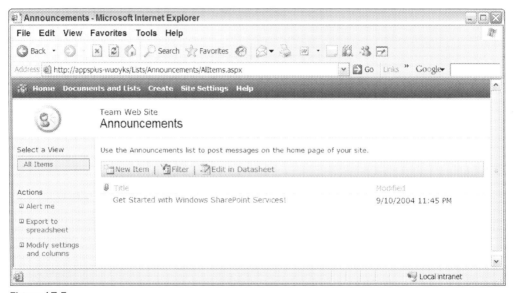

Figure 17-5

2.   Click the New Item link. A blank announcement is displayed.

3.   Fill in the Title, Body, and Expiration date, and then click Save and Close.

4.   Click the Home link, and see your new announcement listed on the home page of the site.

You can go directly to adding a new announcement by clicking Add new announcement from the home page in the Announcements section on the home page.

Other Major Areas

There are a number of other major areas created by default that don't fall into the lists category. They are:

❑   **Document Libraries**: Various shared documents, stored in document libraries. Documents can be anything including Excel spreadsheet, Word documents, XML documents, and .zip files.

❑ **Picture Libraries**: Let you upload and maintain libraries of pictures. Features include tracking the history (copies) of pictures you edit and save in the library; displaying thumbnails, slide shows, and previews; and viewing pictures in Explorer View.

❑ **Discussion Areas**: As with newsgroups, you can set up discussion areas, specifying whether or not you want approval for items listed. Discussions can be viewed either as threads or flat.

❑ **Document Workspaces, Meeting Workspaces, and Sites**: Enable you to create sites under your main site. When you create one of these sites, you specify the title for the site and the location under the main site. You are also given the opportunity to specify one of the many templates to use to create the site.

❑ **Surveys**: You can set up surveys that let you see how users feel about various issues. Surveys can be made up of different types of controls for receiving answers, including drop-downs lists, multiple choice option buttons, check boxes, text boxes, and others.

These are the major areas and lists you can set up and use in your WSS site. If you were to create a Web site that included all these features yourself, it would take quite a bit of work and programming. SharePoint makes creating these sites easy. Before jumping into the integration with InfoPath, take a look at what it takes to customize the WSS site beyond specifying which lists you want to include.

Customizing the Windows SharePoint Services Team Site

Companies can create their own custom site that reflects their business, group, or team's mission just by modifying some properties and adding lists and areas.

As mentioned, with no programming at all you can customize the site to display the features that you need pretty quickly. You have seen all the available areas that you can add to existing lists and areas on the site. You also can customize security, add additional Web parts, and apply themes. To change a site, you have to have administrative privileges and click the link labeled Site Settings. You then see the page displayed in Figure 17-6.

You can see the choices you have on the page displayed in Figure 17-6. Also included on this page, and shown at the bottom of the figure, is Manage My Information. This feature enables you to track various types of user information, including your contact information for the site.

If you click the Go to Site Administration option under Administration, you get a fairly extensive list of options for managing the security of your site.

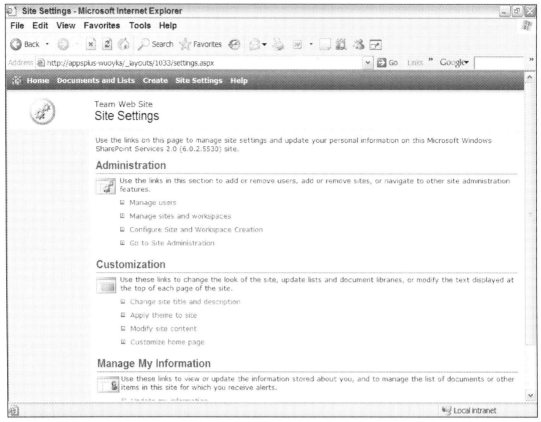

Figure 17-6

Try It Out   Applying a Theme to the Site

Using the default WWS site created by your administrator:

1. Click the Site Settings link.

2. Click Apply theme to site, under the Customization category.

3. Pick the Sky view, as shown in Figure 17-7.

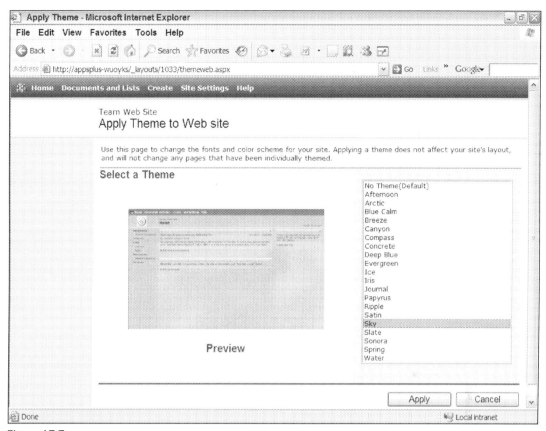

Figure 17-7

Adding Existing Web Parts to Your Site

One of the huge benefits of using WSS to create your site is the use of Web parts. Web parts let you add functionality to your site that would normally take hours to build yourself. If you just need to add a Web part from existing Web parts, you can do so by choosing Site Settings on the WSS site home page.

Choose Customize home page, from the Customization category. The home page will open in a design type mode, and the Web part task bar will open, as shown in Figure 17-8.

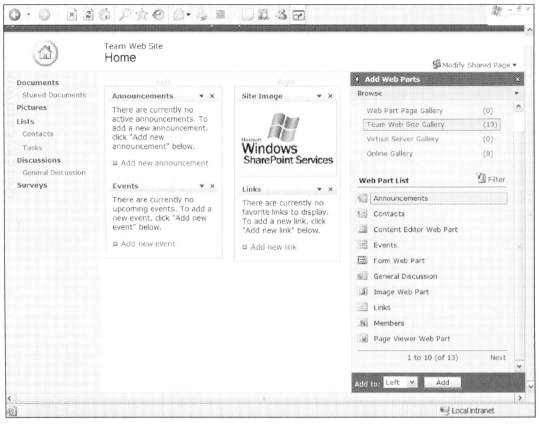

Figure 17-8

As you can see, there are a number of Web part libraries you can choose from. You can even get Web parts from third parties. When you know the Web part you are interested in, you can drag and drop it onto your page.

Creating Your Own Web Parts

However, if you want to create your own Web Parts, or highly modify WWS sites, you will want to learn ASP.NET and use the Software Developer Kit (SDK), which is available for download at http://www.microsoft.com/downloads/details.aspx?FamilyId=AA3E7FE5-DAEE-4D10-980F-789B827 967B0&displaylang=en. To use the SDK, you need to be familiar with .NET, Web services, and ASP.NET. But once you learn them, you have a whole new world of possibilities.

Using InfoPath and SharePoint

By using InfoPath with SharePoint, you can add a great deal of versatility and functionality to your InfoPath forms. You can do a number of tasks such as:

❑ Publish an InfoPath form onto the site for people to fill out with data stored in each table using XML, and publish some of the fields in a list.

❑ Sort the list based on values promoted from the InfoPath form.

❑ Add a Web part to display a graph for each of the values.

You see how to perform these tasks in the following section.

One thing to remember when using an InfoPath form with SharePoint is that if you are using a database for the data source of the InfoPath form, then the user's machine and SharePoint site have to have access to it. For this reason, it is best to use a Web service or simply store the data in XML format when using InfoPath forms with SharePoint.

Publishing an InfoPath Form on a SharePoint Site

You can use any InfoPath form you create on a WSS site, with the data connected, just as you would on your desktop. One of the convenient features of SharePoint is that even if you have your data in separate XML files behind your InfoPath forms, you are able to promote fields to the SharePoint site list, and both sort and query on those fields. The way to put the form up on a WSS site is to publish the form on the site, in a document library. InfoPath creates a new library if you tell it to.

To publish an InfoPath form on a SharePoint site, you need to provide the Publishing Wizard with the HTTP address of the site where you want to publish the form. The Publishing Wizard also provides a means to promote some of the fields into the list and notifies other users about the form being posted.

Try It Out   Publish a Sales Report to a SharePoint Site

To get started, you require a form that you have already created. In this case, one of the sample forms called Sales Report.

1. Open InfoPath, and then click Sample Forms under the Forms Categories.

2. Highlight the Sales Report InfoPath form. The dialog box is shown in Figure 17-9.

3. Click Design this Form. The InfoPath form opens in design view.

4. Choose File ➪ Publish.... The first page of the Publishing Wizard is displayed, as shown in Figure 17-10.

5. Click Next to move to the next page of the Publishing Wizard. This page asks where you would like to publish the form: a Shared folder, SharePoint site, or Web Server.

6. Select the second choice: To a SharePoint form library. The dialog box then looks as it does in Figure 17-11.

Figure 17-9

Figure 17-10

7. Click Next to move to the next page of the Publishing Wizard. The next page asks where on the SharePoint site you would like to publish the form: by creating a new form library or by modifying an existing library. You can see the page in Figure 17-12.

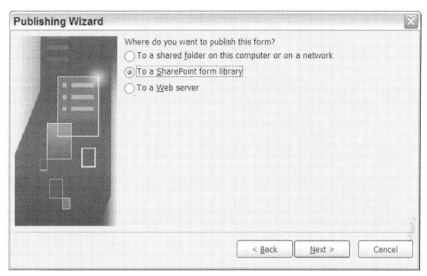

Figure 17-11

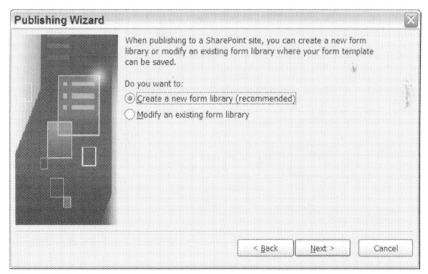

Figure 17-12

8. Click Next to move to the next page of the Publishing Wizard. You are then asked to supply the address of the Web site where you want to publish the form.

9. Type in the address of the Web site. You can see the address used by the author display in Figure 17-13.

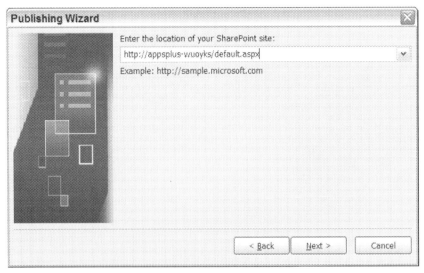

Figure 17-13

10. Choose to Create a new form library, and then click Next. You are then asked to enter the name and description for the new form library.

11. Enter the name and description for the new library You can see an example in Figure 17-14.

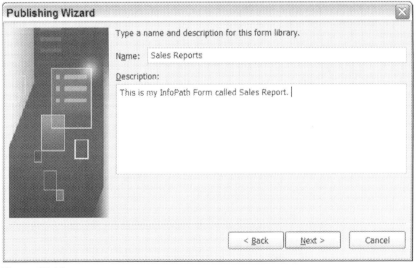

Figure 17-14

12. Click Next. The next page lets you specify the fields you want to promote to the SharePoint site.

13. Choose the field you want to be displayed in the list on the site. You can select multiple fields by holding the Ctrl key and selecting the fields. You also can add additional fields from the data source of the form by clicking the Add button. The form is displayed in Figure 17-15.

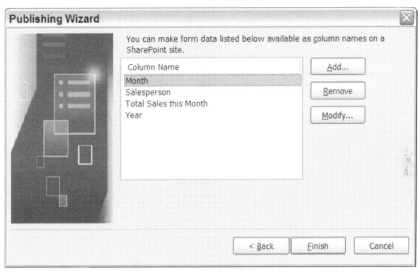

Figure 17-15

14. Click Finish. The wizard adds the form to the list on the site. You are shown the summary page, which asks if you want to notify other users about the new form being added to the site, as shown in Figure 17-16.

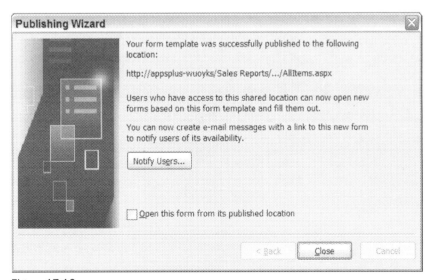

Figure 17-16

15. Click Close.

The new document library has been created and the form uploaded up to the SharePoint site. Remember that although you upload the InfoPath form up onto the site, users will have to have a copy of Microsoft InfoPath on their local machines.

Filling Out InfoPath Forms on the SharePoint Site

Now that you have added the InfoPath form to the SharePoint site, it is time to see how to fill out the form and see the results in the form library list. To accomplish this, return to the SharePoint site and look up the new document library. Once in the library you can view the form's data in list view as well as sort and filter the data.

To look at the data, however, you need to fill out some forms so that the data exists. That is the purpose of this next Try It Out.

Try It Out   **Working with the Form Library**

Using the Windows SharePoint Service site specified throughout this chapter:

1. Click the Documents link, located on the left side of the home page. You see the Sales Reports listed as a new document library, as shown in Figure 17-17.

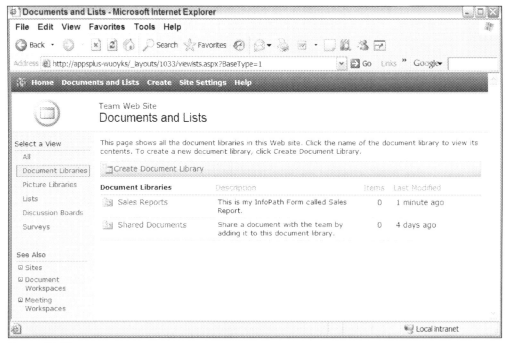

Figure 17-17

2. Click the link Sales Reports. You then see the empty document library with the columns you specified in the previous Try It Out.

3. Click the link Fill Out This Form in the Sales Report document library. InfoPath then opens on the local machine with the form opened for filling.

4. Fill out the form.

5. Choose File ⇨ Save. The Save As dialog box opens with the Sales Report document library displayed, as shown in Figure 17-18.

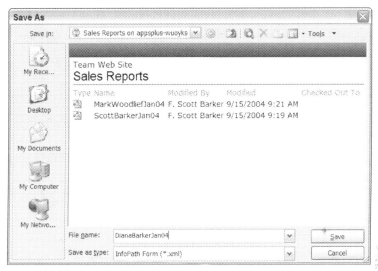

Figure 17-18

6. Type in a meaningful name for the file, because this will be displayed in the library. Figure 17-18 displays this dialog box with a couple of forms already filled out.

7. Click Save. The form is then saved on the WSS site and displayed immediately in the document library list, as shown in Figure 17-19.

The columns displayed in Figure 17-19 have been modified to fit on the screen. You can modify the fields by clicking on Modify Settings and Columns.

You can change the list order in the document library by clicking on the column headings. You can also set filters by clicking on the Filter button, displayed in the toolbar over the list.

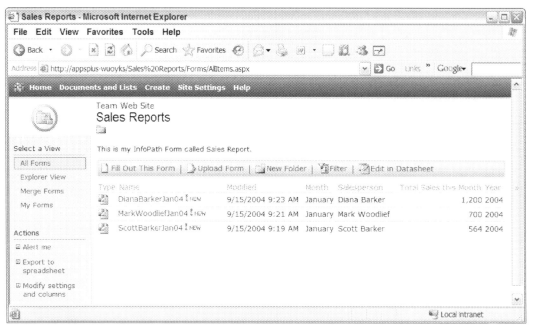

Figure 17-19

Summary

SharePoint products and technologies give companies powerful collaboration tools. Windows SharePoint Services enables users, managers, and administrators to create collaborative Web sites that are perfect for team, department, and company use. SharePoint Portal Services enable multiple WSS sites to be linked with each other and other technologies.

In this chapter, you were given a tour of the SharePoint team site and shown the most common features used on the sites. You were also shown how to modify the site to customize it for your own purposes.

Working with InfoPath forms on SharePoint is extremely powerful and easy. With little or no programming, you can load forms up on a WSS site using the Publishing Wizard included in InfoPath. You can expand the power of both SharePoint and InfoPath by using InfoPath with SharePoint and Web Parts.

Exercises

1.   What operating system is required for installing Windows SharePoint Services?

2.   How do you get Windows SharePoint Services?

3.   What is the term for specifying fields from your InfoPath form to display on the WSS site?

Manufacturing Plant Case Study

All of the earlier chapters in this book have tried to prepare you for completing an InfoPath solution. This chapter ties together many of the lessons and techniques learned, for the purpose of constructing an InfoPath solution that allows maintenance crews to check and report the status of the boiler system associated with a particular building. However, many of the topics in this chapter require an understanding of previously covered concepts, while several will reference code written previously. This chapter also requires some general understanding of data store concepts including Microsoft Access and XML Web Services to deliver the data.

There are many reasons for creating an InfoPath solution for this project, including:

❑ Combining data from multiple boilers into a common data store.

❑ Better analyzing boilers historical data.

❑ Posting results of the boiler system to a Sharepoint portal from better analyzing by staff that does not have InfoPath installed on their computer.

❑ Allowing building maintenance crews to use a tablet PC and InfoPath for more efficient data gathering.

For the purposes of this case study, an Access database will be created using Microsoft Access. This database will be the data store and will be accessed by an XML Web service that that has been created with Microsoft Visual Studio .NET 2003, and the .NET Framework 1.1.

The InfoPath Document

Some of the design of the InfoPath document that is used to collect the data will be described. You can see the final form displayed in Figure 18-1.

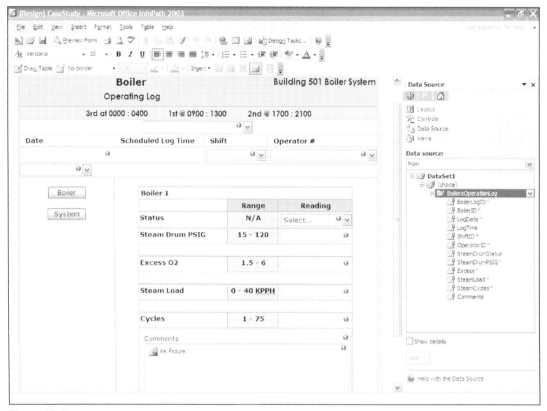

Figure 18-1

When describing the form, you can start by defining the data schema being used. After creating the schema in the InfoPath form to get started, the tables are created in Access with the same fields to hold the data.

Laying out the form in InfoPath is fairly straightforward, using the techniques learned in early chapters to place all of the controls on the form necessary for an inspector to input data.

Creating the Database

When you start to create any database, you need to move the physical world tasks and items, in this case the boiler information, over into the electronic world of the database. To be a good backend or data store, the database, must fulfill several business requirements, in this case to answer the following questions:

1. What boilers are out of the predefined specs?

2. Which boilers are falling out of spec over and over again?

3. How often is the boiler falling out of spec?

4. Which operators are finding the most boilers out of spec?

5. How is the boiler system behaving as a whole?

6. How long is it taking the operators to complete the boiler inspections?

7. Can the InfoPath form expedite data collection?

To answer these questions, a database was created to maintain boiler information. To work with the data in the tables, a plan was created that includes these major tasks:

❏ Designing the Database using Microsoft Access to support the InfoPath frontend

❏ Designing the XML Web service to deliver the data to the clients

❏ Designing the InfoPath document to display or collect data from the Web service

These tasks can be accomplished using a wide array of technologies. For this case study, Access was chosen as the data store for the simple ease of use, without incurring the cost overhead of SQL Server.

> *The preceding bullet points directly reflect how the solution is broken up into three different logical steps in order to create the best overall solution utilizing the best patterns and practices.*

You may find that creating the database first is not where you wanted to jump in. Rest assured that if you start creating an InfoPath form without finely detailed planning, which includes the database, you will run into many problems and your solution will take twice as long to create.

InfoPath was designed to query and populate an existing data store. Unlike working directly in Access, the best practice is to create the complete database first then work on the client side of the application. This will make the InfoPath part of the solution very easy and less time-consuming to create.

The BoilerSystem Data Model

Database modeling and architecture are definitely out of the scope of this book, and there are many books already published covering these two areas extensively.

To keep this case study fairly straightforward, the typical one-to-many type of relationships in the database that will support most real-life situations will be used. If you are interested in more advanced database architecture subjects visit www.wrox.com, and you will see many books on Microsoft Access and/or SQL Server 2000. Following are the tables and fields outlining the BoilerSystem database:

BoilersOperatingLog table

The first table created is the table to hold the actual boiler inspection data. During initial analysis and gathering of the business requirements the BoilerOperatingLog table was found to need 12 Fields. The fields are:

Field Name	Description
BoilerLogID	Autonumber field that will uniquely identify each boiler log record.
BoilerID	Look up field to the Boiler table.
LogDate	Date the inspection took place.
LogTime	Dollar time the log was submitted.
ShiftID	Number of items included in the order.
OperatorID	Lookup field to the Operator table.
SteamDrumStatus	Status of the boilers steam drum.
SteamDrumPSIG	Status of the steam drum PSIG.
Excess	Field to hold the excess PSIG data.
SteamLoad	Steam load of this particular boiler.
SteamCycles	Steam cycle data goes here.
Comments	Any comments the operator may want to make on this inspection are stored here.

SystemLog Table

The SystemLog table will hold the data that is particular to the boiler system as a whole. This will store important information concerning the building and the overall health of the system.

The fields are:

Field	Description
SystemLogID	AutoNumber field that will uniquely identify each system log record.
SteamHeaderPSIG	Steam header PSIG.
SteamFeedWaterHeaderPSIG	Steam water PSIG.
DearatorPSIG	Dearator PSIG.
DearatorTemp	Dearator temperature.
FMACOutsideAirTemp	FMAC outside air temperature.
BlowDownOnlineBoilersLWCO	Status of the boilers steam drum.
ShiftID	Field to hold the excess PSIG data.
LogTime	Steam load of this particular boiler.
OperatorID	Steam cycle data goes here.
Comments	Any comments the operator may want to make on the system inspection are stored here.

Lookup Tables

The following tables are considered lookup tables, they hold static data that doesn't really change that often and are there mostly to provide information to fill in combo boxes or to *look up* data in.

Boilers

This table will hold the individual boiler information. The fields are:

Field	Description
BoilerID	AutoNumber field that uniquely identies each boiler.
BoilerNumber	Boiler number.
BoilerDescription	Description of the boiler.

Shifts

This table will hold the individual boiler information. The fields are:

Fields	Description
ShiftID	AutoNumber field that will uniquely identify each shift.
ShiftName	Shifts name, used for display purposes.
TimeStart	Time the shift starts.
TimeEnd	Time the shift ends.

Operators

This table will hold the individual boiler information. The fields are:

Field	Description
OperatorID	AutoNumber field that will uniquely identify each operator.
OperatorName	Boiler number.
OperatorNumber	Description of the boiler.

The BoilerSystem Relationship Model

When working with more than one table in a database, it is usually more efficient to create one-to-many relationships between the tables. This allows for a more normalized database structure and allows to greater flexibility when creating the Web service and client-side application. Figure 18-2 shows the design of the database with the relationships illustrated:

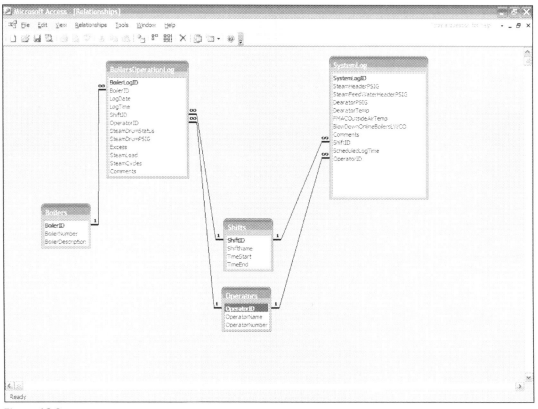

Figure 18-2

Looking at the Boiler Web Service

The Boiler Web service is responsible for handling all transactions between the Access database and the client application, in this case InfoPath. It was created using the XML Web services along with Visual Studio .NET 2003 and C#, as outlined in Chapter 15, "Creating and Working with Web Services."

❑   Start by creating a new C# ASP.NET Web service using Visual Studio

❑   Name the new Web service BoilerWebService

❑   Change the name of `Service1.asmx`, to `DataService.asmx` (make sure you open the `.cs` file and change the name of the class to `DataService` as well, shown here in Figure 18-3

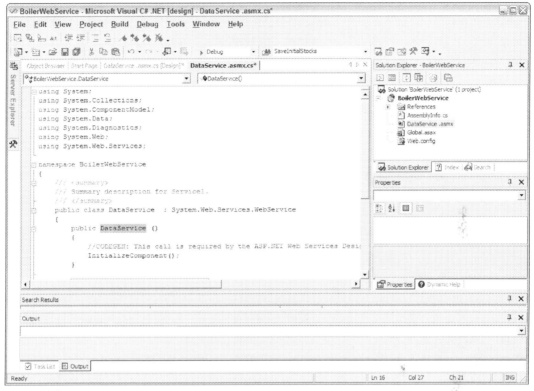

Figure 18-3

Creating the Data Adapters

The ADO.NET OleDbDataAdapters, OleDbDataConnection, and datasets of the System.Data namespace of the .NET Framework were used to create the middle tier of the solution. These components handle all of the interaction between InfoPath and the Access database created for the solution.

OleDbDataAdapters have been created to query the database for specified information. Three were created to handle the lookup tables we have created in the database: daBoilers, daShifts, and daOperators. Two other data adapters were created for daBoilerLog and daSystemLog. You can see all the data adapters in Figure 18-4, along with a oleDbConnection that was created.

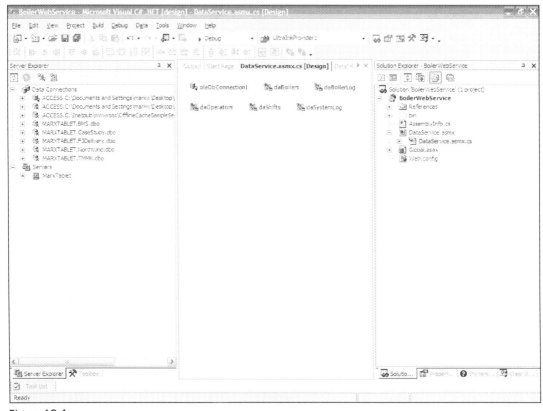

Figure 18-4

Creating the Datasets

The next task was to create the datasets that hold the data for the client application. This was started by creating the dataset that holds the lookup tables. This is a fairly straightforward design-time task and a good place to start with datasets. Using the Generate dataset from the main Visual Studio tool menu, the dataset was created as shown in Figure 18-5.

This dataset was named dsLookups with only the Boilers, Operators, and Shifts tables are added. A repository for the three data adapters that we are using to retrieve the data from the database.

Two more datasets were created using a slightly different approach because they contain relations to other tables as well as hold data.

Figure 18-5

Creating Typed Datasets

These next two datasets are a more advanced type of dataset. These two will by typed datasets that have relationships in them. This will allow you to have one dataset that holds multiple tables that relate to each other.

Using the Solution Explorer, a new DataSet object is added to the project, and named BoilersOperatingLog. Once the dataset is opened, the tables BoilersOperationLog, Boilers, Shifts, and Operators are dragged onto the design surface of the dataset.

A relation object is then dragged onto the BoilerID field in the BoilersOperationLog table in the dataset. The relationship editor inside VS opens. A relationship between the BoilerID field in the BoilersOperationLog table and the Boilers table is then created, as shown in Figure 18-6.

Relationships between ShiftID, OperatorID, and their respective tables have also been created. The last dataset created for this solution was generated using the same methods used to create the BoilerOperatingLog dataset. Two datasets were created to work with the schema of the database.

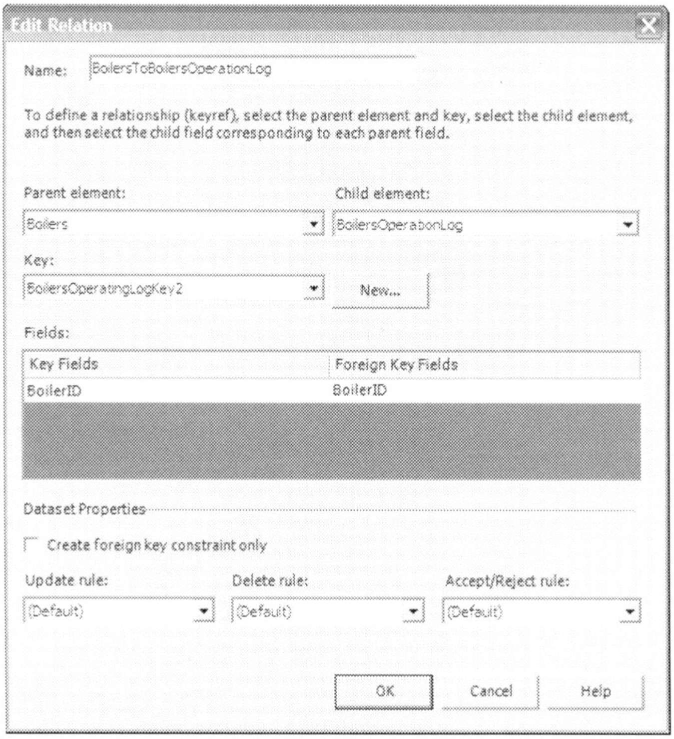

Figure 18-6

Exposing the Datasets

After creating the datasets to work with, you need to add the code necessary to expose these objects to calling applications using a Web service.

❏   In the `DataService.asmx.cs` code file a Web method was created to return the dataset dsLookups from the Web service (and database) that contains the three lookup tables.

❏   At the top of the code file you will add the following `using` statement:

```
using System.Data.OleDb
```

❏   The Web method that follows has three data adapters that go out to the database and fetch all the records to fill up this dataset. The dataset is a container that has the ability to hold many tables and relationships.

```
[WebMethod]
public System.Data.DataSet ReturnLookups()
 {
      OleDbDataAdapter daBoilers = new OleDbDataAdapter("Select * From
           Boilers",this.oleDbConnection1);
      OleDbDataAdapter daShifts = new OleDbDataAdapter("Select * From Shifts",
```

```
            this.oleDbConnection1);
      OleDbDataAdapter daOperators = new OleDbDataAdapter("Select * From
            Operators", this.oleDbConnection1);
      dsLookups ds = new dsLookups();
      daBoilers.Fill(ds,"Boilers");
      daShifts.Fill(ds,"Shifts");
      daOperators.Fill(ds,"Operators");

      return ds;

}
```

Now that the Web method to expose the lookup tables has been described, the InfoPath template will be opened and the datasource added to the form.

❑ Using the Data Connection Wizard a connection to the Web service is created. Because the only method written thus far returns a dataset, something InfoPath is familiar with, you are allowed to use this in the InfoPath document.

❑ Be sure that you select Receive Data, from a Web Service. `http://localhost/ BoilerWebService/DataService.asmx` should be the name of your Web service, type that in the text box, you'll notice right away that the Web method we created earlier shows up in the box on the left, as shown in Figure 18-7:

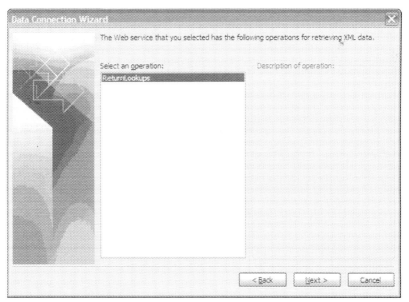

Figure 18-7

❑ This connection was named ReturnLookups.

❑ During design time in the InfoPath document, three drop-down list box controls were dragged onto the InfoPath form.

319

❑ The Web service is used to retrieve the data needed to fill these controls, following the necessary steps to bind the drop-down list box controls to the WebServices dataset.

Inserting Data

Going back to Visual Studio to add another Web method will allow us to submit data from InfoPath, displayed here:

```
[WebMethod]
public void InsertNewBoilerLog(int BoilerID, DateTime LogDate, DateTime LogTime,
int ShiftID, int OperatorID, string SteamDrumStatus, int SteamDrumPSIG, int Excess,
int SteamLoad, int SteamCycles, string Comments)
{
    string sql = "Insert into BoilersOperationLog(BoilerID, LogDate, LogTime,
        ShiftID,OperatorID,SteamDrumStatus, SteamDrumPSIG, Excess,
        SteamLoad,SteamCycles, Comments) values (" + BoilerID + ", " + LogDate +
        ", " + LogTime + ", " + ShiftID+ ", " + OperatorID + ", " +
        SteamDrumStatus + ", " + SteamDrumPSIG + ", " + Excess + ", " +
        SteamLoad + ", " + SteamCycles + ", " + Comments + ");";
    System.Data.OleDb.OleDbCommand cmd = new
        System.Data.OleDb.OleDbCommand(sql,this.oleDbConnection1);
    cmd.Connection.Open();
    cmd.ExecuteNonQuery();
    cmd.Connection.Close();
}
```

Examine the preceding code, notice that the parameters of the Web method directly reflect the fields in the table. The next step is to go back to InfoPath and create the DataConnection used to submit data from InfoPath to this Web service.

Submitting from InfoPath

Switching back to InfoPath to set up the document for submitting its data, we are adding a new data connection to submit data. On the first screen of the wizard, select Submit Data. On the Data Connect dialog box that asks for the Web address of the Web service to use, the following is entered: `http://ocalhost/BoilerWebService/DataService.asmx`.

Under Select an Operation, there are now two Web methods exposed to you. For submitting data, the `InsertNewBoilerLog` method has been used. At one point in the wizard, the ability to match up the parameters of the Web method with the data fields on the InfoPath form is given, as shown here in Figure 18-8.

All of the Web method parameters are matched up with the elements on the InfoPath form. The default name of "Submit"' is left as the name of this data connection.

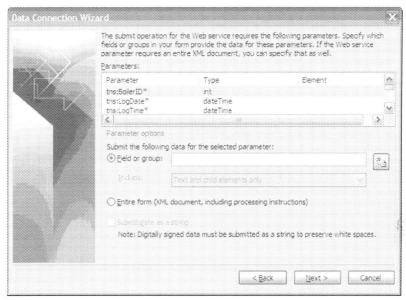

Figure 18-8

Submitting Forms

The last task is to configure the way that InfoPath submits data from the form. Select Submitting Forms... from the Tools menu; the Enable Submit check box is checked. Select the Web service from the drop-down list, and select the Submit data connection for the submit property. Last, check Enable submit on the file menu. The form is now set up to utilize your Web service to submit data.

Then add a button to the form, with the Submit property set.

Situation

The reason for creating this application was that an automotive manufacturing plant needed a way to reduce the paper workflow currently used to collect boiler operation information. There are six boilers spread out around the facility, and this requires constant supervision and safety checks.

Previously the inspectors used a paper-based solution. The inspector would fill out the paper form and then pass it on to someone else to proof read before manually entering the data into the database.

This posed many problems, as you might have guessed. It was becoming more and more difficult to keep track of how the boilers were operating as a whole and which boilers were last inspected and if any work was done to them or not.

Summary

InfoPath was chosen as the primary client application for the data collection. Because this facility wanted to be completely mobile, the tablet PC platform was also chosen to distribute the application on. This allows the users to better analyze and check the data that is going into the system.

As you have seen, through the solution a very mobile workflow has been implemented:

❏   The user picks up a tablet PC and opens up Sharepoint Portal for the Maintenance department.

❏   If one is available, InfoPath gets a new version of the InfoPath form we created.

❏   The user visits each boiler in the facilty and fills out the inspection InfoPath form.

❏   When finished the user submits the boiler inspection data to Access.

❏   The manager comes to work, opens up Sharepoint Portal, or ASP.NET Web page, and gets a list of all boiler inspections that are outside of the normal operating requirements.

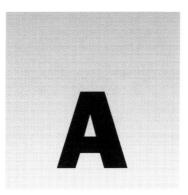

Answers to Exercises

Chapter 1

1. A copy of Microsoft InfoPath must be installed.
2. JScript (default) and VBScript.
3. C# and Visual Basic .NET.
4. 1) Single user use. 2) Published for other's use, or 3) Collaborative efforts.
5. Direct Database, Web Services, and XML Schemas
6. Microsoft Access and Microsoft SQL Server.
7. 1) Create the Data Source. 2) Create the Form. 3) Publish the form. 4) Fill in the Form.
8. Text Box and Drop Down List Box controls.

Chapter 2

1. XML
2. 1) Layout. 2) Controls. 3) Data Sources. 4) Views.
3. Publish Form...
4. Place the cursor on the form where you want the object placed.
5. Drag and drop the control where you want it on the form.

Chapter 3

1. Flat File and Relational.
2. Microsoft Access and Microsoft SQL Server.
3. Primary and Foreign Key fields.
4. The steps are called normalizing your database.
5. XML and XSD.

Chapter 4

1. Text Box control.

2. Repeating Table, Repeating Table with Controls, Repeating Section, or Master/Detail, depending on the data added.

3. 1) Run Query. 2) Submit. 3) New Record. 4) Delete & Submit.

4. 1) Change Database or 2) Edit SQL.

Chapter 5

1. World Wide Web Consortium.

2. HTML and XML standards.

3. XSD.

4. XML and XSD.

Chapter 6

1. Literal Values or Formulas.

2. Conditions and Actions.

3. Clicking the And... button and choosing from the available compounding operators.

4. Standard and Conditional.

Chapter 7

1. Expression Box control.

2. Run Query, Submit, New Record, Delete & Submi, and Rules & Custom Code.

3. 1) Enter the list box entries manually. 2) Look up values in the form's data source. 3) Look up values in a data connection to a database, Web service, file, or SharePoint library or list.

4. Data Connection Wizard.

Chapter 8

1. 1) Repeating Section. 2) Repeating Section with Controls. 3) Repeating Table.

2. Choice Sections and Choice Group Control.

3. Display tab on a repeating table or section.

Chapter 9

1. Click the Add a New View... task on the Views task pane.

2. In the Generals tab of the View Properties dialog, check the "Show on the View menu when filling out the form" check box.

3. The Advanced tab of the Forms Options dialog.

Chapter 10

1. 1) In a shared local area network folder. 2) On a Web Server. 3) In a SharePoint library.

2. All the methods just mentioned require that the user has access to the form template

3. Microsoft WebDAV.

4. Data should appear in Excel.

Chapter 11

1. Microsoft Scripting Technologies and .NET Managed Code.

2. Microsoft JScript and Microsoft VBScript.

3. InfoPath 2003 Toolkit for Visual Studio .NET.

Chapter 12

1. 1) OnBeforeChange 2) OnValidate 3) OnAfterChange

2. XDocument

3. || and &&

Chapter 13

1. 1) Microsoft InfoPath 2003. 2) Visual Studio .NET 2003. 3) InfoPath 2003 Toolkit for Visual Studio .NET.

2. C# and Visual Studio .NET.

3. Windows and Web Installation Programs or Merge Modules.

Chapter 14

1. 1) getDate 2) getFullMonth 3) getFullYear

2. Data Adapter

3. DIV

4. Custom Task Pane area on the Advanced tab of the Forms Options dialog.

Chapter 15

1. XML Web Services.

2. Simplified Object Access Protocol.

Chapter 16

1. 1) Authentication 2) Authorization 3) Data Integrity 4) System Availability

2. A sandbox is a location on your computer that is controlled highly by IE's security settings.

3. 1) SDK Regform Utility 2) MSI

4. 1) CAS (Code Access Security) 2) Role based permissions.

Chapter 17

1. Windows Server 2003

2. Download from http://www.microsoft.com/windowsserver2003/techinfo/sharepoint/wss.mspx

3. Promoting fields.

Beginning InfoPath™ 2003

Index

Web parts, creating, 300
Web parts, existing, adding, 299–300

D

data. *See also* **data source; database**
connected compared to disconnected, 270
connecting to InfoPath, 8
group of, 123
from multiple forms, combining, 5
returning, Web service methods for, 270–274
schema for, 273
Service Pack 1.1 and, 6
views of, generating different, 5
with XML data source, utilizing, 75–80
data connection, specifying for drop-down list box, 115–117
Data Connection Wizard
basing form on Web service, 256–259
default view, creating, 137
exposing datasets and, 319
setting up data connection in, 236, 238
specifying data source for list box, 113, 114
submitting data, 320–321
tasks of, 46–47
using, 47–51
XML document and, 76, 77–78
Data Connections command (Tools menu), 17, 61, 113, 238
Data Field section
adding fields one at a time, 55
adding repeating sections of fields, 55–56
description of, 52
data integrity, 276
data source
adding, 17
adding field as text box, then changing to create drop-down list box, 110
creating, 7
Data Connection Wizard, working with, 46–51
e-mailing form and, 170
multiple tables, choosing, 46

secondary, 47
specifying, 45, 47–51
specifying for list box, 112–114
updating, 61–63
Web service as, 249, 255–262
XML type, 71–73
Data Source task pane
description of, 17–18, 52
displaying fields in, 53
Web service and, 258, 260
data types, 33
data validation conditions, 4
Data Validation dialog box, 198
DataAdapter object, 271
DataAdapters collection, XDocument object, 236
database
Access (Microsoft)
benefits and issues of, 37
exporting to XML from, 70–71
as file-server-based, 36
IT department and, 2
objects used with InfoPath, 37–38
overview of, 36
relationships window, 34
binding choice group to, 127
for case study, creating, 310–311
connecting to existing, 8
customer information, 30
field, 31
file server versus client server, 36
flat file model, 31
frontend and backend, 36
overview of, 29
real-world examples of, 30–31
record, 31
relational model
normalizing data, 35
overview of, 32
referential integrity of data, 34
tables, 32–33
types of relationships, 34
setting up before creating form, 311

F

Z